The Canterbury and York Society

GENERAL EDITOR: PROFESSOR P. HOSKIN

ISSN 0262-995X

CANTERBURY AND YORK SOCIETY VOL. CVIII

Proctors for Parliament

Clergy, Community and Politics,

c. 1248–1539

(The National Archives, Series SC 10)

VOLUME II: 1377–1539

EDITED BY

PHIL BRADFORD & ALISON K. McHARDY

The Canterbury and York Society

The Boydell Press
2018

First published 2018

A Canterbury and York Society publication
published by The Boydell Press
an imprint of Boydell & Brewer Ltd
PO Box 9, Woodbridge, Suffolk IP12 3DF, UK
and of Boydell & Brewer Inc.
668 Mt Hope Avenue, Rochester, NY 14620-2731, USA

website: www.boydellandbrewer.com

ISBN 978-0-907239-81-9

A CIP catalogue record for this book is available
from the British Library

Details of previous volumes are available from Boydell & Brewer Ltd

The publisher has no responsibility for the continued existence
or accuracy of URLs for external or third-party internet websites
referred to in this book, and does not guarantee that any content
on such websites is, or will remain, accurate or appropriate

This publication is printed on acid-free paper

Typeset in Monotype Baskerville by Word and Page, Chester, UK
Printed and bound in Great Britain by TJ International Ltd.

MIX
Paper from
responsible sources
FSC® C013056

For Mark Ormrod
Teacher, Mentor and Friend

PRODUCTION OF THIS VOLUME HAS BEEN ASSISTED
BY GENEROUS GRANTS FROM
THE LINCOLN RECORD SOCIETY
&
THE LATE MISS ISOBEL THORNLEY'S
BEQUEST TO THE UNIVERSITY OF LONDON

CONTENTS

ILLUSTRATIONS

ACKNOWLEDGMENTS

Gwilym Dodd, Hannes Kleineke and Mark Ormrod kindly gave detailed comments on the draft of the introduction, and gave help and advice on other aspects of this second volume. We are also grateful to Charles Fonge, Richard Goddard, Joan Greatrex, Huw Price, Janet Stevenson, Helen Watt and Rob Wheeler for references, support and advice, and to our general editor, Philippa Hoskin, for her learned, kindly and wise support and guidance. Special mention must be made of Robert Swanson for drawing our attention to the material contained in appendices 5 and 6.

ABBREVIATIONS

C&Y	Canterbury and York Society
CCR	*Calendar of Close Rolls*
CFR	*Calendar of Fine Rolls*
CPR	*Calendar of Patent Rolls*
HoP	*The History of Parliament: The House of Commons, 1386–1421*, ed. J. S. Roskell, Linda Clarke and Carole Rawcliffe, 4 vols. (Stroud, 1992)
LP	Letter Patent
ODNB	*Oxford Dictionary of National Biography*
PROME	*Parliament Rolls of Medieval England*
PW	*The Parliamentary Writs and Writs of Military Summons*, ed. Francis Palgrave, 2 vols. in 4 parts (London, 1827–34)
RDP	*Reports from the Lords Committees Appointed to Search the Journals of the House, Rolls of Parliament, and Other Records and Documents, for All Matters Touching the Dignity of a Peer of the Realm*, 5 vols. (London, 1820–9)
RS	Rolls Series (The Chronicles and Memorials of Great Britain and Ireland during the Middle Ages)
TNA	The National Archives

INTRODUCTION

This is the second of two volumes calendaring the contents of series SC 10 in The National Archives, the records of proxy appointments to parliament between *c.* 1248 and 1536, predominantly by the clergy. The first volume contained the information from the start of the series until the end of Edward III's reign in 1377, and the introduction to that volume considered the contents and history of the series, the nature of parliamentary proxies in the Middle Ages, and the men and institutions who appointed proctors. This volume calendars the remaining appointments from the accession of Richard II until the end of the series, while the introduction considers in greater detail the men who acted as proctors in the medieval and early Tudor parliaments.

In the three centuries covered by SC 10, at least two thousand men were appointed as proctors of the clergy in parliament. These account for more than 5,800 proxy appointments made in the 2,731 letters which come from the clergy and the single surviving enrolled set of proxies,[1] but in all cases these are minimum figures. Several documents have names which are illegible, and in some cases the decay is such that it is impossible even to determine how many proctors were appointed. There may have been many more appointments made; as was discussed in Volume 1, we have no way of knowing how many documents have been lost from the collection which now forms SC 10. Since there is a large gap in the records between 1447 and 1523, in addition to the lost letters from other periods, it is very likely that considerably more than two thousand individuals were named in proxy letters. We must also take into account the names we can obtain from sources such as the Lords' Journals, bishops' registers and other survivals in various archives, some of which have been included as appendices to this volume.

Hence a considerable number of men received a proxy appointment from a member of the clergy in the later Middle Ages. Even if not all attended, they still constituted a significant element of the membership of parliament in these years. True, many had a distinctly transitory role in the institution, at least in their capacity as clerical proctors, and all the standard problems of medieval prosopography apply.[2] Ninety-five per cent of those found as proctors in SC 10, accounting for some two-thirds of the total appointments, were named ten times or fewer.[3]

---

[1]   These figures discount the fifty-two letters from secular peers in SC 10 and four misfiled letters, but include details found in the *Vetus Codex* for 1307, as well as stray letters from C 49, C 146, C 219 and C 270; for a discussion of the contents of SC 10, see the introduction to Volume 1.

[2]   It is not always easy to distinguish between two men of the same name – for example fathers and sons or uncles and nephews – whose careers overlapped. When it comes to unrelated men with identical names, establishing whether one or more individuals are involved is more often than not a matter of plausibility. Where there is doubt about an identification, we have recorded all possibilities in the biographical details in Appendix 7.

[3]   There are 5,828 appointments involving 2,078 individuals (subject to the caveat about

Roughly three-fifths of the individuals have only one surviving proxy appointment to their name. That is not to say that these single appointees were necessarily insignificant, since amongst their number can be found the earls of Stafford, Northumberland and Huntingdon,[4] as well as several bishops and even one archbishop of Canterbury.[5] Of course, such men would have been present in parliament in any case, and it has to be conceded that a number of the proctors appointed just once, and in several cases those appointed more than once, are obscure figures. However, it is also worth stating that a surprising amount can be known about many of the men named, even when their career as a clerical proctor was brief. Among the proctors can be found monks, abbots and priors, current and future bishops and deans, chancery and other royal clerks, members of parliament (both knights of the shires and citizens and burgesses), lay officers, and other members of the ecclesiastical and county communities. The clerical proctors represent a cross-section of later medieval political society, a reminder that the firm stratification of parliament into rigid houses took place relatively late. Until well into the Lancastrian period, and very possibly into the Yorkist era, members summoned by personal writ to sit among the Lords were appointing to represent them men who had no personal right to sit among the parliamentary peerage. The proctors serve as a reminder that many people had diverse roles in parliament, which brought its members together in overlapping interests, and should caution us against viewing the medieval assembly in accordance with more rigid later practice.

Moreover, a considerable amount can be learned from fewer than a hundred men who between them accounted for a third of the total proxy appointments. If some individuals made fleeting appearances on the parliamentary scene, there were others who received numerous proxy appointments and also had other parliamentary duties. Twenty-nine men, the overwhelming majority of them chancery clerks, were appointed twenty or more times, with five receiving fifty or more appointments. Thomas Evesham, a chancery clerk from Worcestershire,[6] is named in 114 letters across a twenty-eight-year period (1313–41), making him by some distance the most frequently appointed proctor in SC 10, far ahead of the seventy-five appointments of second-placed John Rome between 1381 and 1414. Such men played a significant part in parliamentary history, albeit one which has tended to be overlooked and undervalued. The general neglect of SC 10 has resulted in this element of the parliamentary membership being overlooked, not least because many proctors were also present in parliament in another capacity.

---

the difficulty with confidently distinguishing between those with identical names) that can be identified in SC 10 (clergy letters only), the *Vetus Codex*, C 49, C 146, C 219 and C 270, although this discounts damaged and illegible entries where no details can be obtained: 1 appointment – 1,223 men; 2 – 334; 3 – 154; 4 – 85; 5 – 57; 6 – 55; 7 – 35; 8 – 21; 9 – 15; 10 – 12; 11 – 15; 12 – 12; 13 – 3; 14 – 6; 15 – 6; 16 – 5; 17 – 5; 18 – 3; 19 – 3; 20 – 3; 22 – 4; 23 – 2; 24 – 1; 25 – 3; 29 – 1; 32 – 1; 35 – 1; 36 – 3; 28 – 2; 40 – 1; 42 – 1; 46 – 1; 50 – 1; 53 – 1; 62 – 1; 75 – 1; and 114 – 1.

[4]   Edmund Stafford, earl of Stafford, proctor of the bishop of Coventry and Lichfield in 1402 (41/2028); Henry Percy, earl of Northumberland, appointed by the bishop of Hereford in 1442 (50/2463); and George Hastings, earl of Huntingdon, named by the prior of Coventry in 1532 (51/2520).

[5]   The bishops and abbots who acted as proctors will be discussed in detail later in this introduction.

[6]   B. Wilkinson, *The Chancery under Edward III* (Manchester, 1929), p. 151, traces Evesham's career.

PATTERNS OF APPOINTMENT

Given that SC 10 spans 288 years (1248–1536), it is unsurprising that the pattern of proxy appointments varied across such a large period, with a discernible shift in the type of men who were appointed and the number of proctors each sender named. This information reveals much about changing attitudes to parliament as well as reflecting broader and more fundamental political shifts between the reign of Henry III and that of Henry VIII.

Tables 1 and 2 show how many proctors were named in each proxy letter found in SC 10 (as well as those misfiled in other classes); Table 1 contains data only from the letters, whereas Table 2 also includes data from the list of proxies enrolled in the *Vetus Codex*.[7]

As Tables 1 and 2 demonstrate, around half of all proxy letters across the period covered by SC 10 named two proctors to represent the sender, with more than ninety per cent naming three or fewer proctors.[8] In some ways, this is unsurprising. The number of proctors technically allowed to the lower clergy was prescribed by the *praemunientes* clause, which commanded that the diocesan clergy choose two proctors and the cathedral chapters one. While the clergy were generally quite obedient and for the most part restricted themselves to two proctors (and quite often just named one), the chapters proved disinclined to send only one proctor, especially from the mid-fourteenth century. Furthermore, there were no guidelines for how many proctors other clergy should appoint, not least because they were not meant to be naming proctors in the first place, but instead should have attended parliament in person.

These bare statistics mask some significant trends, in which the pattern of the fourteenth and sixteenth centuries is notably different from that of the fifteenth. Under Edward I, the practice was to appoint one or two proctors and never more than four (although it should be acknowledged that the majority of these figures derive from the *Vetus Codex*, at the very end of the reign, and may thus be atypical). This pattern continued under Edward II, where slightly fewer than nine in every ten letters name one or two proctors. More senders appointed three or four proctors than in his father's reign (although the number of surviving appointments is considerably greater), with just one instance – William Greenfield, archbishop of York in 1313 (2/91) – where five proctors were chosen. The same trend is found broadly under Edward III, although increasingly senders were naming three men to represent them in parliament, and there is the first instance of six proctors being appointed (28/1355). Richard II's reign is the first in which there are no surviving letters which name no proctors,[9] and the proportion of documents in which only a

---

[7] The figures in the tables do not take account of the fact that some letters are duplicates, with more than one copy surviving for the same parliament, although not all cases where multiple letters survive from the same sender actually name the same number of proctors. For the purposes of these tables, every letter has been counted where information can be obtained from it.

[8] In the case of a few damaged documents, it is possible that the number of proctors named is a minimum figure, although in most cases the number can be identified even when the names can no longer be read.

[9] As noted in Table 1, the letters in which no proctors were named were usually letters close to the king excusing the absence of bishops or abbots. Corresponding proxy appointments survive for some, but by no means all, of these.

TABLE I. NUMBER OF PROCTORS APPOINTED PER LETTER IN SC 10

	0	1	2	3	4	5	6	7	8	9	U
Henry III	4	2	1	0	0	0	0	0	0	0	0
Edward I	0	8	2	0	0	0	0	0	0	0	0
Edward II	18	194	250	38	3	1	0	0	0	0	2
Edward III	5	241	615	170	30	7	1	0	0	0	9
Richard II	0	27	191	135	57	7	3	0	0	0	0
Henry IV	0	8	75	67	28	16	7	1	2	1	2
Henry V	0	6	53	54	15	12	1	4	6	1	0
Henry VI	0	12	69	38	21	15	4	1	0	0	1
Henry VIII	3	18	16	6	0	0	0	0	0	0	4
Unknown	*2*	*11*	*7*	*0*	*2*	*0*	*0*	*0*	*0*	*0*	*21*
Total	**32**	**527**	**1279**	**508**	**156**	**28**	**16**	**5**	**8**	**2**	**39**

This table covers all the letters in SC 10 which derive from the clergy (excluding those misfiled documents which belong in other classes) as well as the stray letters from C 49, C 146, C 219 and C 270 which belong in SC 10. The numbers in the top row represent the number of proctors named in each letter. The letters in which no proctors were named were usually letters close to the king, a response to the summons serving as an excuse for absence. U = unknown.

TABLE 2. NUMBER OF PROCTORS APPOINTED PER LETTER
IN SC 10 AND *VETUS CODEX*

	0	1	2	3	4	5	6	7	8	9	U
Henry III	4	2	1	0	0	0	0	0	0	0	0
Edward I	2	65	40	4	2	0	0	0	0	0	0
Edward II	18	194	250	38	3	1	0	0	0	0	2
Edward III	5	241	615	170	30	7	1	0	0	0	9
Richard II	0	27	191	135	57	7	3	0	0	0	0
Henry IV	0	8	75	67	28	16	7	1	2	1	2
Henry V	0	6	53	54	15	12	1	4	6	1	0
Henry VI	0	12	69	38	21	15	4	1	0	0	1
Henry VIII	3	18	16	6	0	0	0	0	0	0	4
Unknown	*2*	*11*	*7*	*0*	*2*	*0*	*0*	*0*	*0*	*0*	*21*
Total	**34**	**584**	**1317**	**512**	**158**	**28**	**16**	**5**	**8**	**2**	**39**

In addition to the letters recorded in Table 1, this table includes the proxy appointments found in the Vetus Codex (TNA C 151/1) for the parliament at Carlisle in January 1307. The numbers in the top row represent the number of proctors named in each letter or enrolled entry. U = unknown.

single proctor is appointed falls dramatically. Two or three had become standard, with a few more choosing to appoint between four and six men than in his grandfather's time.

The accession of Henry IV brought a significant change. The majority of letters still name two or three proctors, with those containing a lone proxy appointment now a tiny proportion of the total. However, it is notable that a quarter of those sending proctors chose four or more names, with the bishop of Coventry and Lichfield naming nine men in 1404 (41/2035). The trend continued in the reign of Henry V, where letters containing seven or eight names are not isolated examples. There are cases in which the rules were flagrantly ignored: in April 1414, both the chapter and the clergy of Carlisle named eight proctors rather than the stipulated one and two (45/2210 and 45/2213). Not until Henry VI does the pattern change again, with most appointers reverting to the later fourteenth-century habit of naming two or three proctors, and none appointing more than seven. It is unclear what happened under the Yorkist kings and Henry VII, but by the reign of Henry VIII the numerical pattern is very similar to that of the late thirteenth and early fourteenth century; letters are once more found in which no proctors are appointed, and the majority of senders name just a single proctor, with no more than three names found in any one letter.

Change is found in qualitative as well as quantitative terms, with a considerable difference in the type of men chosen as proctors. These men will be discussed in more detail shortly, but a general trend is apparent across the period. For most of the fourteenth century, nearly all proctors were clerics or religious, with almost no laymen being selected for the role beyond a very occasional MP or lawyer. Most of those sending proctors made use of clerks in royal service, especially chancery clerks, who – not least because they were certain to be in parliament – were by far the most frequently appointed group of men in SC 10. Abbots and priors in this period often sent one of their monks to represent them in parliament, frequently alone in the earlier years. The list of proctors sent by bishops might occasionally be quite impressive, such as when the appointer or the proctor was the archbishop of Canterbury,[10] but even then it tended to consist of other bishops. Laymen become more common as the century progresses, but aside from cases where there were special circumstances (such as St Benet of Hulme in the 1370s),[11] they continued to account for a tiny minority of the parliamentary proctors of the clergy. The principal difference between the earlier part of the fourteenth century and the reign of Richard II lies in the increasing number of proctors of higher status under Richard than in earlier years.

[10]   In 1319, Walter Reynolds named the bishops of Ely and Winchester (6/282); in 1333 Simon Meopham selected the bishops of London, Ely, Lincoln and Hereford (17/830); and in 1371 Simon Islip appointed the bishops of London, Worcester and St Davids (30/1452 and 30/1453). Strangely, in 1330 Meopham twice chose relatively minor clerks as his proctors for parliament (13/640 and 13/649). Simon Islip was the bishop of Exeter's proxy in 1362 (28/1392) and William Courtenay was named by the clergy of Colchester archdeaconry in 1384 (35/1735).
[11]   The case of St Benet's in the 1370s is discussed in greater detail below, in the section on laymen as proctors.

Once again, the fifteenth century, and more particularly the usurpation of Henry IV, marks the point of change.[12] There was no dramatic change of personnel after 1399 – many names are found either side of Richard II's deposition and Henry IV's usurpation – but a large number of new names begin to appear. The majority of proctors continued to be clerics, but it is much rarer to find lone monks appointed, or indeed for anyone to become a sole proctor. Men denoted as 'layman', 'literate', 'gentleman', 'citizen', 'knight', or even 'earl' begin to appear amidst clerks, monks, canons, archdeacons, deans and bishops, with an increase in the number of clergy higher up the ecclesiastical hierarchy. As Henry IV's reign advanced, it became more typical to appoint a wide spread of proctors, in numbers and of status very rarely found in the fourteenth century. In 1404, the bishop of Coventry and Lichfield named the dean of Hereford, a canon of Wells, three canons of Lichfield, a rector from his diocese, a knight and two esquires (41/2035). In 1410, the bishop of Worcester appointed Lord Beaumont, the abbot of Winchcombe, the archdeacon of Buckingham, a knight and four gentlemen (44/2162). If anything, this trend grew more apparent during Henry V's reign: in April 1414, the bishop and archdeacon of Carlisle chose the same eight clerks (44/2192) while the prior of Coventry named the archdeacon of Canterbury, two chancery clerks, two laymen who served as MPs and three monks of his priory; and in 1420, the bishop of St Asaph selected the bishops of St Davids, Llandaff and Bangor, the dean and two canons of St Asaph, the examiner-general of the court of Canterbury and two 'literate gentlemen' (47/2310). In the case of this particular bishop of St Asaph, Robert Lancaster, it is likely that the desire to choose large numbers of appropriate men was a conscious display of loyalty, given that his predecessor had defected to Owain Glyn Dŵr in 1404.[13]

The shift in patterns of representation took place in the context of other developments. The early fifteenth century was apparently a period in which the parliamentary representation of the clergy and the appointment of proctors was an important and debated topic. In November 1414, the abbot of Thorney informed the king in his letter of appointment that he did not hold of the king by barony, but by pure and perpetual alms (45/2230). The question of whether the higher clergy were summoned to parliament in feudal terms, by virtue of being tenants-in-chief, or in political and religious terms as the leading churchmen with important roles in the realm, is one which has never been satisfactorily determined.[14] The *Modus Tenendi Parliamentum* states that 'to parliament ought to be summoned and come archbishops, bishops, abbots, priors, and other higher clergy who hold by earldom or barony by reason of such tenure'.[15] It is worth noting, however, that all the bish-

---

[12]   A. K. McHardy, 'Henry IV: The Clergy in Parliament', in *The Reign of Henry IV: Rebellion and Survival, 1403–1413*, ed. Gwilym Dodd and Douglas Biggs (York, 2008), pp. 136–61.

[13]   On John Trevor's role in the Glyn Dŵr Revolt, see R. R. Davies, *The Revolt of Owain Glyn Dŵr* (Oxford, 1995), pp. 116, 213–14. Trevor (also Trefor or Trevaur) had himself served as a proctor for his predecessor as bishop of St Asaph, Laurence Child, in 1388 (37/1803).

[14]   For a more detailed discussion of this question, see P. J. Bradford, 'Parliament and Political Culture in Early Fourteenth Century England', unpublished University of York Ph.D. thesis (2007), pp. 71–3 and 81–2.

[15]   *Parliamentary Texts of the Later Middle Ages*, ed. Nicholas Pronay and John Taylor (Oxford, 1980), p. 80. See also Helena M. Chew, *The English Ecclesiastical Tenants-in-Chief and Knight Service, especially in the Thirteenth and Fourteenth Centuries* (Oxford, 1932), pp. 168–79; and M. V.

ops were summoned even though not all held in such terms; the bishops of Carlisle held nothing from the king, while the Welsh bishops and the bishop of Rochester held their temporal lands from the archbishop of Canterbury, yet all were summoned to parliament.[16] In case of a vacancy in a see, the writ of summons was sent to an ecclesiastical official, the guardian of spiritualities. It seems likely, therefore, that the feudal justification for summoning bishops was a secondary consideration, even if their role in parliament was not typically a spiritual one. The question of tenure seems to be more relevant in the case of the heads of religious houses, since there were abbots and houses who sought to be spared the trouble and cost of parliamentary representation, especially under Edward III. Those abbots and priors who successfully applied to have their parliamentary obligations removed did so on the grounds that they held nothing in chief of the king, while several who hopefully made this claim had their applications dismissed.[17]

Quite why Thomas Charwelton, the abbot of Thorney, decided to raise this matter in 1414 is obscure, since he had been appointing proctors for a decade and continued to do so for the rest of his abbacy (he died in 1426). It hardly seems likely, therefore, that he was seeking to have his house removed from the list of summons. It is apparent that since Henry IV's usurpation, some of the higher clergy had been investigating the place of the clergy in parliament. In around 1406, the section concerning the summoning of the clergy to parliament in the *Modus Tenendi Parliamentum* (written in the 1320s)[18] was copied into Archbishop Arundel's register.[19] It is interesting that the archbishop looked back to a text written some eighty years earlier to find this information, a reminder that for all its inaccuracies and the significant changes to parliament in the fourteenth century, the *Modus* is the only known 'manual' in this period which explicitly covered the practicalities and theoretical justification for parliament. It is less clear why Arundel (or his registrar) felt the need to copy the text at this stage. There were tensions between the king and some of the clergy in Henry IV's reign, not least in the events which led to the execution of Archbishop Scrope of York in 1405, but for the most part Henry and

---

Clarke, *Medieval Representation and Consent: A Study of Early Parliaments in England and Ireland, with Special Reference to the* Modus Tenendi Parliamentum (London, 1936), pp. 15–32.

[16] Chew, *Ecclesiastical Tenants-in-Chief*, pp. 1–36; Susan Reynolds, *Kingdoms and Communities in Western Europe, 900–1300* (2nd edition: Oxford, 1997), p. 307.

[17] Chew, *Ecclesiastical Tenants-in-Chief*, pp. 174–6; Aloyse Marie Reich, *The Parliamentary Abbots to 1470: A Study in English Constitutional History*, University of California Publications in History 17 (Berkeley and Los Angeles, 1941), pp. 348–9; J. S. Roskell, 'The Problem of the Attendance of the Lords in Medieval Parliaments', *Bulletin of the Institute of Historical Research* 29 (1956), p. 202; Enoch Powell and Keith Wallis, *The House of Lords in the Middle Ages* (London, 1968), pp. 342–6. Among those who successfully sought exemption from parliamentary summonses under Edward III were the abbots of Beaulieu (1341), St Augustine's, Bristol (1343), Thornton (1343), Osney (1346) and Leicester (1352), and the priors of Sempringham (1343), Spalding (1343) and Lewes (1365).

[18] The justification for this dating of the *Modus* can be found in Bradford, 'Parliament and Political Culture', pp. 186–98.

[19] Lambeth Palace Library, Reg. Arundel I, f. 561v.; cf. *Parliamentary Texts*, ed. Pronay and Taylor, pp. 67–8. This entry in Arundel's register is found after the section for writs which covers October 1399 to January 1406, which suggests a date of 1406, although the entry itself is undated.

Arundel had a respectful, cooperative relationship.[20] It is possible that the lengthy parliamentary sessions of 1406 caused unease among some of the clergy around long absences in Westminster and the associated costs, causing a particular problem for struggling bishops and monasteries who had to pay for proctors. The archbishop may thus have been seeking a clear reminder of the theoretical basis for the clergy's role in order to respond to such questions, especially in the uncertainty caused by the king's ill health. At around the same time Philip Repingdon, bishop of Lincoln, had a formulary drawn up to record how to respond to writs of summons and elect proctors, and how to do this after a prorogation.[21] Of Henry IV's ten parliaments, five were summoned for dates which were subsequently delayed, and of these four also changed location.[22] This habit of proroguing parliaments in both time and place presumably led Repingdon to have these instructions drawn up to help his clerks ensure that they complied with the requirements. These survivals from Canterbury and Lincoln are clear evidence that the matter of the clergy's place in parliament, and the correct legal forms associated with the clerical presence, became important issues in the early fifteenth century, not least with a changing relationship between parliament and convocation.

The developments of Henry IV's reign can probably be explained by the anxiety surrounding the dynastic change.[23] Raised as a nobleman rather than a prince in training for kingship, Henry's approach to parliament was notably different from that of his fourteenth-century predecessors.[24] Recent research has tended to view him as a relatively successful manager of parliament, at least in his ability to procure taxation and manage the commons and the political community.[25] However, Henry's management of his household and parliament could not mask the fact that his title to the throne was insecure, and he faced serious challenges in the period 1403–6 in particular.[26] The complete absence of Welsh material in SC 10 for Henry's reign, in a series in which Wales is otherwise unusually well repre-

---

[20]   Chris Given-Wilson, *Henry IV* (London, 2016), p. 366.

[21]   York Minster Library MS 22, ff. 72–72*v*. This text is printed as Appendix 6 of this volume.

[22]   The parliament originally summoned for 27 October 1400 at York met on 20 January 1401 at Westminster; that due to convene on 15 September 1402 was delayed until the 30th; the assembly planned for 3 December 1403 was moved to Westminster on 14 January; the 1406 parliament was first summoned for 15 February at Coventry, was changed to 9 February at Gloucester, and actually met on 1 March at Westminster; and the 1410 parliament was first called for Bristol before being moved to Westminster.

[23]   McHardy, 'Henry IV: The Clergy in Parliament', p. 142.

[24]   Phil Bradford, 'A Silent Presence: The English King in Parliament in the Fourteenth Century', *Historical Research* 84 (2011), pp. 209–10.

[25]   A. J. Pollard, 'The Lancastrian Constitutional Experiment Revisited: Henry IV, Sir John Tiptoft and the Parliament of 1406', *Parliamentary History* 14 (1995), 103–19; Gwilym Dodd, 'Conflict or Consensus: Henry IV and Parliament, 1399–1406', in *Social Attitudes and Political Structures in the Fifteenth Century*, ed. Tim Thornton (Stroud, 2000), pp. 118–49; Douglas Biggs, 'The Reign of Henry IV: The Revolution of 1399 and the Establishment of the Regime, 1399–1406', in *Fourteenth Century England* I, ed. Nigel Saul (Woodbridge, 2000), pp. 195–210; Douglas Biggs, 'The Politics of Health: Henry IV and the Long Parliament of 1406', in *Henry IV: The Establishment of the Regime, 1399–1406*, ed. Gwilym Dodd and Douglas Biggs (York, 2003), pp. 185–205; Given-Wilson, *Henry IV*, pp. 434–6.

[26]   Recent scholarship is most handily summarised in Given-Wilson, *Henry IV*.

sented, is one testament to this; the bishops of both the northern Welsh dioceses of Bangor (Louis Byford) and St Asaph (John Trevor) joined Glyn Dŵr in 1404, which presumably had an impact on their cathedral chapters and clergy. Under these circumstances, it is perhaps to be expected that those appointing proctors during and after Henry's reign chose a variety of men of different standing to represent them, in order to avoid investing too much in agents who might prove to be unreliable or politically suspect. It is also worth remembering that Lollardy was a cause of investigation and fear in Henry's reign, which might have caused some to avoid being tainted with suspicion.

What is more surprising is that the pattern continues and if anything grows more pronounced after Henry V's peaceful accession in 1413. Of course, the mythology of Agincourt and Henry's military successes have tended to mask the continued challenge to the Lancastrian regime, demonstrated not least in Oldcastle's Rebellion and the Southampton Plot.[27] Although no longer seen as a genuine threat, Owain Glyn Dŵr did not die until 1415 or 1416, and some Welsh resentment continued to smoulder, even if the four (English) bishops in Wales were now all loyal to the English crown.[28] As SC 10 reflects, there is a greater continuity between the reigns of Henry IV and Henry V than is sometimes realised, and faced with this uncertainty, in appointing proctors the clergy continued to show the same caution after 1413 as before. Only once Henry VI had peacefully ascended the throne was it clear that the dynasty was relatively secure, something manifested in SC 10, where the clergy began to name fewer proctors to represent them on each occasion. It would be fascinating to see what effect the Wars of the Roses had on proxy appointments, but the documents have been lost in intervening centuries and we can only speculate.

What is clear is that the Yorkist and early Tudor period did see major changes in approaches to parliament. By the time the SC 10 series resumes under Henry VIII, after a seventy-six-year gap, the pattern of appointment had changed dramatically, with a far smaller number of proctors drawn from a much more restricted group.[29] From the clergy, nearly all of the proxy appointments we have for the Tudor period are from bishops and abbots, the lower clergy having almost disappeared from the records.[30] The higher clergy were exclusively appointing other

---

[27] Christopher Allmand, *Henry V* (London, 1992), pp. 74–68, 294–304; Maureen Jurkowski, 'Henry V's Suppression of the Oldcastle Revolt', in *Henry V: New Interpretations*, ed. Gwilym Dodd (York, 2013), pp. 103–29; T. B. Pugh, 'The Southampton Plot of 1415', in *Kings and Nobles in the Later Middle Ages: A Tribute to Charles Ross*, ed. Ralph A. Griffiths and J. W. Sherborne (Gloucester, 1986), pp. 62–89; T. B. Pugh, *Henry V and the Southampton Plot* (Southampton and Gloucester, 1988).

[28] The exact date of Glyn Dŵr's death is unknown, but probably occurred before the commission issued in February 1416 to receive his submission. See Davies, *Revolt of Owain Glyn Dŵr*, pp. 326–7, and Llinos Smith's article in the *ODNB*.

[29] It is worth noting that proxy appointments for convocations do exist for the period where the SC 10 evidence is lacking, for example from the prior and chapter of Durham for convocation in York Province.

[30] There are extant appointments from Durham Cathedral. On 17 January 1504, the subprior and chapter named Ralph Colyngwod [Collingwood] and Thomas Swallwell [Swalwell], monks of Durham, and John Batmanson, doctor of laws, as their proctors. On 29 May 1536, the prior appointed Cuthbert [Tunstall], bishop of Durham as his proctor, while the subprior and chapter named Sir Edward Tempest, Edward Hyenmers,

lords to represent them. This reflects the fact that the concept of a parliamentary peerage had become much more clearly defined by the Tudor period (and quite possibly under the Yorkist kings), and within the House of Lords it was presumably unacceptable by this stage for a proctor to be someone who was not entitled to sit amongst the peers in their own right.[31] The first surviving Tudor letters in SC 10 date from 1523, but earlier proxy appointments survive in the journals of the House of Lords for 1510, 1512 and 1515. What is notable about these appointments is that the spiritual and temporal lords were using one another as proctors interchangeably; in 1512, for example, the bishop of Carlisle named the bishop of Durham and Lord Dudley, while the earl of Oxford appointed the bishop of Winchester and the earl of Surrey.[32] For the 1512 assembly, as well as the February and November sessions of the 1515 parliament, nearly all those appointing proctors, laymen and clergy alike, named both a lay lord and a bishop or abbot as their proctors. At this stage, there was clearly a perceived overlap in the interests of the temporal and spiritual elements within the House of Lords.

After 1515, the next proxy appointments are those in SC 10 for 1523, and in the intervening years there had been a marked change. The remaining letters in SC 10 and the journal entries until the dissolution of the monasteries in 1539 show that lay and spiritual lords were now appointing only their own kind as their proctors. Even amongst the clergy, bishops tended to appoint only other bishops, and abbots other abbots, although there were some exceptions. It is hard to be certain exactly what had caused this sudden and abrupt division between secular and clerical proxy appointments, although the most likely single cause is the Hunne Affair of 1514–15.

The suspicious death of Richard Hunne in the Lollards' Tower in December 1514, while awaiting trial for heresy, and his post-mortem conviction and burning at the stake, aroused considerable anger against the clergy in London and provoked a political and religious crisis.[33] Attempts were made in parliament to have Hunne's property (forfeited to the crown as he was a condemned heretic) restored to his family, and even to introduce a murder charge. Parliament in 1515

---

and Robert Davell, doctor of laws. See Durham University Library, Durham Cathedral Muniments Register V, ff. 75*v* and 260*v*.

[31] The development of the House of Lords in the late Lancastrian, Yorkist and early Tudor periods is outlined in Powell and Wallis, *House of Lords*, pp. 451–542. See also P. R. Cavill, *The English Parliaments of Henry VII, 1485–1504* (Cambridge, 2009), pp. 106–17.

[32] *Journal of the House of Lords, 1509–1793*, 39 vols. (London, 1767–1830), vol. I, pp. 11–12, calendared in Appendix 2 of this volume.

[33] Eliza Jeffries Davis, 'The Authorities for the Case of Richard Hunne', *English Historical Review* 30 (1915), 477–88; Arthur Ogle, *The Tragedy of the Lollards' Tower* (Oxford, 1949); John Fines, 'The Post-Mortem Condemnation for Heresy of Richard Hunne', *English Historical Review* 78 (1963), 528–31; Richard Wunderli, 'Pre-Reformation London Summoners and the Murder of Richard Hunne', *Journal of Ecclesiastical History* 33 (1982), 209–24; Richard Marius, *Thomas More* (London, 1984), pp. 123–41; Sybil M. Jack, 'The Conflict of Common Law and Canon Law in Early Sixteenth-Century England: Richard Hunne Revisited', *Parergon* 3 (1985), 131–45; Peter Gwyn, *The King's Cardinal: The Rise and Fall of Thomas Wolsey* (London, 1990), pp. 34–41; G. W. Bernard, *The Late Medieval English Church: Vitality and Vulnerability before the Break with Rome* (New Haven, CT, 2012), pp. 1–16; Richard Dale, 'The Death of an Alleged Heretic, Richard Hunne (d. 1514), Explained', *Reformation and Renaissance Review* 15 (2013), 133–53.

met in these acrimonious circumstances, with hostility against benefit of clergy, praemunire, and the independence of the Church in general raised as issues which would return with new vigour in 1529.[34] The efforts to enact legislation to restrict benefit of clergy were strongly opposed by certain of the lords spiritual in both convocation and parliament in 1515.[35] With clergy privileges under attack in the House of Lords as well as in the wider realm, after 1515 the clergy apparently closed ranks and began to appoint only their clerical colleagues to represent their interests as proctors in parliament.

From the resumption of the evidence in 1523, however, there is a clear variance between the bishops and the abbots. Although bishops were now generally appointing other bishops and abbots other abbots, the difference was that the bishops generally knew their fellow-bishops because they were frequently brought together in both political and ecclesiastical forums and by affairs of state. Even if they did not function as a harmonious group, they were largely aware of the identity of their colleagues and hence their proctors. The abbots had no such collegiality, and the interests of one house often came into conflict with another, presumably reasons why in the fourteenth and fifteenth century abbots almost never appointed other abbots to represent them, relying on monks of their own houses, chancery clerks or local notables. Whereas in the fourteenth and fifteenth century there is usually a discernible logic in the choice of proctors, in the 1520s there is a sense that the higher clergy, abbots in particular, were growing desperate and simply covering themselves by naming anyone of the same status who might conceivably attend parliament. Only in the 1530s, as the Church came under grave threat and the break with Rome was effected, did the higher clergy (especially the abbots) start to take parliamentary attendance seriously. It is notable that a comfortable majority of abbots were present in 1539 and were complicit in making themselves redundant.

These trends give us an insight into the relationship between clergy and parliament across almost three centuries. As with the nature of parliament itself, the patterns of proctorial representation changed and evolved, especially in response to events and times of particular uncertainty in the political climate. There was a gradual but discernible shift in the type of men who were chosen to serve as proctors of the clergy during the period covered by SC 10, and any full understanding of the series requires some study of the individual proctors. For convenience, they are discussed in categories, although it is worth noting that while these groups allow for easier discussion of trends and individuals, they are not exclusive. The boundaries of the categories are fluid and some men could easily be placed in two or more, since ecclesiastical preferment entailed many serving as proctors in more than one capacity during a career and often in the same parliament.

---

[34]   Stanford E. Lehmberg, *The Reformation Parliament, 1529–1536* (Cambridge, 1970), pp. 6–7.
[35]   P. R. Cavill, 'A Perspective on the Church-State Confrontation of 1515: The Passage of 4 Henry VIII, c. 2', *Journal of Ecclesiastical History* 63 (2012), 655–70. On the wider theme of anticlericalism in parliament, see P. R. Cavill, 'Anticlericalism and the Early Tudor Parliament', in *Managing Tudor and Stuart Parliaments: Essays in Memory of Michael Graves*, ed. Chris R. Kyle, book issued as *Parliamentary History* 34.1 (2015), pp. 14–29.

THE PROCTORS

1. King's Clerks

'King's clerks' is a term which incorporates an amorphous group, from those holding permanent positions as clerks of the chancery, exchequer, privy seal or household, to those who fulfilled particular roles at given times or held occasional benefices at the king's gift. Such clerks were the most numerous of the proctors and the men most consistently used from Edward II's reign until the late 1440s when the SC 10 evidence fails. From about 1330 their presence among the proctors becomes more notable for several reasons: increasingly elaborate crown administration meant that the number of its clerical servants was growing; Edward III found them very useful as links to the provinces, and essential in many aspects of his war effort; some had established links with members of the lay aristocracy;[36] and their work in parliament was not diminished by the changes in geographical recruitment which followed Archbishop Scrope's execution in 1405. There is, however, a need for a note of caution before these men are discussed. Some of them, especially *magistri*, were not career civil servants but pursued 'portfolio careers' in which they moved into, and out of, crown service. These were especially valued on diplomatic missions and on specialised commissions of enquiry where their legal training made them useful. Furthermore, men of high status, including kings, would sometimes describe someone as 'our dear clerk' when the link between them was tenuous.[37]

Chancery Clerks

Chancery clerks represent by far the greatest number of appointments in SC 10 as a whole, even if their importance diminished during the fifteenth century and had disappeared by the sixteenth. Men such as Thomas Evesham (114 appointments, 1313–41), John Rome (75, 1381–1414), John Frank (62, 1386–1442), Robert Farrington (53, 1376–1404) and Peter Barton (53, 1363–97) feature repeatedly in letters of appointment across the course of several decades each. Although there was exchequer involvement in the early days, from the 1330s it was clerks of the chancery who provided parliament's administrators, so it is not surprising that so many were chosen as the clergy's representatives.[38] Some proctors are known to have held such positions as clerk of parliament, under-clerk, or receivers of petitions. Ironically, chancery clerks are less easy to identify than are exchequer clerks, whose wages appear on the issue rolls, so it is likely that more chancery clerks were

---

[36] This was first pointed out by Wilkinson, *Chancery under Edward III.*, pp. 178–9, and taken further by Charles W. Smith, 'A Conflict of Interest? Chancery Clerks in Private Service', in *People, Politics and Community in the Late Middle Ages*, ed. Joel Rosenthal and Colin Richmond (Gloucester, 1987), pp. 176–91.

[37] For the difficulty of interpreting this phrase see A. Hamilton Thompson, 'The College of St. Mary Magdalene, Bridgnorth', in *Archaeological Journal* 84 (2nd series 34) (1927), p. 28.

[38] Three articles by A. F. Pollard give details of this: 'The Clerical Organization of Parliament' and 'The Clerk of the Crown,' *English Historical Review* 57 (1942), 31–58 and 312–33; and 'The Mediaeval Under-Clerks of Parliament', *Bulletin of the Institute of Historical Research* 16 (1938–9), 65–87.

proctors than have been identified. Many individuals are described only as 'king's clerk', usually when presented to an ecclesiastical benefice, and some of these were probably chancery clerks. It is also clear, from detailed study of one successful individual, that leading chancery clerks were really the heads of small businesses, employing others who were not paid directly by the crown but who were essentially king's clerks at one remove.[39] Such men might later move into direct and more readily identifiable crown employment. Richard Tretton and Thomas Haxey were two proctors whose careers illustrate this.[40] Despite the difficulty in identifying those of lesser rank, it is chancery clerks who have received most attention from scholars.[41]

Chancery clerks can be found as proctors between 1306, with the appointment of Hugh Normanton by Bishop Dalderby of Lincoln (1/15), and 1447, when Thomas Kirkby was one of the abbot of Ramsey's proctors (50/2478).[42] Numerous chancery clerks were appointed in the intervening years, and as has already been noted, some of them received a large number of proctorial appointments.[43]

Though the numbers are smaller from the fifteenth century, the concentration of commissions in the hands of chancery mandarins continued. Simon Gaunstead, with thirty-two appointments from 1393 to 1423, was employed by an exceptionally wide range of men: the abbots of Battle, Ramsey, St Albans, and St Mary's, York; the deans and chapters (either together or separately) of Lincoln, London and York; the archbishop of York; and the bishops of Durham, Lincoln and Winchester. By contrast, John Rotherham's twenty-four commissions from 1390 to April 1414 were nearly all from houses in Lincolnshire and Cambridgeshire. John Wakering, like Gaunstead, had wide contacts; by the time he received the last of his seventeen commissions, from Bishop Edmund Stafford of Exeter on

---

[39] Alison McHardy, 'John Scarle: Ambition and Politics in the Late Medieval Church', in *Image, Text and Church, 1380–1600: Essays for Margaret Aston*, ed. Linda Clark, Maureen Jurkowski and Colin Richmond (Toronto, 2009), pp. 68–93, esp. p. 85; T. F. Tout, *Chapters in the Administrative History of Mediaeval England*, 6 vols. (Manchester, 1920–33), V, pp. 78–80.

[40] Richard Tretton, acting twelve times for Peterborough between 1362 and 1386, had once been a household clerk of Robert de Thorp (chancellor 1371–2), before moving into direct crown service. Thomas Haxey was a clerk of John Waltham (keeper of the privy seal), but later that year became keeper of the rolls and writs of common pleas, a post in which he succeeded Tretton: Tout, *Chapters*, IV, p. 19n.; *CPR 1381–86*, p. 226; *CPR 1385–89*, p. 314.

[41] Studies are found in Tout, *Chapters*; Wilkinson, *Chancery under Edward III*; Malcolm Richardson, *The Medieval Chancery under Henry V*, List and Index Society, Special Series 30 (1999); Smith, 'Conflict of Interest?'; Charles W. Smith, 'Some Trends in the English Royal Chancery: 1377–1483', *Medieval Prosopography*, VI (1985), 69–94; Douglas Biggs, 'The Appellant and the clerk: the assault on Richard II's friends in government, 1387–9', in *The Reign of Richard II*, ed. Gwilym Dodd (Stroud, 2000), pp. 57–70.

[42] This was the last year in which Kirkby was clerk of parliament; he was appointed in 1438. He was keeper of the rolls 1447–61, and lived until at least 1476: Richardson, *Medieval Chancery*, p. 117.

[43] Several long-serving clerks, each working for forty years and more, have been identified: Nicholas Wymbyssh, who entered in 1394 and who was working almost to his death in 1461, is the longest-serving, but others among the proctors include John Bate (1421–69), John Frank (1388–1438, although it is possible that there are actually two different men of this name who overlapped), John Hartlepool (1388–1429) and Henry Shelford (1388–1439). See also Smith, 'Some Trends', esp. 71, 87.

7 March 1416 (45/2231), this talented administrator and fervent Lancastrian had already been elected bishop of Norwich.[44]

Not surprisingly, some men received multiple appointments to one parliament. John Rome had nine in 1404, while Thomas Kirkby and William Prestwick had five apiece in 1439. Prestwick also had eight in 1432 and Kirkby had seven in 1442. Not only were clerks of parliament and receivers of petitions obvious and popular choices throughout the fourteenth and fifteenth centuries,[45] but the variety of king's clerks lessened during the fifteenth century, and chancery men, always in the majority, became even more predominant from the 1420s. Yet despite the many commissions which some received, they should not be viewed as professional proctors but as crown servants who undertook additional private services, such as giving advice and support to some of the king's subjects, especially members of the lay aristocracy and major religious houses. Acting as parliamentary proctor was just another strand of their diverse business.

Other King's Clerks

Chancery clerks, with their links to parliament's administration, were the pre-eminent and obvious proctors among the king's clerks, but were by no means the only ones. The most unusual example was Nicholas Colnet, Henry V's physician, whose commissions came from the prior and chapter of Worcester in 1414 (44/2191 and 45/2216). The prior concerned was John Fordham (1409–38) a contemporary of Colnet's at Oxford.[46] Nicholas Colnet was greatly valued by Henry V; he was a beneficiary of the king's will of 1415, and went on the Agincourt campaign.[47] Another unlikely proctor was William Brewster, whose career was in the administration of the royal kitchen from 1425. The year 1442, when he received his two commissions from Thorney (50/2435) and Ramsey (50/2456), was perhaps the high point of his ecclesiastical career, when he added a prebend in St Paul's to those he already held in Chichester and Lincoln. Adam de Chesterfield, appointed in 1376 (31/1524), was for twenty years (1355–75) controller of works at the Tower of London and the palace of Westminster.

---

[44]   His first commission was in 1402 (41/2002); see also the entry by R. G. Davies in *ODNB*. Under Wakerying the Norwich bishop's register was much more clearly set-out, and his successors continued to use his innovations.

[45]   On particular clerks of parliament, see W. M. Ormrod, 'On – and Off – the Record: The Rolls of Parliament, 1337–1377', in *Parchment and People: Parliament in the Middle Ages*, ed. Linda Clark, book issued as *Parliamentary History* 23 (2004), 39–56; and Michael Hicks, 'King in Lords and Commons: Three Insights into Late Fifteenth Century Parliaments, 1461–85', in *People, Places and Perspectives: Essays on Later Medieval & Early Tudor England in Honour of Ralph A. Griffiths*, ed. Keith Dockray and Peter Fleming (Stroud, 2005), pp. 131–53 on John Faukes. Hicks' discussion demonstrates why clerks of parliament might be attractive choices as proctors, not least the access they had to the king while parliament was in session. See also the relevant biographies in *HoP* for the period 1386–1421.

[46]   A. B. Emden, *A Biographical Register of the University of Oxford to A.D. 1500*, 3 vols. (Oxford, 1957–9), I, p. 469 and II, p. 705.

[47]   C. H. Talbot and E. A. Hammond, *The Medical Practitioners in Medieval England: A Biographical Register* (London, 1965), pp. 220–2; Alison K. McHardy, 'Religion, Court Culture and Propaganda: The Chapel Royal in the Reign of Henry V', in *Henry V*, ed. Dodd, pp. 131–56, esp. pp. 133 and 135 n.29.

Every other department of government is represented among the proctors, for they included men who were, or who would become, or who had been, clerks of the wardrobe and household, such as William Gunthorpe (who later moved to the exchequer), Robert Baldock, John Carp, Thomas Clopton, Robert Cottingham, Thomas Cross, Nicholas Hungate, William Kilsby, and Roger Waltham, all named before October 1377, and John Sleaford standing as a later example. Exchequer examples are balanced between those before Richard II's reign (Willliam Brocklesby, Henry Greystoke, John Hildesley, John Houton, Robert Sadington and Robert Wyclif), and those who became proctors later (Arnold Brocas, Richard Chesterfield, John Findern, John Legburn, Richard Pirton, William Ward and Roger Winter). These served as exchequer clerks, as opposed to exchequer barons, whose careers were often in other courts or departments (and were very often laymen); William Ward was one example of a man who moved from being an exchequer clerk (remembrancer) to exchequer baron, while Adam Harvington was unusual because he served in the exchequer of Ireland, between 1324 and 1330.

Administrative developments, and a rise in the department's prestige, perhaps resulted in more privy seal clerks occurring during the later period, but they are not easily identified. Even John Winwick, who crowned a distinguished career in that department with five years as keeper of the privy seal (1355–60), is never identified by department in any of his eleven proxy appointments between 1344 and 1358, but instead as 'canon of Wells', 'canon of Lichfield', or 'treasurer of York', depending on who made the appointment. Later privy seal clerks included Thomas Field, Richard Prentys, Henry Ware and John Wellingborough, one of three men of that name who were privy seal clerks.[48] The later period also saw the rise of the post of king's secretary, five of whose holders are found among the proctors, though only William Pilton was described as such (in 43/2140), with others not actually holding the office when named. John Stone was described as 'secretary' (42/2208); John Stopyndon as 'keeper of the rolls' (50/2455); Thomas Langley twice as 'keeper of the privy seal' (41/2012 and 42/2088) and once as 'archdeacon of Norfolk' (when chosen by the bishop of Norwich in 42/2090); while Richard Andrew was given no description in the letter appointing him (50/2477).

Administrators from the central law courts were occasionally chosen, among them Hugh Aston, clerk of common pleas (26/1297), and Robert Foxton, chirographer of the court of king's bench (4/189 and 10/496). There were also four who at one time held the post of keeper of the writs and rolls in common pleas: Peter Luddington, Richard Tretton, William Sandford and Thomas Haxey. This brief survey indicates that king's clerks of every kind may be found among the personnel of SC 10. However, any such analysis is somewhat artificial because some men, especially the more successful, moved from one department to another and held multiple portfolios.

Notaries

A group which falls into no one category was the small number described as notaries. At least one was William Fakenham, whose appointers identified him as

---

[48] Tout, *Chapters*, V, pp. 70, 72 n., 76, 81, 89, 93, 98, 101–5, 112.

such (28/1380, 29/1402 and 30/1456), and as a clerk of the bishop of Durham. At the time (1362 and 1363), the bishop was Thomas Hatfield, whose register is incomplete and damaged. By contrast, John Giffard, whose two appointments were for parliaments in 1328 (12/227, 12/590 and 12/600), was a canon of York and a choice of colleagues in the chapter, and was also in crown employment.[49] So too was William Ferriby the younger, a loyal servant of Richard II.[50] On the two occasions when Ferriby the younger was chosen he was acting for William Ferriby the elder, archdeacon of Cleveland (29/1426 and 31/1508). Notaries were also to be found among chancery clerks, though they cannot usually be identified from the SC 10 material; John Braintree is a notable example, while John Thoresby, archbishop of York and an appointer of proctors, had been a notary in his earlier career.[51]

King's Clerks: General Observations

One striking fact to emerge from this general survey of king's clerks is that some of the most frequently named proctors had extremely wide geographical links, with connections stretching over county, diocesan and provincial boundaries. However, their reach was not ubiquitous; there was not so much a north-south divide as an east-west one, for on the evidence of SC 10, their presence was less evident in Exeter, Carlisle, Hereford and Wales. This may perhaps be accounted for in the value of the endowments which funded the prebends which so many held, which made certain of them more desirable; those in York, Lincoln and Salisbury, and to a lesser extent Lichfield and London, were much richer than those of Exeter, Hereford and the Welsh cathedrals.

Acting as a parliamentary proctor sometimes ran in families. The three Stratfords, Henry, John and Robert, were kinsmen. The Thoresby-Ravenser-Waltham clan formed an outstandingly successful kinship group.[52] The Chesterfields were part of a civil service family.[53] Examples could be multiplied, though with so much royal recruitment centred on the north-east midlands and Yorkshire in the fourteenth century, apparent kinsmen may simply have been neighbours. Names can sometimes be misleading, as John Islip, steward of Thorney Abbey, came from Islip in Northamptonshire, while Simon Islip, the future archbishop of Canterbury, came from Islip in Oxfordshire. An interesting puzzle is posed by the leading chancery clerk and frequent proctor John Rome, and Thomas Rome, a monk of Durham. Thomas Rome's duties included being present at the trial of the Lollard Richard Wyche at Auckland Castle in about 1401.[54] His very varied tasks and

[49]   Tout, *Chapters*, III, p. 34 n.2; V, pp. 276, 285.
[50]   Chris Given-Wilson, *Chronicles of the Revolution 1397–1400* (Manchester, 1993), pp. 50, 228; David R. Carlson, 'Letters of Richard II (1397–8) in the authorship of William Ferriby', *Historical Research* 87 (2014), 574–80.
[51]   Pierre Chaplais, 'Master John de Branketre and the Office of Notary in Chancery, 1355–1375', *Journal of the Society of Archivists* 4 (1971), 169–99, reprinted in Pierre Chaplais, *Essays in Medieval Diplomacy and Administration* (London, 1981), chapter XXII.
[52]   For their family connections see Tout, *Chapters*, III, pp. 215–16.
[53]   Tout, *Chapters*, III, p. 215 n.1; V, p. 105.
[54]   Emden, *Biographical Register*, III, pp. 1587–8; Anne Hudson, 'Which Wyche? The Framing of the Lollard Heretic and/or Saint', in *Texts and the Repression of Medieval Heresy*, ed.

constant travelling took him all over the north-east of England, and to Oxford, London, Pisa and Rome. As the house's proctor he went to parliament and convocation, and was an envoy to the earls of Northumberland and Westmoreland, the archbishop of York, the royal court, and the Benedictine General Chapter. In over forty years he can have had little time for prayer and contemplation except when on a horse.[55] The coincidence of dates makes it likely that he was a kinsman, perhaps brother, of John Rome. Family ties among proctors were not restricted to clerks. The layman Thomas Ingleby was the brother of Henry Ingleby, a privy seal clerk and recipient of seven commissions between 1337 and 1358. Among laymen, Robert and William Babthorpe were described in their commission as brothers (43/2145). Ralph Babthorpe is likely to have been a kinsman. Albin and Thomas Enderby were father and son.

Most of the king's clerk proctors, like the others, were doubtless paid in cash, whether as occasional payments or as regular fees for business and legal advice. They might also receive payments in kind. A few, though, had sufficiently permanent connections (with abbeys at least) to be granted a living in the house's gift, though for benefices they were competing with others who gave advice and support to such patrons.[56] There is scope for further work in this area, but some pointers may be offered here. Ramsey Abbey's rectory of Over (Cambridgeshire) was granted to several men who were also the abbey's proctors. These included Thomas Potterspury (17/814), who was presented to the rectory during the first year when he is known to have been a king's clerk,[57] and Robert Muskham, whose eighteen commissions between 1366 and 1385 were not all from Ramsey.[58] Abingdon, Bury St Edmunds, Glastonbury and Peterborough were other abbeys whose proctors received livings in the house's gift.[59] The greatest source of patronage was, of course, the crown, and kings' clerks were ideally placed to take advantage of this bounty.

It is rarely possible to add human interest to these accounts of civil service careers, but Adam Horsley's life is an exception. This exchequer clerk was controller of the great or pipe roll from 1375 to 1382, and foreign apposer of the exchequer from 1382 to 1385.[60] He was rector of St John the Baptist, Stamford, from 1369, seems never to have intended to serve his cure in person, and in 1377 was described as 'not resident' in the clerical poll tax assessment, a label unique in the arch-

---

Caterine Bruschi and Peter Biller (York, 2003), pp. 221–37; Anne Hudson, 'Wyclif and the North: the evidence from Durham', in *Life and Thought in the Northern Church c. 1100–c. 1700: Essays in Honour of Claire Cross*, ed. Diana Wood, Studies in Church History subsidia 12 (1999), pp. 87–102.

[55] He entered religion in 1383 and died in 1425. See Emden, *Biographical Register*, III, pp. 1587–8; and the biography by A. J. Piper in *The Durham Liber Vitae*, ed. David and Lynda Rollason (London, 2007), III, pp. 302–4.

[56] 'Clerks had at least seven major sources of generating income', of which Richardson identified benefices as the first: Richardson, 'Chancery', pp. 38–49, esp. pp 39–42.

[57] A. K. McHardy, 'Some Patterns of Ecclesiastical Patronage in the Later Middle Ages', in *Studies in Clergy and Ministry in Medieval England*, ed. David M. Smith (York, 1991), pp. 20–37, esp. pp. 26–7 and nn. 33 and 34.

[58] Tout, *Chapters*, III, p.361. The first and last appointments were from St. Albans.

[59] McHardy, 'Some Patterns of Patronage', pp. 20–37, esp. pp. 22–8.

[60] Apposers were auditors of the sheriffs' accounts. The post was abolished in 1833.

deaconries of Lincoln, Leicester and Stow. Yet behind this career was a soul in torment, and during the 1380s Horsley corresponded with the Augustinian canon Walter Hilton, who acted as his spiritual counsellor. In March 1385 Adam Horsley resigned his rectory and left crown employment. In or after 1386 he became a Carthusian and entered the Charterhouse of Beauvale in Nottinghamshire, where he was said to have lived 'praiseworthily' (*laudabiliter*), an accolade very sparingly bestowed.[61] This would explain why Horsley's appointment as a proctor, for the abbot of Peterborough in 1383 (35/1713), was not repeated.

2. Bishops

Although they frequently appointed proctors to represent them, bishops themselves received relatively few proxy appointments. The first extant appointment of a bishop as a proctor is found in 1314, when the bishop of Llandaff named the bishop of Bangor as one of his proctors for an assembly at York (3/129). From then until 1442, just thirty-two bishops received proxy appointments in the surviving documents, of which nineteen appear only once.[62] However, not all of these episcopal proctors were novices in this regard; around a third of the thirty-two had acted as proctors before being elevated to the episcopate. Nicholas Bubwith, for example, was a proctor only once during his episcopate, when – as bishop of Bath and Wells – he was one of four bishops named by the bishop of Rochester in 1411 (44/2176). However, prior to his consecration as bishop of London in September 1406, he had had an active career as chancery clerk, ecclesiastic and royal official, and between January 1401 and February 1406 he received sixteen proxy appointments, roles such as king's secretary and keeper of the privy seal presumably making him an attractive choice. One of Henry IV's earlier secretaries, Thomas Langley, was named as proctor six times while bishop of Durham, but prior to his consecration in 1406 he had already been given seven proxies as another man busy in royal and ecclesiastical service. Bubwith and Langley were amongst the ecclesiastical favourites of Henry IV, part of a group of men whose elevation to the episcopate the king actively sought, even at the risk of conflict with the papacy; as such, they were politically safe options as proctors.[63] It might not be coincidental, for example, that Bubwith made his sole appearance as a proctor for the chapter of York Minster in the parliament of 1406 (43/2102), with one of his two fellow proctors being John Prophet, another of Henry's secretaries for whom the king tried (and failed) to obtain a bishopric.[64] In the aftermath of Archbishop Scrope's rebellion and execution,[65] with the loyalty of York in question, it would

[61]   Joy M. Russell Smith, 'Walter Hilton and a Tract in Defence of the Veneration of Images', *Dominican Studies* 7 (1954), pp. 180–214; A. K. McHardy, 'Superior Spirituality *versus* Popular Piety in Late-Medieval England', in *Elite and Popular Religion*, ed. Kate Cooper and Jeremy Gregory, Studies in Church History 42 (2006), pp. 89–98, esp. 91–5.

[62]   1442 is the last date on which a bishop appears as a proctor in SC 10 before the series fails in 1447. As Appendix 4 shows, bishops continued to be used as proctors after this date, and by the Tudor period their appearance in this role was common.

[63]   On Henry IV's episcopal appointments, see Richard G. Davies, 'After the Execution of Archbishop Scrope: Henry IV, the Papacy and the English Episcopate, 1405–8', *Bulletin of the John Rylands Library* 56 (1977), 40–74; and Given-Wilson, *Henry IV*, pp. 354–60.

[64]   Given-Wilson, *Henry IV*, p. 359.

[65]   See the various articles in *Richard Scrope: Archbishop, Rebel, Martyr*, ed. P. J. P. Goldberg

be understandable that the city's cathedral chapter might opt to be represented by two clerics from the king's circle whose loyalty to Henry was unquestioned. The keeper of the spiritualities of York, *sede vacante*, also opted judiciously for Bubwith and Prophet, along with the chancery clerk John Rome (43/2127).

Yet if several episcopal proctors were named to the role with proctorial experience predating their consecrations, it remains true that bishops are infrequently named in extant letters appointing proctors. Just fifteen bishops are recorded as proctors in the fourteenth century, with none known before 1314 or from the 1320s, 1340s, 1350s, 1360s or 1390s. In the fourteenth century, only bishops named other bishops as their proxies, and even then it was very unusual. With the exception of Simon Meopham's unusual appointment of low-ranking clerks in March and October 1330 (13/640 and 13/649), on the rare occasions that archbishops of Canterbury named proctors they tended to opt for a selection of other bishops; thus Walter Reynolds in 1319 (6/282, two bishops), Simon Meopham in 1333 (17/830, four bishops) and Simon Sudbury in 1371 (30/1452 and 30/1453, three bishops). Just once did an archbishop of Canterbury receive a proxy from another bishop, when Simon Islip was named by John Grandisson, bishop of Exeter, in 1362 (28/1392), while there is no record of an archbishop of York being appointed. After Adam Houghton of St Davids twice named John Gilbert of Hereford as his proctor, in 1384 and 1388 (35/1730 and 37/1810), there were then no surviving appointments in which bishops received a proxy until 1410. In the fourteenth century, it was thus largely the archbishops of Canterbury – whose absences from parliament were in any case atypical, given the significance of the position – who made use of his suffragans to serve as proctors. Otherwise, bishops appointed proctors but did not customarily receive the proxies of others.

After 1410, under Henry V and Henry VI, it became more common for bishops to be named as proctors. The numbers were still not large, especially considering that in Henry V's reign notably more proctors were being named in many letters of appointment, but there is a discernible increase. Whereas on the surviving evidence no fourteenth-century bishop was selected as a proctor more than twice, in the first half of the fifteenth-century several members of the episcopate received a handful of appointments each.[66] Benedict Nicolls (Bangor, 1408–17 and St Davids, 1417–33) was named a proctor on ten occasions between 1416 and 1432, eight of which appointments came from his Welsh neighbour Robert Lancaster, bishop of St Asaph. Nicolls does not seem to have been a proctor prior to becoming a bishop, yet was an assiduous attender of parliament, commendable given that both of his dioceses were about as far from Westminster as was possible. This tends to suggest that he was heavily involved in government affairs, or perhaps not especially interested in his dioceses. Thomas Langley (Durham, 1406–37) received four of his six proxies in the period 1411–23 from Henry Bowet, archbishop of York, although his prior proctorial service while dean of York and chancellor has already been noted. John Stafford (Bath and Wells, 1425–43 and Canterbury, 1443–52) and Philip Morgan (Worcester, 1419–26 and Ely, 1426–35) were both named five times each in the period 1425–32, although both had been in royal service and

(Donington, 2007); and W. Mark Ormrod, 'The Rebellion of Archbishop Scrope and the Tradition of Opposition to Taxation', in *Henry IV: Rebellion and Survival*, ed. Dodd and Biggs, pp. 162–79.

[66] For the careers of the men discussed in this paragraph, see Appendix 7.

had also served as proctors prior to their consecrations. Henry Beaufort (Lincoln, 1398–1405 and Winchester, 1405–47) was appointed four times by Henry Bowet of York between 1419 and 1423, while William Barrow (Bangor, 1418–23 and Carlisle, 1423–9) was likewise named four times (all alongside Benedict Nicolls) by Robert Lancaster of St Asaph in 1419–22. A few bishops were named on single occasions, but the six fifteenth-century bishops who received several proxy appointments mainly seem to have had significant careers prior to joining the episcopate and were all involved (to some degree) in royal service. All were additionally diligent in attending parliament.[67] Thus although bishops remained unusual choices as proctors in the fifteenth century, those who had a background in royal service and were active parliamentary bishops were viewed as appropriate choices by at least some of their colleagues who were less keen or able to undertake their responsibilities in parliament.

Given that the pool from which proctors could be chosen had shrunk to members of the House of Lords by the time surviving proxy records resume in 1510, it is not surprising that Tudor bishops were called on more frequently, and not merely by their episcopal colleagues. The early years of Henry VIII's reign saw a variety of bishops employed in proctorial service. In 1510, the bishops of Bangor and St Davids were named by their colleague at St Asaph, while the bishops of Durham and Ely were named by abbots.[68] 1512 saw four bishops (Coventry and Lichfield, Durham, Llandaff and Winchester) receive appointments from a mixture of bishops, abbots and lay lords.[69] Six bishops (Durham, Lincoln, London, Norwich, Winchester and York) were appointed proxies in February 1515, but only Richard Fox of Winchester (representing Lord Audley) was chosen from the episcopal bench in the November session of the same year.[70] Only two appointments survive from 1523: the bishop of Salisbury named his colleagues from Exeter and Winchester (50/2479), while the abbot of Peterborough selected the bishops of Ely, Lincoln and Norwich (50/2480). During the Reformation Parliament, however, few bishops were chosen as proctors. John Salcot (*alias* Capon), who had been elected abbot of St Benet of Hulme through the influence of Thomas Wolsey and found royal favour by siding with Henry VIII over the question of his divorce from Catherine of Aragon, served as proctor in several sessions of this parliament in his successive roles as abbot of St Benet's, abbot of Hyde near Winchester, and bishop of Bangor.[71] As a regular attender of parliament, in favour with the king, he would have made a logical choice. Otherwise, however, only a handful of bishops make very occasional appearances in the proxy lists prior to the dissolution of the monasteries.

---

[67]   See the tables in Richard G. Davies, 'The Attendance of the Episcopate in English Parliaments, 1376–1461', *Proceedings of the American Philosophical Society* 129 (1985), pp. 79–81.

[68]   *Journal of the House of Lords*, vol. 1, pp. 3–4.

[69]   *Journal of the House of Lords*, vol. 1, pp. 11–12.

[70]   *Journal of the House of Lords*, vol. 1, pp. 19–25, 44.

[71]   Salcot was believed by contemporaries to have owed his appointment to Bangor to the influence of Anne Boleyn, or at least the Boleyn faction: Eric Ives, *The Life and Death of Anne Boleyn* (Oxford, 2005), p. 261. He seems to have been motivated by a concern to retain the favour of the governing regime rather than by any deep religious principle, since he willingly accepted the various changes of Henry VIII's and Edward VI's reign, but then (as bishop of Salisbury) reverted to Roman Catholicism under Mary. His career is summarised in the article by Angelo J. Louisa in the *ODNB*.

From 1539, bishops almost exclusively chose their episcopal colleagues when appointing proxies, and from 1626 they were required to do so.[72] In the Middle Ages, however, a much wider group of people could be used as proxies, and the numerous official duties which encumbered many bishops in parliament – such as acting as triers of petitions or serving as chancellor or one of the other officers of state – presumably made them unappealing choices compared to chancery clerks, monks and officials whom those appointing proctors would know more intimately and could entrust with their interests. Even in the early Tudor period, abbots and secular peers could be chosen as well as bishops. It was thus not until circumstances compelled the bishops to choose only from their colleagues on the bench, after the end of the evidence in SC 10, that bishops began to feature consistently as parliamentary proctors.

3. Abbots

If bishops were a rarity as proctors in the medieval parliament, abbots were almost non-existent. As was discussed in the Introduction to Volume 1, the heads of religious houses easily account for most extant proxy appointments in SC 10, but they do not themselves seem to have been used as proctors. The appointment of an abbot as a proctor in surviving records from the Middle Ages is exceptional: John Sherburn of Selby was named by Archbishop Alexander Neville of York in 1382 and 1383 (34/1690 and 34/1684), and William de Bradley of Winchcombe was nominated by Bishop Thomas Peverel of Worcester in 1410 (44/2162). It is notable that in both cases these abbots were nominated by their diocesan bishops. Otherwise, even though there is clear evidence that a small minority of abbots (especially the abbot of Westminster) did attend parliament, at least occasionally, their almost complete absence from the list of proctors suggests that they were simply not considered suitable for the role. As will be discussed below, abbots tended to prefer to send their own monks or people about whom they had some personal knowledge. The abbots did not form a coherent group and there was little need for an abbot to know the heads of other houses, and in any case the often conflicting interests of various foundations meant that it is unlikely many abbots would have entrusted their proxy to a colleague.

By the Tudor period, abbots had abandoned (or been forced to abandon) the use of monks, chancery clerks and local officials. In the earlier years of Henry VIII, they could choose bishops and secular peers, but after 1515 they became increasingly dependent on other abbots. Forced to rely on colleagues about whom they knew little or nothing, there is something almost comical about some of their appointments. On 5 April 1532, the abbot of Glastonbury appointed the abbot of Colchester as one of his two proctors without naming him, presumably unaware that Thomas Barton had died eleven days earlier and not yet been replaced (51/2510). The sender of 50/2489 is sadly illegible, but on 24 November 1529 his letter proceeded to name 'John, bishop of London' (the bishop was actually Cuthbert Tunstall) as the first of his three proctors, then leaving a large gap for the name of the abbot of Waltham, presumably in the futile hope that someone might find out his identity before the letter was sent. The abbot of St Mary's, York, clearly did not know the name of his colleague at St Benet of Hulme in 1533,

[72] *Journal of the House of Lords*, vol. 3, p. 507.

with another space for a name being left unfilled (51/2512), while the abbot of Bardney was similarly unaware of the identity of the abbot of Waltham in 1536 (51/2518). For the same parliament, the abbot of Ramsey simply gave up and left a large space in which no proctors were entered (51/2522).[73] A year later, the abbot of Evesham appointed the abbot of Peterborough, presumably unaware that his proctor had himself elected to be absent from parliament and named his own proctors.[74] Clearly some information was filtering back to the abbots from parliament, enough for them to know which abbots were receiving proxies and being active, but it was then a case of appointing these people in complete ignorance of who they were and what they might do.

This notwithstanding, there does appear to have been a small group of 'parliamentary' abbots in the early sixteenth century, who were frequently deployed as proctors. In February 1515, John Islip of Westminster and Richard Kidderminster of Winchcombe collected four proxies apiece, while in the November 1515 session only one of the nine men appointing proctors did not name either Islip or Kidderminster.[75] These were clearly known to be active lords spiritual, with unusual evidence existing of Kidderminster's political activity in his vocal opposition to attempts to restrict benefit of clergy in 1515.[76] Islip was also named in the Reformation Parliament sessions of 1529, 1531, January 1532 and April 1532. John Salcot (*alias* Capon) was a popular choice as abbot of St Benet of Hulme and then Hyde near Winchester; he continued as abbot of Hyde after his consecration as bishop of Bangor in 1534, and continued to hold the two posts until Hyde Abbey was dissolved and he was translated to Salisbury in 1539. His successor at St Benet's and the future bishop of Norwich, William Repp (*alias* Rugg) was another common selection in the mid-1530s. In January 1534, among their other appointments, Salcot and Repp were appointed as a pair by several abbots.[77]

For more than two centuries, most abbots seem to have avoided attending parliament whenever they could, with only the odd exception appearing on the list of triers of petitions.[78] This is not to say that they were politically inactive, since there is evidence of them being used in royal service for the wider church; for example, Thomas Spofforth, abbot of St Mary's, York, was one of the English delegates at the Council of Pisa in 1409. However, personal attendance at parliament was not something with which abbots generally concerned themselves. Through necessity, their attendance record improved in the sixteenth century, although it was still not outstanding. Yet when it came to the dissolution of the monasteries, the abbots – having been promised suitable inducements for their own futures – suddenly found

---

[73]   1536 is the only parliament for which SC 10 letters can be compared against enrolled entries, since a fragment of the journal for this assembly has survived in a manuscript now in the British Library. The enrolled list reflects these omissions in the original letters: British Library Harley MS 158, ff. 144–144*v*. The list is calendared in Appendix 3.

[74]   *Journal of the House of Lords*, vol. 1, p. 58.

[75]   *Journal of the House of Lords*, vol. 1, pp. 19, 43.

[76]   Cavill, 'Perspective on the Church-State Confrontation of 1515', p. 656.

[77]   *Journal of the House of Lords*, vol. 1, p. 58.

[78]   Although see Martin Heale, *The Abbots and Priors of Late Medieval and Reformation England* (Oxford, 2016), pp. 212–18, where it is argued that the heads of religious houses developed a renewed enthusiasm for public service from the 1450s (something which we cannot trace in SC 10 as the evidence is lacking for this period.)

the energy to attend parliament to vote themselves out of existence. Seventeen abbots are marked as present on the list for the first day of parliament in 1539,[79] a high attendance rate which continued throughout the parliament. Only two abbots were registered as absent in the proxy lists, one of whom was the recalcitrant Richard Whiting of Glastonbury, later to be executed.[80] Notably, the only two other abbots to be executed – Thomas Marshall (*alias* Beche) of St John's, Colchester and Hugh Cook of Reading – were present for most of the session, including for the readings of the bill to suppress the monasteries. On 28 June, 1539, sixteen abbots were present as parliament was prorogued,[81] after which, their jobs and parliamentary status having been abolished, they departed for the final time. After centuries of evading parliamentary duties, the abbots finally appeared in force only in order to forever relieve themselves of the need for attendance.

4. Monks

The first named proctor in SC 10, Brother Philip of Cirencester in a letter probably dating from 1248 (1/2), was a monk, and more than 300 monks were subsequently named by their abbots, cathedral priors or cathedral chapters to act as their parliamentary proctors in the period up to 1447. As with other categories, most of these monks – more than 250 – are only found once or twice in the surviving documents, but a handful of men were named on several occasions. Monks would never be numerous in the medieval parliament, but the evidence of SC 10 suggests that there was at least a handful in most assemblies, since many abbots would appoint one monk (and on rare instances more) to represent them.

The priors and chapters of monastic cathedrals also used their fellow-monks as proctors, but to a much lesser extent. Evidently cathedral communities, even if regulars, had much greater links with the outside world – secular clerks and laymen – than did rural abbeys.[82] Only around forty of the extant names of monks appointed as proctors come from this source. Nevertheless, SC 10 provides evidence for monks being appointed by the priors of nine of these ten cathedrals, while other evidence demonstrates that the exception – Canterbury Cathedral – also made use of monks.[83] There are only a few isolated examples from Bath, Carlisle, Norwich, Rochester and Winchester, but during the fourteenth century the priors and chapters of Coventry, Durham, Ely and Worcester used some of their monks regularly (if infrequently). Roger Wentbridge (Coventry, 1362–79) received six appointments covering five parliaments, otherwise there is no evidence for any cathedral monk being named to more than three parliaments (although as the prior and chapter sometimes appointed the same people separately, some feature in more than three surviving letters). It was clearly less important to cathedral

---

[79] *Journal of the House of Lords*, vol. 1, p. 104.

[80] *Journal of the House of Lords*, vol. 1, p. 103.

[81] *Journal of the House of Lords*, vol. 1, p. 125.

[82] For the context, see Joan Greatrex, *The English Benedictine Cathedral Priories: Rule and Practice, c. 1270–c. 1420* (Oxford, 2011).

[83] Although there are no letters from Canterbury Cathedral in SC 10, the register of the prior (preserved in Cambridge University Library) shows that numerous appointments, many involving monks of the cathedral, were made by the prior and chapter. See the tables in J. H. Denton and J. P. Dooley, *Representatives of the Lower Clergy in Parliament, 1295–1340* (London, 1987), pp. 103–21.

priors and chapters than it was to abbots to have their interests represented by a fellow-monk.

The reasons for sending a monastic subordinate are not hard to discern. Economy was one of them. For example, when the abbot of Peterborough sent a messenger bearing his excuses for failure to attend the Coventry parliament of 1404, the man (a lay servant) took two horses. When monks journeyed away on business they usually took two, three or four horses; when the abbot went travelling he took twenty-two.[84] Youth and fitness might be another qualification. John Berton was a proctor for the chapter of Norwich cathedral priory in 1324 (9/432), over twenty years before his next occurrence in records of the house.[85] His colleague John Clippesby was similarly youthful, being only recently out of Oxford where he had been a student from around 1317 to 1322 or 1323. This was not Clippesby's first time as a parliamentary proctor, for he was one of two so acting in July 1321.[86] Nicholas Enford was a very junior man when appointed by the chapter of Worcester in 1325, the year in which he was forty-fifth in order of seniority in the house (10/487).[87] William Halloughton was only eight years into his monastic career on his first appointment by the prior of Coventry in 1411 (44/2174). Economy and geographical usefulness were occasionally combined, as in 1402 when the abbot of St Mary's, York included among his proctors William Dalton, 'the prior of our cell of Rumburgh, our fellow-monk' (41/2018). Rumburgh, in Norfolk, was more convenient for Westminster than York. When William Appleby was a proctor for Durham in October 1404 (42/2078), he was warden of Durham College, Oxford, having been appointed the previous August.[88]

Into the 1330s, it was common for an abbot or prior to appoint a monk as their solitary parliamentary proctor. Although it became less frequent thereafter, the practice continued throughout the medieval period, and there were some heads of religious houses – such as Abbots Thomas Pethy (Hyde near Winchester, 1362–80) and Thomas Prestbury (Shrewsbury, 1399–1426) – who continued to show a slight preference for sending lone monks to parliament. The last recorded instance of a monk being entrusted with a sole proxy is in 1439, when the prior of Bath named William Salford to represent him (49/2436). Considerably less common was sending only monks when more than one proctor was appointed; there are several examples of pairs of monks being entrusted with proxies, although most date from the late thirteenth or early fourteenth century and the last recorded instance was in 1354, when Thomas de la Mare of St Albans sent two of his monks to parliament in his stead (26/1281). There are even instances of three monks receiving a proxy, although usually alongside a chancery clerk or similar outsider, as in 1404 when the prior and chapter of Durham Cathedral named three of their monks alongside the chancery clerk John Rome (42/2078).

---

[84] *Account Rolls of the Obedientiaries of Peterborough*, ed. Joan Greatrex, Northamptonshire Record Society 33 (1984), pp. 129–30, 171. The abbot's journey was to the installation of Philip Repingdon as bishop of Lincoln in 1405.

[85] In 1345–6 and 1348–9: Joan Greatrex, *Biographical Register of the English Cathedral Priories of the Province of Canterbury c. 1066–1540* (Oxford, 1997), p. 483.

[86] Greatrex, *Biographical Register*, p. 496.

[87] Greatrex, *Biographical Register*, p. 689.

[88] *Durham Liber Vitae*, III, p. 299.

Several abbots had particular monks whom they appointed repeatedly. Thomas Bury of Peterborough was sent by his abbot, Henry of Overton, to be his proctor on fourteen consecutive occasions between 1372 and 1388. Richard Hethersett of St Albans was employed by Richard of Wallingford for eleven of the abbot's fourteen appointments (1328–34). At the same house later in the century Thomas de la Mare used his monk (and in later years, prior) John Mote six times in a row (1354–72), followed by another of his monks, Robert Chestan, for at least eleven of his remaining sixteen appointments (1373–95).[89] John Grantham (Crowland, 1376–85) was nine times named as his abbots' proctor, while John Greatford (Ramsey, 1330–40), John Horkesley (St John's, Colchester, 1390–1432), Ralph Thurlaston (Leicester, 1335–44) and Richard Appleton (St Mary's, York, 1372–80) received eight proxies apiece from the heads of their houses.

A few monks very probably gained advancement through their parliamentary service, or at least their service marked them as candidates for advancement. Some who were employed as proxies by their abbot(s) would themselves later be appointed to head their house. Geoffrey Gaddesby was used a total of twelve times by John Wistow II and John Heslington before assuming the abbacy of Selby in 1342. On each of these occasions, Gaddesby was named alongside the chancery clerk (and clerk of parliament) Thomas Brayton,[90] although on one occasion Brayton and Gaddesby served with another monk of the abbey, Richard Athelmaslet (18/890). Alan Kirkton of Thorney was also named on twelve occasions by Thomas Charwelton between 1404 and 1425, before he succeeded Charwelton as abbot in 1426. (Charwelton himself had been sent to parliament on four occasions by his predecessor but one, John Deeping, in the period 1385–90.) Kirkton was typically the last named of two or (more usually) three proctors, following one or two clerks. John Tintern was employed by William of Badminton in 1313 before being used as one of Adam de la Hok's proctors in nine of his thirteen extant appointments, before his own elevation to the abbacy of Malmesbury in 1330. Five of these appointments were alongside the chancery clerk Thomas Evesham. One of Tintern's successors at Malmesbury, Walter Camme, used Thomas Chelsworth as his first-named proctor for his last seven appointments, before Chelsworth assumed the abbacy following Camme's death in 1396. Around a dozen other men also became abbot of their house, or prior of a monastic cathedral, having held at least one appointment by a predecessor as a parliamentary proctor. In one unusual case, a future abbot represented a different house to the one on whose behalf he would later appoint his own proxies: Walter of Winforton, a monk of Worcester Cathedral who three times represented the chapter, was then elevated to the abbacy of Winchcombe.

It is noteworthy that once they had become abbots, these men themselves often became frequent appointer of proctors, and it is plausible that the role of parliamentary proctor may have been seen as a comparatively low-status assignment, perhaps less prestigious than convocation.[91] It should be remembered, however,

[89] 36/1799 is damaged and at least one name has been lost, so it is possible that Chestan was also named in this letter.

[90] On Brayton's role in parliament, see Ormrod, 'On – and Off – the Record', 39–56. The village of Brayton is around a mile south-west of Selby, which makes it likely that Thomas was a native of the area and used by the abbots of Selby for that reason.

[91] In 1433–4 the bailiff of Peterborough (Thomas Wydeville) and Ralph Joliff, who was

that monks used as proctors were typically younger than those appointing them, and long journeys were thus presumably less of a trial for them. A monk could also travel more economically than an abbot or prior with the accompanying retinue. Whether experience in parliament would later pave the way to an individual's smoother elevation to an abbacy is an intriguing possibility which cannot be tested.

On the other hand, attending parliament was evidently just one of the jobs which able, energetic, and fit monks were commissioned to do. Accounting at the exchequer for tax money when their abbot had been appointed a collector was another task which brought some monks into contact with government. John Bedford, monk of Ramsey and proctor in 1379 and 1380 (33/1609 and 33/1633) later accounted at the exchequer for taxation collected by his abbot in 1384 and 1386,[92] while John Hainton, monk of Bardney, accounted at the exchequer for taxation in 1377,[93] and then acted as proctor in 1380 and 1384 (33/1650 and 35/1727). Abbots of Benedictine houses were called to chapter meetings of the order's English province, and were also reluctant attenders at those gatherings. So the Durham monks John Butterwick (c. 1338), William Appleby (1405) and Thomas Rome (1411 and 1417) represented their priors at provincial chapters, with the Peterborough monks Walter Friskney (1414, 1423, 1429 and 1444), Richard Harlton (1414, 1417 and 1426) and Thomas Fannell (1417) also acting for their abbot.[94]

Where their lives can be traced these monk-proctors performed a variety of roles both within their houses and outside. Emeric Lumley, whose career probably began in the thirteenth century, was guest master and sacristan at Durham, and spent many years between 1326 and 1344 as master of Jarrow.[95] William of Masham, whose Durham career was essentially in farming, apparently died in the course of his parliamentary duties: appointed to parliament in April 1357, he died in the south of England before late August.[96] Among Worcester monks Robert Weston, whose life as a religious began in 1323 and continued until at least 1362, was a regular traveller; in addition to his five appointments to parliament (1340–52), there was one to convocation (1342), and journeys on business to London, Leicester, and Bath.[97] Walter of Winforton, a monk of Worcester from 1339, was cellarer (1353–5, 1356–8 and 1359–61), but interspersed these years with periods of constant travel on the prior's behalf. His appointment as abbot of Winchcombe in 1360 may have been a relief after so many journeys.[98] At Durham John Butterwick, who was born shortly after 1275, held various positions in the house, from registrar (1319), to chancellor (1321), to prior's official (1322) and librarian (1323). From 1329,

next in rank among the abbey's lay administrators, went to parliament in London: *Account Rolls of the Peterborough Obedientiaries*, p. 171. Joliff, but not Wydeville, was a parliamentary proctor: British Library Add. MS. 25288, ff. 128, 139, 142, 143v, 145. In some dioceses (such as Rochester and Winchester) the care with which affairs of convocation were entered in the bishops' registers is notable.

92   TNA E 359/15, mm. 10, 17.
93   TNA E 359/15, m. 6.
94   *Documents Illustrating the Activities of the General and Provincial Chapters of the English Black Monks 1215–1540*, ed. W. A. Pantin, vol. III, Camden Third Series 54 (1937), pp. 210, 212, 214.
95   *Durham Liber Vitae*, III, p. 226.
96   *Durham Liber Vitae*, III, pp.258–9.
97   Greatrex, *Biographical Register*, pp. 891–2.
98   Greatrex, *Biographical Register*, p. 899.

when he first became almoner, a post he held intermittently until 1345, his life was one of almost constant travel and included attending the Benedictine general chapter at Northampton and convocation at York in 1338, as well as numerous journeys to Durham properties, mainly in Yorkshire.[99] In later generations William Appleby (entered religion *c.* 1373, died. *c.* 5 April 1409) and Thomas Rome (monk 1381, died between June 1424 and May 1425) also led lives which combined posts at Durham with regular travelling. The difference between them and earlier parliamentary proctors for Durham Cathedral was that both were wardens of the house's college at Oxford (Appleby in 1404–9 and Rome in 1409–18).[100]

From the later fourteenth century, and more prominently in the fifteenth century, monks were most typically named as one of a group of proctors. As already noted, the number of proctors each sender named began to increase, and like others, abbots appointed a wide range of people to ensure that their interests were properly represented. Consequently, monks were named alongside chancery clerks and layman as just one element in a group of proctors. It was in Henry IV's reign that the proportion of monks among the proctors declined sharply, though probably as a result of social and ecclesiastical changes rather than for political reasons.[101] Yet if their importance was reduced, it is significant that abbots and priors continued to make use of members of their houses, presumably as men who could be fully trusted with the interests of the monastery or cathedral. With the failure of the evidence, it is unclear at exactly what stage monks ceased to be a part of parliament, but for at least two centuries they were an omnipresent – and frequently overlooked – feature of the assembly.

4. Canons, Cathedral Clergy, Archdeacons, Secular Clergy and Ecclesiastical Officials

It may seem somewhat strange to link the canons of secular cathedrals, archdeacons and other secular clergy together in one group. However, pluralism was common in the medieval church and there is often considerable overlap amongst the men who held these offices. It was not impossible, for example, for the same man to be a rector of a benefice, a non-residentiary canon of a cathedral, and an archdeacon, as well as a chancery or other type of royal clerk. The proxy letters themselves can sometimes disguise this, since they usually only give the proctor one of their titles. Yet in some cases this information incidentally enhances knowledge of the career of a particular cleric, pushing back the known date of his appointment, or supplies the name of a previously unknown dean, canon or archdeacon.[102] Although not a unified group, many of the proctors found in this category share important traits and remind us that for all the diversity of titles they bear in the appointments, the most important source of proctors was the royal chancery or other government departments.

---

[99] *Durham Liber Vitae*, III, pp. 231–3.

[100] *Durham Liber Vitae*, III, pp. 302–4.

[101] McHardy, 'Henry IV: The Clergy in Parliament', p. 143.

[102] For example, 10/489 teaches us that the dean of Bangor in 1325 was Madoc ap Nova, while C 219/5/17/3 supplies the otherwise unknown names of an archdeacon and a canon of Bangor.

Cathedral Canons

Many of the letters of appointment explicitly describe proctors as canons of one
(or more) of the secular cathedrals. However, in most cases, this did not denote a
direct relationship between the proctor and the cathedral (or other church) named,
since the men so identified were non-resident canons.[103] For the most part, these
canonries were sinecures, conferring ecclesiastical status on men whose more significant role was that of chancery clerk or other government official. The richest
prebends tended to be held by such men, especially at York Minster, since a significant number of royal clerks were Yorkshiremen during the fourteenth century.[104]
For example, it is likely that being a Yorkshireman caused John St Pol to receive a
canonry at York and be used as a proctor by their chapter, but with one exception
he is named as 'canon of York' only in letters of appointment by the chapter of
York Minster.[105] He was simultaneously a canon of Exeter Cathedral (although it is
only the bishop of Exeter who used that title in appointing St Pol), which indicates
that it was as (a very senior) chancery clerk that St Pol was first and foremost attractive as a proctor.

Stating that he was a canon of a secular cathedral (or that he held another prebend) may thus have provided a link between the cathedral or diocese concerned
and the man they had named as a proctor. It is notable, however, that it was generally a chancery clerk or other royal official who was a non-resident canon who was
chosen, rather than a residentiary canon who had no national prominence. Geog-
raphy could be a factor in places other than York; for example, Thomas Capen-
hurst, a canon of St Asaph hailing from neighbouring Cheshire,[106] was employed
exclusively by the dioceses of St Asaph and Bangor, largely by bishops. Yet it seems
that these 'native sons' were adopted only once they had acquired status within
the chancery or royal administration which made them worth cultivating. Some
letters specifically mention that the proctor was a canon of more than one place;
men such as Richard Haversham and John Carlton, for example, are occasionally
designated 'canon of Wells and Llandaff'.

One interesting man falling into this category is the chronicler Adam Usk,
named as a proctor seven times between 1416 and 1423. With the exception of one
appointment by the abbot of Cirencester (45/2235), all of these were by Bishop
Robert Lancaster of St Asaph, and all six of his letters refer to Usk as a canon of
St Asaph.[107] All but one (46/2287) also mention his legal qualifications, although
46/2272 calls him a 'bachelor of both laws' instead of 'doctor of laws', as found
correctly in the remaining four documents. It is likely that it was this expertise
which led to Usk's appointment, but it is notable that only Lancaster of the Welsh
bishops seems inclined to have made use of it. By this stage, Usk was an ageing
man who can have had no hope of ecclesiastical preferment, given his colour-
ful history of collusion with the Avignon papacy and Welsh rebels in the hope

---

[103]   On non-resident canons in the fourteenth century in particular, see Kathleen Edwards,
The English Secular Cathedral in the Middle Ages (Manchester, 1949), pp. 84–96.
[104]   A. Hamilton Thompson, 'The Medieval Chapter', in *York Minster Historical Tracts
627–1927* (London, 1927), pp. 12–15; Edwards, *English Secular Cathedral*, p. 86.
[105]   On St Pol's career, see Wilkinson, *Chancery under Edward III*, pp. 155–7.
[106]   Wilkinson, *Chancery under Edward III*, p. 164.
[107]   44/2247, 46/2260, 46/2272, 46/2287, 47/2310 and 47/2349.

of securing a bishopric.[108] Thus he was not a man whose proxy appointments demonstrate him ascending the ecclesiastical ladder, but neither was he a stranger to parliament. He had certainly been present in assemblies at the end of Richard II's reign and the start of Henry IV's, providing especially lengthy accounts in his chronicle of the parliaments of 1397–8 and 1401.[109] His chronicle also gives evidence for his earlier presence in convocation. It is thus a pity that by the time of his proxy appointments, Usk's chronicle is very sketchy, and of the assemblies in which he was named a proctor only the two of 1416 even merit very brief mention in his text, and his own presence (if he was indeed there) is passed over in silence.[110] Yet Usk's career, as someone whose promising rise had been frustrated and ended in a period of excommunication and outlawry, is a reminder that for certain proctors, such appointments (both canonries and proxies) could be signs of trust marking a return to respectability after time in the wilderness.

Although the majority of canons fall into the non-residential category whose main importance was their royal service, there are plenty of instances of members of the residentiary chapter being appointed as proctors. There are forty-four letters (accounting for forty-two proxy appointments, two being from the same source for the same assembly) in which the dean of one of the secular cathedrals is named as a proctor. There are also six instances on which the subdean of Lincoln was given a proxy appointment.[111] In most cases, especially in the earlier years covered by SC 10, deans were named by their diocesan bishops or their own chapters.[112] For the chapters, the value of having their dean (who was meant to be personally present in parliament in any case) as their representative are obvious. Likewise, a bishop who found the dean of his cathedral to be reliable and someone with whom he could work had a handy proctor who presumably would know at least something of diocesan affairs. Later, there are examples of bishops appointing the dean of a different cathedral, or of deans being named by abbots. In large part, deans chosen in this later manner were significant as royal clerks or in national governance in another capacity, men such as John Prophet or Thomas Langley. As proctors, cathedral deans were never numerous (especially once we discount men such as Prophet and Langley who were chosen more as royal servants than as deans), and even when present in their own right seem to have made little impact

---

[108] Chris Given-Wilson provides a detailed summary of Usk's life in the introduction to his Oxford Medieval Texts edition of the chronicle: *The Chronicle of Adam Usk 1377–1421*, ed. and trans. C. Given-Wilson (Oxford, 1997), pp. xiv–xxxviii, with the Avignon flirtation covered on pp. xxix–xxxiii.

[109] *Chronicle of Adam Usk*, pp. 20–40 and 120–6. For discussion of the source used by Usk in addition to his own experience for the first of these assemblies, see C. Given-Wilson, 'Adam Usk, the Monk of Evesham and the Parliament of 1397–8', *Historical Research* 66 (1993), 329–35.

[110] *Chronicle of Adam Usk*, pp. 262–5. Usk deals with the second of the 1416 parliaments under 1417, a dating error addressed by Given-Wilson on p. 265, n. 5.

[111] These appointments were by the bishop of Lincoln in 1316 (4/196); by the dean and chapter of Lincoln in 1410 (44/2154); by the 'president' and chapter of Lincoln Cathedral in 1414 and 1416 (45/2228 and 45/2246); and by Hugh Hanworth, archdeacon of Stow, in 1414 and 1416 (45/2223 and 45/2243).

[112] Intriguingly, in 1407 the chapter of York specifically noted that they were making the proxy appointments in the absence of the dean (John Prophet), before continuing to appoint him as one of their proctors (43/2135).

on the records of parliament in the middle ages. Slightly over fifty letters name the
chancellor, precentor or treasurer of the cathedral, presumably men who could be
entrusted with representing the cathedral's interests.

Archdeacons

A similar pattern can be discerned among archdeacons. A little under two hundred extant letters include an archdeacon among the named proctors, but in many
cases these were also royal clerks of some form. Offices were held in plurality, so
that it is not uncommon to find the same man simultaneously holding an archdeaconry and one or more canonries, yet for only one of these titles to be used
in the proxy appointment. In many cases, archdeacons were appointed primarily
as royal clerks of some form and would receive appointments from more than
one source. To take the parliament of 1373 as an example, five archdeacons are
known to have received proxy appointments. John Blaunchard of Worcester was
the proxy for three men or institutions within the diocese of Worcester: the prior
and chapter of Worcester Cathedral, acting separately, and the abbot of Evesham
(30/1483, 30/1491 and 31/1507). However, he was also named by the bishop of
Salisbury, who additionally appointed Roger Clun, archdeacon of Salisbury, to
represent him (30/1486). The bishop of Norwich named William Swinefleet, the
archdeacon of Norwich, as one of his proctors (30/1487), while the chapter of
York Minster chose Archdeacons Humphrey Charlton (Richmond) and Richard
Ravenser (Lincoln) amongst their representatives (30/1489). It is notable that these
last two were additionally identified as canons of York. This small sample demonstrates the overlap of local and national interests; Clun was certainly a royal
clerk and Ravenser had a significant career in the chancery and royal household.
Nepotism and collegiality also had a place in the choice of archdeacons. In 1316,
Bishop Gilbert Segrave of London appointed Stephen Segrave, archdeacon of
Essex (in London diocese) and presumably a kinsman, as his sole proctor (4/182
and 5/225). Familial ties are similarly likely between Thomas of Nassington, prior
of Spalding, and his proctor of the same name, archdeacon of Exeter, in 1337
(20/1000). John Freton, archdeacon of Norfolk, served in 1377 as the proctor of
Roger Freton, dean of Chichester (31/1538).

Since an archdeaconry was also often a sinecure or a step on the career ladder
for a cleric, we should not be surprised to see that it was their role as royal clerk
that was often more important, which accounts for such instances as the abbot of
Winchcombe naming the archdeacon of Colchester as a proctor (35/1705), or the
bishop of Coventry and Lichfield selecting the archdeacon of Dorset (42/2094).
However, it is important not to overlook the geographical links which were significant in other cases, especially in the large diocese of Lincoln and in Wales. In 1423,
the subdean and chapter of Lincoln Cathedral appointed three diocesan archdeacons – Oxford, Stow and Bedford – amongst their four proctors (48/2354). Not all
archdeacons were royal clerks, and some of those found in SC 10 as proctors are so
obscure that even their dates of office are not known for certain. It is true that these
local links were probably an important factor in the choice of some archdeacons
to act as proctors. The Welsh dioceses quite often used one of their archdeacons
to represent them, and several abbots would occasionally appoint their local archdeacon as a proctor. It is worth remembering that as archdeacons were meant

to be personally present in parliament, they would be an obvious choice when considering proctors, especially in cases where they had local allegiances to the individual or institution nominating them.

Other Benefice Holders

In the course of the fourteenth century, over 250 appointments designate the rector of a benefice as a proctor, with twenty-five men named as vicars of some form in the letters. There is a notable change in the fifteenth century, when those termed 'rectors' account for fewer than thirty appointments, and just one vicar is explicitly chosen. There was some overlap with those discussed previously in this section, since chancery clerks could hold benefices in plurality with their cathedral canonries and other offices, but only the most important office (or the one most relevant to the appointer) tends to be listed in the letters of appointment. There are several examples of bishops appointing royal clerks under the title of a benefice held in their diocese. Where there is no evidence of outside interests, it seems that in general those rectors chosen as proctors held local benefices. In the first half of the fourteenth century, from which the majority of these appointments date, rectors were chosen most often in the diocese of Carlisle, Durham, St Davids, Worcester and York, although there are plenty of examples from elsewhere. Although not significant on a national scale (and perhaps not even on a local one), these men are a reminder of the variety of clergy who served as proctors in medieval parliaments.

Ecclesiastical Officials and Clerical Lawyers

In the fourteenth century, a small group of men were chosen as proctors because of their place within the household of the bishop of abbot appointing them. The practice became less common as the century progressed and extremely rare by the fifteenth century. Men specifically designated as the official, steward, chancellor, chamberlain or some other post in episcopal or abbatial households were never more than a tiny handful of the proctors available in any single parliament, but they do not generally fit into any of the ecclesiastical categories previously discussed. It seems natural that a bishop or abbot may on occasion wish to have a trusted member of his household to represent him, although there is little discernible pattern in those appointments which do survive.

A number of proctors are specifically recorded as doctors of civil or canon law (or both laws). As these qualifications are not always recorded, it is probable that more ecclesiastical lawyers are found among the proctors than the evidence now suggests, but to our knowledge they were never a large group in parliament. Some had other roles, such as an archdeaconry, which more readily explain their appointment. Once again, the number of clerical lawyers declines over the period, with almost none explicitly designated as such in the fifteenth century. The increasing number of secular lawyers being used, as well as the turn towards a greater number of more varied proctors amidst the nervousness over the change of regime in 1399, can to some extent explain the decline of both officials and clerical lawyers. Even under the first three Edwards, few had anything amounting to a parliamentary career, and we can only speculate about their occasional appearance as proctors.

6. Laymen

Although extremely rare in the early period covered by SC 10, the use of laymen as proctors grows more frequent as we move through the series. It is important to note that laymen are not always as easily identifiable as one might think. Anyone not described as 'dominus' or 'magister', might well be a person who was not in orders, but only one man in the whole series is precisely and explicitly described as 'layman'.[113] Early in the fourteenth century an individual could have an ecclesiastical career and be classed as the clerk in episcopal service, yet later serve the crown as a justice in one of the central courts, a role which soon came to be undertaken exclusively by laymen. Such was Thomas Hepscott (9/422 and 9/423), prebendary of Lanchester 1318, rector of Appleby 1325–31, rector of Morpeth 1331, and justice of the bishop of Durham 1334–9, who was also an advocate of the court of common pleas, of which he became a judge in 1341.[114] Sometimes on one occasion an individual would seem to be a layman, but on others, someone who is clearly the same man has the title 'clerk'. Thus Robert Aston, described as 'clerk' when chosen as one of the proctors for the abbot of Cirencester in 1315 (3/139), was not so described when he was again chosen in 1320 (7/303). Enquiry shows that a Robert Aston was the steward of the abbey's estates in 1321. Was this the same Robert Aston who was a justice of the peace and gangster in 1327, an MP for Gloucestershire in 1328, and a retainer of the earl of Lancaster in 1333?[115] A similar problem is posed by the name Robert Waryn. Brother Robert Waryn, monk of the house, was appointed by the abbot of Ramsey in 1373 (30/1499). Both earlier, in 1371, and later, in 1376, Robert Waryn, not described in any way, was also a Ramsey proctor (29/1451 and 31/1528). However, in 1377 and again in 1382, 'Robert Waryn, esquire' was a Ramsey proctor, and a Robert Waryn was proctor in 1379, 1380 and 1394 (33/1609, 33/1636 and 34/1929). All these commissions were from two successive abbots of Ramsey, Richard Shenington (1349–78) and Edmund Ellington (1378–96), and apparently refer to two individuals who cannot be easily disentangled. In 1407 the abbot of St Benet of Hulme named two deputies, one of them William Champneys (43/2132). Was this the life retainer of Henry IV, or a chancery clerk of the same name? Since the other proctor was a (married) chancery clerk, James Billingford, the latter alternative seems more likely. Confusingly, there were two Robert Gilberts, one a distinguished clerical diplomat and prolific pluralist who became bishop of London (44/2187, 44/2188, 45/2201A, 45/2228 and 45/2246), the other an MP for Gloucestershire eight times between 1415 and 1432, but who was only once a proctor (46/2253). This is a familiar problem. R. L. Storey was sometimes similarly perplexed when trying to decide the status of men in royal service during the first half of the fifteenth century, a time when the distinction between clerics and laymen was becoming increasingly blurred.[116]

---

[113]   John Deerhurst, appointed four times by the abbot of Winchcombe between 1391 and 1395: 37/1848, 38/1878, 38/1900 and 39/1942.

[114]   *Durham Liber Vitae*, III, p. 105; John Sainty, *The Judges of England 1272–1990*, Selden Society, supplementary series 10 (1993), p. 64 (as Heppescotes).

[115]   Nigel Saul, *Knights and Esquires: The Gloucestershire Gentry in the Fourteenth Century* (Oxford, 19198I), pp. 88, 153, 182, 275.

[116]   R. L. Storey, 'Gentleman-bureaucrats', in *Profession, Vocation and culture in Later Medieval England: Essays dedicated to the memory of A. R. Myers*, ed. Cecil H. Clough (Liverpool, 1982), pp. 110–29.

Laymen were present, albeit in small numbers, from the early fourteenth century. In 1307 Warin Martyn, knight, a professional soldier, was appointed a proctor by both the bishop of St Davids and by the archdeacon of St Davids. The fact that the bishop concerned was called David Martin perhaps indicates why this proctor was chosen, but Warin Martyn was also desirable because he was used to making long journeys. In 1298 he had been commissioned to array 2,500 Welsh foot soldiers to fight in the Scottish war, and five years later was pardoned for the 'homicides and other crimes' which his Welsh levies had committed while marching over England and Wales.[117] Another early example came in April 1319 when the coadjutors acting on behalf of the aged Bishop Dalderby of Lincoln commissioned a triumvirate of proctors, one of whom was Sir Simon Chamberlain, a past and future MP for Lincolnshire.[118]

During the rest of the fourteenth century the numbers and proportion of laymen increased, and in February 1371 came the first commission to laymen alone, to John Harling and George Felbridge by the abbot of St Benet of Hulme (29/1449), which will be discussed in greater detail shortly. This was exceptional, and all-lay appointments never became normal. From October 1380 the designation 'knight' can be found (33/1647, 33/1650 and 34/1652), which was applied, until 1414, to a miscellaneous group including members of the royal household, MPs and lawyers. Thereafter the title 'gentleman' was applied to the same sorts of men, doubtless as a result of the Statute of Additions of 1413.[119] Laymen were of many categories and classes: members of parliament, local gentry, merchants, lawyers, the administrators of ecclesiastical estates, tenants, courtiers, urban politicians and members of the lay peerage. These groups were not, of course, mutually exclusive. In particular, many members of parliament were evidently lawyers, and there was no division between their legal and parliamentary roles.

Estate Administrators, Lay Servants and Tenants

This is a somewhat elusive group, and perhaps included some employees of modest rank. In November 1322 Geoffrey Fromond, abbot of Glastonbury, chose William Seles as one of two proctors (9/417), but five years later his successor employed Seles on a different matter. Glastonbury was in dispute with the bishop of Bath and Wells over the maintenance and repair of a bridge at Wookey, Somerset, and the abbot was alleged to have employed ten named men, and others, to break the bishop's half of the bridge. Seles was among the miscreants, and his employment in such direct action, as well as his position well down the list of perpetrators, suggests that he was a comparatively lowly person.[120] John Islip (of Islip, Northamptonshire), who had three appointments from Thorney between 1324 and 1334, was bailiff of the abbey's estates.[121]

---

[117] *CPR 1292–1301*, p. 343; *CPR 1301–7*, p. 177.

[118] Lincolnshire Archives Office, Reg. 3 (John Dalderby, Memoranda), f. 416*v*.

[119] *Statutes of the Realm*, 11 vols. (London, 1810–28), vol. II, p. 171.

[120] Commission of *oyer and terminer* on this matter, 18 Sept. 1327: *CPR 1327–30*, p. 208.

[121] Sandra Raban, *Estates of Thorney and Crowland: A Study in Medieval Monastic Land Tenure*, University of Cambridge Department of Land Economy Occasional Paper 7 (1977), p. 45, n.8.

Estate managers were generally of a higher social ranking, and they form the earliest identifiable group of laymen, occurring from the 1320s. Robert Grantchester, 'our steward', represented the abbot of Crowland in February 1324 (9/426), and 'the prior's steward' acted for the prior of Spalding in 1332 (17/820). Few appointments included such helpful information, but we know that William Bradwell (7/343) was steward of the Winchcombe estates; Robert Aston (3/139 and 7/303) and Richard Urdeleigh (27/1311) were stewards of Cirencester's; Robert Palet (26/1277, 27/1302 and 28/1386) was steward of the abbey estates of St Peter's, Gloucester, as was Sir John Cassy (35/1733, 36/1762, 36/1792 and 37/1814); while William Cheltenham was steward of the bishop of Worcester's estates (20/983, 22/1059, 22/1091, 24/1151 and 25/1213).[122] Ironically, these proctors did not all represent the house which employed them. The bishop of Worcester's steward was the proctor for the abbot of Gloucester, while Cirencester's steward was a proctor for the abbot of Malmesbury. These were all found in one county, Gloucestershire, and it seems likely that some men so far unidentified served monastic, or episcopal, estates elsewhere. Monastic stewards had been rising in status since the early thirteenth century and during the fourteenth their posts became 'honourable and lucrative sinecures'.[123] Our proctorial stewards illustrate this well: Trehampton, Bradwell and Cheltenham were MPs, and Sir John Cassy's career was crowned with eleven years as chief baron of the exchequer.

Perhaps because their senior servants may have been considered too grand to act as proctors in parliament, one abbey certainly sent a second-rank lay employee to parliament. This was Ralph Jolyff, chosen by John de Deeping, abbot of Peterborough.[124] Jolyff was not the abbey's bailiff but was evidently an important and energetic servant. In 1414, when his wages were 10 shillings a term, he went at least twice to London, and also to France and Southampton.[125] Another Peterborough administrator was William Tresham, three times a proctor in the period 1427–32, and important in the house's administration, though probably of lower rank than Jolyff.[126] Some of the more obscure laymen were evidently monastic tenants. Among the Durham proctors Gilbert Elvet paid rent for a toft and twenty-one acres of land to Durham priory in 1396–7.[127] John Killinghall, proctor for Durham (either the prior and chapter, or the two parties acting separately) thirteen times throughout Richard II's reign, was probably another.[128] It is likely that other unidentified men could be connected to property owned by the religious house which sent them to parliament, and were either tenants or servants, or both.

---

[122] Saul, *Knights and Esquires*, p. 88.

[123] David Knowles, *The Religious Orders in England. Volume II: The End of the Middle Ages* (Cambridge, 1955), pp. 284–5.

[124] British Library, Add. MS. 25288, ff. 128, 139, 142v, 143v, 145m 147v, 156.

[125] *Account Rolls of the Obedientiaries of Peterborough*, pp. 148, 150, 152, 153.

[126] British Library, Add. MS. 25288, ff. 139, 143v, 145.

[127] In West Merrington in Auckland parish, county Durham: *Durham Cathedral Priory Rentals Volume I: Bursars' Rentals*, ed. R. A. Lomas and A. J. Piper, Surtees Society 198 (1989), p. 119.

[128] In 1396–7 a William Painter paid 10 shillings for the tenement 'formerly of John Killinghall' in Elvet, Durham: *Durham Cathedral Priory Rentals*, p. 119.

Members of Parliament

Almost by definition, most bishops were men with wide contacts who also had in their cathedral chapter a pool of 'persons duly qualified for the service of God in church and state'.[129] The focus of monastic outlook was usually much more local, and hence nearly all the proctorial MPs were chosen by parliamentary abbots. Appointing a man who was going to parliament as member for a borough or county constituency would seem not only economical but soundly practical, and many who appear in SC 10 can be identified as MPs. However, not all were elected representatives to the parliaments for which they were appointed as proctors. Some were future members, while others were past MPs, and in this way they extended their parliamentary careers. In such cases the economic advantage was less obvious, but their appointments reveal something of the local and normally hidden relations between lay politicians and clerics, especially the religious. Nor did MPs always represent the county in which the house lay. For example, William Bradwell was a member for Worcestershire in 1322 but also represented the abbot of Winchcombe in Gloucestershire (7/343). Starting in 1325 the abbots of Crowland in south Lincolnshire began a tradition of choosing MPs for Rutland and Northamptonshire to act on their behalf (10/485), which continued into the 1440s at least (50/2472). The earliest of these, Hasculf Whitewell, was in 1328 granted a fee of five marks a year for life, for his past and future service.[130] Over time the number of men with parliamentary connections who were chosen increased. During the years between 1307 and 1377 forty-four MPs appear, while in a similar seventy-year period, from 1377 to the end of the sequence in the mid-1440s, there were over sixty.

Local MPs were especially valued by heads of religious houses who were not summoned to parliament frequently. In 1322 the abbot of Buckland, a house otherwise absent from SC 10, chose Robert Chisbridge, one of his local Devon MPs (8/351). A decade later several West Country houses were represented, and chose local lay members; the priors of St Germans and Bodmin, for example, both named as their sole proctor John Billoun, an experienced MP, though he did not sit for a lay constituency that year (15/750 and 16/764).[131] Reasons of economy probably explain the local members who were commissioned by clergy, of all ranks and kinds, of Carlisle diocese, though interestingly, most were chosen in the first half of our period. There were six between 1324 and January 1377, but none thereafter.

Some men were more notable in local politics than as MPs. Such was Sir John Pulteney, a wealthy merchant who had four times been mayor of London (1331, 1332, 1334 and 1337), as well as representing the city at royal councils in 1328 and 1345. Sir John was named proctor in 1340 (23/1111), just as he started to build his great hall at Penshurt Place, Kent.[132] William Wygge, modestly described as 'citizen of Winchester' in his appointment of 1404 (42/2064), had once been MP for the city, but more notably was its mayor five times, dying in office in 1413.

---

[129] This phrase is part of the bidding prayer to be used by a preacher before a sermon, which is today Canon B19 of the Church of England.

[130] E. D. Jones, 'The Church and "Bastard Feudalism": The Case of Crowland Abbey from the 1320s to the 1350s', *Journal of Religious History* 10 (1978–9), 142–50, esp. p. 145.

[131] For discussion of the unusual circumstances of 1332, see volume I of this work, pp. xli–xlii.

[132] Anthony Emery, *Greater Medieval Houses of England and Wales, 1300–1500. Volume III: Southern England* (Cambridge, 2006), pp. 386–94.

County Officials and Other Local Commissiaries

Appointment as representatives of the clergy enabled some men to attend parliament who otherwise could not have done so. Sheriffs and escheators were
understandable choices. Richard Foxcote, who was appointed by the abbot of
Hailes in 1315 (3/142), would later become sheriff of Gloucestershire. Thomas
Faversham (9/409) was keeper of the Cinque Ports in the early 1330s, while John
Brune was a deputy sheriff of Worcestershire in 1335 (6/288). Stephen Donet,
acting for St Augustine's, Canterbury in 1332 (16/791) was one man who received
local commissions but rose no higher. Four men, Richard Albert of Yaxley, John
Stukeley, Nicholas Styuecle and John de Harrowden, were commissioners to keep
the Statute of Labourers of 1355.[133] All were associated with East Anglian houses,
while Harrowden and Styuecle held county posts. Edward Acton was proctor
for the abbot of Shrewsbury in 1386 (36/1784) and sheriff of Shropshire in the
1380s, but did not rise to become an MP. The Lincolnshire family of Enderby was
unusual in providing proctors from a non-parliamentary base. Albin Enderby was
the recipient of numerous local commissions and had links with both Crowland
and Bardney, being a proctor for those houses between 1385 and 1402. Twice (in
1393 and 1394) he acted for both abbots. In 1402 a proctorial colleague was his
son Thomas (the only father and son appointed together in the extant records),
and the younger Enderby continued the family tradition. In 1404 he represented
both houses, and in 1406 and 1410 Crowland alone. Thomas was a parliamentary
elector of Lincolnshire in 1411 and was probably a lawyer.[134]

Courtiers

Whereas most laymen had a local connection to the men appointing them, a small
group were notable for their links to central authority. Not many proctors could
be described as 'courtiers', but they merit a mention, and there is one especially
notable case from Norfolk. In the parliament of 1371, and again in 1372, the abbot
of St Benet of Hulme appointed two men whose source of power was the court in
the later days of Edward III, when it was heavily criticised for its corruption. The
choice of two laymen would by itself make their appointment noteworthy at this
stage, but John Harling and George Felbridge were also unusual in being newcom-
ers to Norfolk county society. This unpleasant pair, 'hardly less notorious' than
the king's mistress Alice Perrers, had acquired a collection of lucrative positions
in East Anglia, and now found a way into parliament as clerical proctors.[135] It is
hard to believe that their parliamentary appointment was anything but the result
of their political power, though to what extent they intimidated the abbot cannot
be known. The abbot in question, William Methwold, then appointed Harling
on three more occasions in Edward's reign, once acting alone and twice with

---

[133]   *CPR 1354–58*, pp. 294–6; *Calendar of Fine Rolls 1353–60*, pp. 270, 341. A Nicholas Styuecle
was a proctor on thirteen occasions between 1352 and 1376, although it is possible that the
appointments are of two different men, father and son.

[134]   Alan Rogers, 'Parliamentary Electors in Lincolnshire in the Fifteenth Century',
Lincolnshire History and Archaeology 3 (1968), pp. 37–8.

[135]   Their careers are noted in W. Mark Ormrod, *Edward III* (New Haven, CT, 2011),
p. 535, which is also the source of the quotation.

John Holkham, a justice of the peace in Norfolk. Harling continued to be used in Richard II's reign, twice more with Felbridge, making his last appearance as Methwold's proctor in November 1381. On this final occasion, Harling was appointed jointly with the chancery clerk and archdeacon of Norfolk, John Freton. For the next parliament, in October 1382, Freton appears alone, as he does again in 1384 before Methwold employed another chancery clerk, James Billingford, from 1385. It is of interest that between the 1381 and 1382 parliaments, St Benet's Abbey had been a key location in an attempted rising in Norfolk. The house had already been besieged twice during the Peasants' Revolt in 1381, on one occasion because it was assumed that Bishop Despenser of Norwich was inside.[136] In the autumn of 1382, the conspirators saw the abbey as a suitable stronghold in the event of their rebellion being successful.[137] How far St Benet's had become a target because it had become entangled with unpopular courtiers is hard to determine, but it seems that the abbey became ensnared in the murky world of Norfolk politics in the 1370s, acting as the platform for two unsavoury characters to find a place in parliament. Whether the events of 1381–2 persuaded – or permitted – Abbot Methwold to free himself of the influence of troublesome courtiers is an open question, but since Harling's decade as a proctor for the abbey came to an end at this point, it is not implausible. It is a highly unusual case, but it does show how the proxy system was open to manipulation for wider political ends.

Thomas Saville, twice a choice of the prior of Coventry (38/1890 and 39/1924), was certainly associated with the monarch, being one of a group of four men who slept outside Richard II's chamber from 1378–9 until the end of the reign.[138] Another Coventry choice, in 1402, was Ralph Rochford (41/2026) who occurred as a chamber knight in 1402–3 and 1405–6. There seems no local connection, as Rochford was a Lincolnshire man, who was appointed chief steward and master forester of the Isle of Axholme in 1405, commissioner of the peace in Kesteven in 1411, and commissioner of array in Holland in 1436.[139] His colleague, John Littlebury, sheriff of Lincolnshire in 1398–9 and a chamber knight in 1401, represented Crowland in 1406 (43/2114). Littlebury was a survivor, for he was closely linked to Richard II and his more abrasive servants in the last years of the reign, yet by 1408 was clearly deep in Henry IV's confidence.[140] Two members of the Babthorpe family, Robert – a king's esquire – and his brother William, were proctors for Selby in 1410 (43/2146). Described as 'gentlemen', the same two served in 1414 (45/2214). A William Babthorpe also served Selby in 1417 and Ramsey in 1429 (46/2278), while William Babthorpe, clerk, was a Selby choice in 1439 (49/2444). Finally, Ralph Babthorpe (proctor for Selby in 1447, 50/2476) served both Henry V and Henry VI, being a king's esquire by January 1433 when he was granted the keeping of Scarborough castle (worth £20 a year) for good service, and continuing until at least June 1437.[141] He combined this with posts in East Yorkshire, such

---

[136] TNA KB 9/166/1, mm. 44*v*, 97 and 103.

[137] For the events of September 1382 in Norfolk, see Herbert Eiden, 'Norfolk, 1382: A Sequel to the Peasant's Revolt', *English Historical Review* 114 (1999), 370–7.

[138] Chris Given-Wilson, *The Royal Household and the King's Affinity: Service, Politics and Finance in England 1360–1413* (New Haven, CT, 1986), p. 54.

[139] *CPR 1405–08*, p. 18; *CPR 1408–13*, p. 482; *CPR 1429–31*, p. 521.

[140] Given-Wilson, *Royal Household*, pp. 195–6, 249.

[141] *CPR 1429–36*, p. 251; *CPR 1436–41*, p. 63.

as commissioner of banks and ditches (1433 and 1435), steward of the forest of Galtres (1437), and keeper of the peace (1437–41), ending as a commissioner of array in 1446.[142] A Ralph Babthorpe was a squire of the household in 1451–2 and was one of those expelled from court following a parliamentary petition in 1451;[143] this was perhaps his son. Though this sample is small the impression gained is that men linked to the court were chosen in times of political uncertainly, especially later in our period.

Although not, strictly speaking, courtiers, one sub-group of proctors calls for mention: past or present servants of the house of Lancaster. Twenty-seven have been identified among the proctors in SC 10. Most were laymen, although five clerks can be found in their number. Fourteen were not MPs,[144] but thirteen were.[145] Only one began as a proctor in the fourteenth century, Thomas Skelton.[146] Two were proctors under Henry VI: Robert Andrew and Roger Flore.[147] All the others appear in Henry IV's reign, and the first three years of Henry V. Even though these men were not technically courtiers, their political connections were surely significant.

Lawyers

Lawyers of every rank are represented among the proctors. At one level we have men who were described as 'skilled in law' (*iuris peritus*). Among these were John Percy for the archdeacon of Cleveland in January 1377 (31/1550), Richard Yanworth for the abbot Cirencester in October 1377 (32/1567), William Bryan for the bishop of Coventry and Lichfield in November 1384 (35/1724), and Thomas Hornby and William Cheney acting for the abbot of Hyde near Winchester in January 1404 (41/2047). We can often deduce why these men were chosen. Percy, an otherwise obscure man, was probably a northerner, as was Ferriby, a king's clerk. Yanworth was an employee (*menour*) of the abbot of Cirencester, and was a far from spotless character.[148] The link between lawyers and locality is discernible from Edward II's reign; Roger Hillary, a rising star of the legal profession, whose family had property in Warwickshire and Staffordshire, was appointed by the prior of Coventry in 1342 (10/451).[149] His links to the abbot of Ramsey,

---

[142]   *CPR 1429–36*, pp. 280, 524; *CPR 1436–41*, pp. 63, 593; *CPR 1446–52*, p. 238.

[143]   Ralph A. Griffiths, *The Reign of King Henry VI* (London, 1981), p. 326.

[144]   Robert Babthorpe, Nicholas Bradshaw, Roger Dokwra, Thomas Hornby, John Kyme, John Morpeth, John Springthorpe, John Stanley (senior), John Thoralby, Thomas Tickhill, Robert Tirwhite, Thomas Wace, John Wakering and John Woodhouse.

[145]   Robert Andrew, Roger Flore, Robert Gilbert, John Grevell, Roger Leche, William Newport, John Pelham, Peter de la Pole, Thomas Rempston, Thomas Rokeby, John Russell, Thomas Skelton and John Thornbury.

[146]   Chief steward of the southern and Welsh parts of the duchy of Lancaster *c.* 1393–1405, *HoP 1386–1421*, vol. 4, p. 380. Skelton was untypical of the group in every way, someone who acquired links to the duchy through one of his several advantageous marriages.

[147]   Andrew was steward of the duchy of Lancaster estates in Berkshire, Dorset, Hampshire, Oxfordshire, Somerset and Wiltshire, 1415–37: *HoP*, vol. 2, p. 35. Flore was steward of the northern parts of the duchy of Lancaster, 1416–27, and chief steward of the duchy estates in Lancashire and Cheshire, 1417–25.

[148]   Saul, *Knights and Esquires*, pp. 185–6.

[149]   See the entry by J. S. Bothwell in *ODNB*.

from whom he had a proxy appointment two years earlier – in which he was described as 'clerk' – are less clear (9/403). Illard Ousefleet, who occurred as a serjeant at law from 1354 to 1366, was appointed by the abbot of Selby four times between 1352 and 1362.[150] Ousefleet, on the south bank of the Ouse, is some fifteen miles from Selby, and in an area where the house had extensive properties. Robert Charlton hailed from Wiltshire, from a village close to Malmesbury, whose abbey he represented eight times between 1370 and 1384, and where he evidently had a kinsman, William, among the monks (named in 34/1694). His links spread outwards so that he received commissions from other West Country abbots: Gloucester, Cirencester (where the abbot in 1320–35 was a Richard Charlton) and Winchcombe. His successful judicial career also brought him links to Westminster and St Albans.[151]

The first appointment of only lawyers was made by the abbot of St Peter's, Gloucester, to Robert Charlton and John Cassy in November 1384, with the second to the same two in October 1385 (35/1733 and 36/1762). Charlton was then a serjeant at law and Cassy evidently a rising lawyer; they were both members of the commissions of the peace and *oyer* and *terminer* in Gloucestershire in 1382.[152] In the next two commissions from the same abbot, September 1386 and January 1388, the two judges were joined by William Horbury, clerk (36/1792 and 37/1814). Doubtless the reason for these unusual commissions was the dispute between Gloucester Abbey and Vale Royal Abbey in Cheshire over the church of St Padarn in Llanbadarn Fawr, Cardiganshire. This can be traced from the early 1380s and came before the king's council in 1387, when the chancery clerk William Horbury was described as the abbot of Gloucester's attorney,[153] and before both parliaments of 1388 as the subject of petitions. The abbot of Gloucester could be described as a good judge of character, since Robert Charlton was appointed chief justice of Common Pleas in the first parliament of 1388, and John Cassy became chief baron of the exchequer in 1389.

In East Anglia, similar useful links between abbot and proctor may be observed. William Witchingham, presumably a Norfolk man, had a long legal career, first as a serjeant at law (1354), king's serjeant (1361–5), and then as a justice of common pleas from 1365 to 1377; he was still alive in 1379.[154] His parliamentary links with St Benet of Hulme lasted from 1348 until 1354, though he continued to be useful to the house after this period in which he served as a proctor. The abbey needed legal help, since it was in dispute with the countess of Norfolk over a fishery, as well as suffering assaults to its members from local gentry.[155] In 1372 Witchingham headed a commission of *oyer* and *terminer* following an alleged ambush and chase of the abbot and a monk by a local knight and his son.[156]

[150]   J. H. Baker, *The Order of Serjeants at Law*, Selden Society, supplementary series 4 (1984), p. 542 (surname Usflet). Illard, or Hillard, was later a justice of assize on the midlands circuit, 1362–6: TNA JUST 4/4/56.
[151]   See Gwilym Dodd's article in *ODNB*; Baker, *Serjeants*, p. 404; Sainty, *Judges of England*, p. 56.
[152]   *CPR 1381–85*, p. 251.
[153]   TNA SC 8/212/10590.
[154]   Baker, *Serjeants*, p. 546; Sainty, *Judges of England*, p. 66.
[155]   For the fishery dispute with the countess see TNA C 14/77/6 and TNA SC 8/26911. For a complaint of assault, *CPR 1348–50*, p. 3.
[156]   *CPR 1370–74*, p. 242.

Further examples can be found in the following century. The abbot of Hyde's decision to include two lawyers among his proctors in 1404 (41/2047) was perhaps because he was in dispute with the crown over the manor of Piddletrenthide, in Dorset. His choices were shrewd, for Thomas Hornby had been retained by the former Henry Bolingbroke in 1392–3 when an apprentice at law, and William Cheney was evidently an able man who would later rise to be chief justice of king's bench.[157] At Crowland, top lawyers were prominent among the proctors of the 1420s and 1430s. William Babington, chief exchequer baron, was appointed in 1421 (47/2334). In 1425, now chief justice of common pleas, he was again chosen, along with James Strangeways, a fellow judge of that court (48/2390). In the next two decades Nicholas Dixon, the exchequer baron, was a Crowland proctor in 1435, 1442 and 1447 (49/2422, 50/2452 and 50/2472). On the first occasion he was joined by John Ellerker, described as a serjeant at law. A colleague of Dixon's in the 1440s was William Tresham. In selecting him Abbot Litlington was following an established Crowland tradition of appointing MPs for Northamptonshire as proctors. Tresham himself was a lawyer, a crown servant from 1415, and already an experienced parliamentarian by 1442, and both in that year and 1447 was speaker of the Commons.[158] The abbot's interest in naming high-profile lawyers to represent him was simple: the house was involved in a series of disputes with its tenants in the south Lincolnshire fens – an area of marshland where disputes about boundaries were common – and needed powerful legal support.[159]

William Donnington was described as 'literate' when commissioned by the prior of Coventry in 1411 (44/2174), and is perhaps to be identified with the Coventry hosier of that name, but is probably to be distinguished from a namesake who was the prior's choice between 1433 and 1445 (49/2420, 49/2435, 50/2459 and 50/2469). This William Donnington was recorder of Coventry from April 1434 to September 1448, and was apparently still alive in 1450 when he was a member of the Drapers' Guild.[160] He was one of the last two identifiable lawyers among the proctors, along with John Vampage, the attorney-general, who was proxy for the abbot of Evesham in 1435, 1442 and 1447 (49/2427, 50/2460 and 50/2473). Donnington was comparatively lowly in legal terms, and it was probably a general rule that abbots chose highly placed lawyers as their parliamentary proctors when their house was facing serious legal cases. Whether such proctors demanded higher fees is a question which is, as yet, unanswerable.

Lay Peers

A final group of laymen comprised members of the lay peerage or members of the aristocracy. The earliest example is Bishop Grandisson of Exeter's choice of William Montague, second earl of Salisbury, and his brother John in September

---

[157]   TNA C 44/22/15; Robert Somerville, *History of the Duchy of Lancaster, vol. I, 1265–1603* (London, 1953), p. 386; Baker, *Serjeants*, p. 504; Sainty, *Judges of England*, pp. 8, 26.

[158]   Henry Summerson in ODNB.

[159]   See Rose Graham in *VCH Lincolnshire*, pp. 114–15; *CPR 1429–36*, p. 219; TNA C 1/12/53; TNA SC 8/308/1533; TNA DL 41/1065.

[160]   *The Records of the Guild of the Holy Trinity, St. Mary, St. John the Baptist and St. Katherine of Coventry*, vol. II, ed. Geoffrey Templeman, Dugdale Society, XIX (1944), pp. 11, 170.

1363 (29/1407). The two young men were the bishop's kinsmen, since their mother Katherine was a daughter of William, first Lord Grandisson, and the bishop had been a friend and correspondent of the first earl. This appointment tells us more about Grandisson's aristocratic outlook than anything else, for among his other choices when choosing proctors were the archbishop of Canterbury and the bishop of Bath and Wells. The next example could not have had more different motivation. In September 1402 John Burghill, bishop of Coventry and Lichfield, named Edmund, earl of Stafford as his first proctor (41/2028). Burghill had been a courtier bishop under Richard II and remained loyal to him to the end, for he was the only bishop to attend the former king's interment at Langley. By 1402 he was elderly, and clearly felt vulnerable under the new regime, which explains his choice of Stafford, a close associate of Henry IV. What might have been a promising connection giving security was cut short by the earl's death at the battle of Shrewsbury the following year.

The turbulent politics of Henry VI's reign doubtless explains the rise in the number of upper-class proctors in the mid-fifteenth century. In 1442 the bishop of Chichester chose Viscount Beaumont (50/2462), the bishop of Hereford chose the earl of Northumberland and Lord Scrope (50/2463), and the abbot of St Mary's, York also named Lord Scrope (50/2464). Here, it seems, we can observe the start of nervousness caused by political uncertainty. Just at the point when the files of SC 10 fail us, other evidence suggests that this practice became more common. Thomas Beckington of Bath and Wells appointed John Stourton, Lord Stourton in 1453 and 1456, and chose Ralph Butler, Lord Sudeley in both 1459 and 1463.[161] This practice continued into the Tudor period, at least until the events of 1515 discussed previously. In 1512 Bishop Richard Mayhew of Hereford chose George Neville, Lord Bergavenny along with Lord Herbert, the king's chamberlain, and in 1515 appointed Bergavenny alone.[162] His successor Charles Booth chose Walter Devereux, Lord Ferrers (of Chartley) in 1523.[163] Finally, Thomas Wyford, prior of Coventry, named George Hastings, earl of Huntingdon one of three proctors in the 1532 session of parliament (51/2520). It seems evident that from Henry VI's later years onwards, some clerical peers found it prudent to appoint prominent courtiers who had local connections.[164]

CLERICAL PROCTORS IN PARLIAMENT: CONCLUSION

As the foregoing discussion has demonstrated, the men appointed as proctors in the medieval parliament were a varied group, the overlapping roles and allegiances often making it difficult to categorise them tidily. Some were present in parliament purely as a result of their nomination as a proctor. Others were primarily present in another capacity, as a member of the secretariat or as a member of the assembly in their own right, and only secondarily as a proctor for others. The

---

[161] *The Register of Thomas Bekynton Bishop of Bath and Wells 1443–1465*, ed. H. C. Maxwell-Lyte and M. C. B. Dawes, Somerset Record Society 49 (1934), pp. 221, 264–5, 331, 385.

[162] *Registrum Ricardi Mayew, episcopi Herefordensis, A.D. 1504–1516*, ed. A. T. Bannister, C&Y 27 (1919), pp. 146, 209.

[163] *Registrum Caroli Bothe, episcopi Herefordensis, A.D. 1516–1535*, ed. A. T. Bannister, C&Y 28 (1921), p. 139.

[164] All the proctors discussed in this paragraph have entries in the *ODNB*.

letters appointing proctors gave them wide but vague powers, and it may be that part of their role was to witness and assent to measures formulated by the king and his intimates and presented by councillors and ministers. Unlike in the Stuart and Hanoverian period, when proctors were members of the House of Lords and could thus cast up to two proxy votes in addition to their own, we have no evidence that there were formal divisions in the medieval parliament or that proctors had voting rights in this sense. One important question has thus far not been addressed: what did the proctors do? We can offer only pointers here, but there is still scope for considerable research in this area.

The medieval parliament was an event as much as an institution. It is clear that much went on in and around parliamentary sessions which went unreported in the rolls of parliament, and from some of the appointments we get some hints about some of these unrecorded events. The choice of able and important lawyers by abbots whose houses were engaged in lawsuits suggests that lobbying in specific causes was a consideration. Even aside from legal cases religious houses had many reasons to petition the crown.[165] Further evidence comes from the chapter accounts of Lincoln cathedral. For much of the fourteenth century the chapter was engaged in a dispute with the citizens of Lincoln which culminated (successfully for the chapter) in 1390, with the appointment of an arbitrator (John of Gaunt) who was well disposed towards the cathedral and came down strongly on the chapter's side. Capitular representation was even able to effect legislation which censured the mayor and bailiffs for failing to cooperate with king and council in this case.[166] This was not the only matter of concern to the chapter in these years: the filling of a prebend was also of the subject of representation. Indeed, the exercise of ecclesiastical patronage was of concern to any, whether individual or corporation, with benefices at their disposal.[167] Thus petitioning and the less formal business of lobbying shaded into one another, and though it was not necessary to be present in parliament to present petitions, the personal touch could have been crucial. The informal contacts and activities which went on during parliamentary sessions are lost to us. The account of MPs wrestling and playing football in the cloister of Gloucester Abbey during the parliament of 1378 is a rare glimpse of what went on when parliament met.[168] It is therefore reasonable to conclude that the duties of proctors included being present, lobbying, and keeping a watching brief on the interests of their principals.

The most celebrated of all the clerical proctors, and the only one who has attained the fame of being mentioned as such in general histories, was Thomas Haxey, a man with a diverse and unusually dramatic career.[169] The petition he presented to the first parliament of 1397 complaining, among other things,

---

[165] *Petitions to the Crown from English Religious Houses c. 1272–c. 1485*, ed. Gwilym Dodd and Alison K. McHardy, C&Y 100 (2010). The selection printed in this volume still represents only a small proportion of the surviving material.

[166] See Alison K. McHardy, 'The Representation of the Clergy in Parliament', in *Fourteenth Century England* 10, ed. Gwilym Dodd (Woodbridge, 2018), pp. 47–66.

[167] TNA SC 1/12/133 and SC 1/16/65 are examples of letters written by Thomas Corbridge, archbishop of York, on this very matter in 1304.

[168] *Historia et Cartularium Monasterii S. Petri Gloucestrae*, ed. W. H. Hart (London, 1863), vol. 1, pp. 52–4.

[169] Tout, *Chapters*, IV, pp. 17–19; Nigel Saul, *Richard II* (New Haven, CT, 1997), pp. 369–70.

about the personnel of the court, roused Richard II's ire and caused Haxey to be condemned as a traitor and, for a few days, he was in mortal danger. Although the episode appears in no chronicle, it was extensively reported in the rolls of parliament.[170] As reported, though, the petition was unusual in not naming the petitioner. Haxey's basic relationship was with Selby Abbey, the source of five of his twelve proxy appointments, the last of them being in 1397. A canon of both Lincoln and Lichfield, Thomas Haxey had been a proctor for the bishop of Lincoln, John Buckingham, in 1393 (38/1871), while Richard Scrope, bishop of Coventry and Lichfield, chose him two years later (39/1944). He also had two commissions from the chapter of Lincoln during the next century and under the next dynasty in 1404.

It is hard to see Thomas Haxey's highly political critique of Richard II's regime as originating from disgruntlement at Selby Abbey. It seems much more likely that it had its origins among discontented king's clerks, for the crown service, and especially the chancery, was partisan and divided, especially in the 1380s and 1390s.[171] However, we do know of one service to Selby which Haxey performed. After his unmasking and brush with the taint of treason, Haxey apparently retreated to Rampton, in Nottinghamshire, the rectory of his prebend in Southwell Minster, and the abbot of Selby was forced to turn elsewhere for his parliamentary representation.[172] But from Rampton Haxey continued to be in contact with the abbot of Selby; he sent a messenger to the abbey in March 1399, and in September that year he gave advice to the abbot through the porter sent to consult him. The nature of 'the business of the lord abbot' is not stated, though was likely connected with the recent landing of the exiled Henry Bolingbroke.[173] Though neither the abbot nor Haxey were in parliament, such advice is surely an extreme example of the help which a proctor might give his principal at a time of revolution.

These are just some of the human stories which lie behind series SC 10. In these two volumes, we have sought to provide the extensive evidence which demonstrates the presence of an entire cross-section of the clergy and their representatives, often in large numbers, in the medieval parliament. SC 10 is a valuable body of material, and hopefully making its contents more readily available will encourage further study of the important place the clergy occupied in medieval English politics. It is also worth remembering that although it is by far the most significant resource, the series does not provide the only evidence for the parliamentary clergy. We have located and calendared some letters outside SC 10, which have strayed into other series in The National Archives, or are found in other archives and registers, but

---

[170] See Richardson, 'Chancery', pp 92–4; A. K. McHardy in *ODNB*; A. K. McHardy, 'Haxey's Case, 1397: The Petition and its Presenter Reconsidered', in *The Age of Richard II*, ed. James L. Gillespie (Stroud, 1997), pp. 93–114; Gwilym Dodd, 'Richard II and the Transformation of Parliament', in *Reign of Richard II*, ed. Dodd, pp. 71–84. The source is discussed in A. K. McHardy, *The Reign of Richard II* (Manchester, 2012), p. 317. For Haxey's links to Southwell see 'Thomas Haxey and the Collegiate Church', in *Minster People*, ed. Stanley Chapman and Derek Walker (Southwell, 2009), pp. 34–41.

[171] Biggs, 'The Appellant and the Clerk'; McHardy, 'John Scarle'.

[172] To Alexander de Stayndrop, the abbot's attorney in the court of Common Pleas, who was his proctor in the 1399 parliament: J. H. Tillotson, *Monastery and Society in the Late Middle Ages: Selected Account Rolls from Selby Abbey, Yorkshire, 1398–1537* (Woodbridge, 1988), pp. 55, 64.

[173] Tillotson, *Monastery and Society*, pp. 61, 70.

the material calendared in these volumes will not be exhaustive. Given the nature and sheer size of the records of the English medieval administration, it is almost certain that there are further strays lying in other parts of The National Archives, the British Library, and elsewhere. That said, such documents are likely to be isolated examples which will simply add to the records published here. Unless there is a very well-hidden source lying in an obscure archive, the calendars in these two volumes make available the overwhelming majority of records for medieval parliamentary proxies.

This evidence gives an insight into aspects of the medieval English parliament which have largely been overlooked. From the Tudor period onwards (and probably this reflects changes which had begun or even happened under the Yorkist kings), the proxy records are of a different nature, the appointers peers and their proctors drawn from the small number of fellow-members of the House of Lords. These might tell us about certain dynamics within the Lords, but they are far less informative about wider parliamentary politics than are the medieval records. Proctors may have been an anachronism by the time they were abolished in the nineteenth century, but they were an essential part of the medieval parliament. What SC 10 and associated evidence demonstrates is the fluidity of politics in the later Middle Ages. Parliament was a continually evolving institution in the medieval period, lacking the rigidity of membership it would later come to acquire. The clerical proctors found in parliament are a cross-section of political society, demonstrating how deeply the church was interwoven into all aspects of that society. Men could be present in multiple capacities, and indeed as proctors have a role in assemblies they would otherwise have had no right to attend. Royal clerks gained experience and connections. Relationships were formed between those who repeatedly attended parliaments. Careers were launched or advanced as people were noticed in this national forum. The clerical proctors were an integral part of the parliamentary world. In giving us a window into this world, SC 10 is a clear and firm reminder of the role of these men and of the important place of the clergy within the medieval parliament.

EDITORIAL PRACTICE

The same practice has been used in this volume as was employed in volume 1 for calendaring, spelling and editorial insertions (see volume 1, pp. liii–liv).

IDENTIFICATION

An asterisk after a proctor's name identifies those proctors for whom further details are provided in Appendix 7 of this volume.

ABBREVIATIONS USED IN THE CALENDAR

En   The document is in English.

F   The document is in French.

LP   The document is a letter patent.

MP   Member of Parliament for the parliament in question, with the constituency noted. Where a proctor was an MP in a parliament other than the one for which he was a proctor, this is noted in Appendix 4.

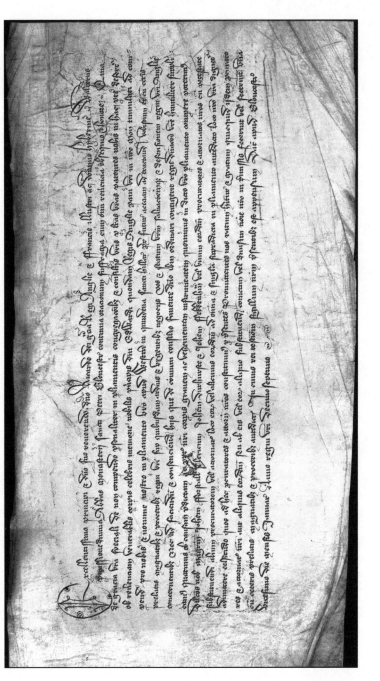

SC 10/39/1901. In excusing himself from the parliament of January 1394 Walter Froucestre, abbot of Gloucester, reminds Richard II that his great-grandfather, Edward II, was buried in the abbey church. Richard visited Gloucester in 1378, when parliament met in the abbey, and later made several attempts to have Edward II canonised, the first two in 1387 and 1392.

SC 10/42/2070. From the early fifteenth century a number of letters show that whoever drew them up was unsure of the names, or numbers, of the proctors to be appointed. Here, in the abbot of St. Augustine's, Canterbury letter of 1404, the proctors' names have been added later, with insufficient space for their description, 'clerks'. Roger Paternoster and Roger Eastwell are so far unidentified.

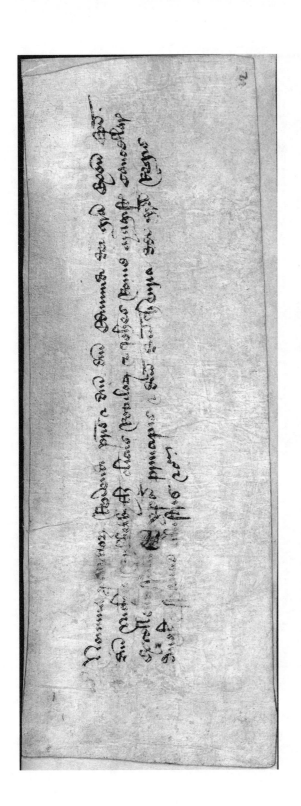

SC 10/42/2051. This is the smallest document in the class, only 16.5 cm. wide x 6 cm. high – most are 25–30 cm. wide x 12–14 cm. high. This was almost certainly written in December 1403 or January 1404, for the parliament which finally met at Westminster on 14 January 1404, and resembles 'instructions to a secretary', from Edmund Stafford, bishop of Exeter. It represents a unique survival of a type of document which must once have been very common, and illustrates the early stage in the production of the documents which survive in SC 10.

SC 10/43/2138. This letter patent of 1407 shows the sophisticated finished product which Bishop Stafford's chancery could produce. His three proctors, Wakering, Rome, and Hartlepool were distinguished men in crown service, while the bishop himself, Edmund Stafford, was a former keeper of the privy seal and chancellor: in person when summoned through the bishop, this is one of several examples of them appointing proxies to be found in SC 10.

SC 10/43/2147. In 1410 the abbot of Bardney's clerk
left too much space for the names of the three proctors, John Rotherham, John Kyme, and William
Friskney a monk of the house, in this letter patent.
Putting the monastic colleague last was unusual.

SC 10/46/2274. Letter patent, 1417. The clergy of Carlisle diocese used the seal of the Officiality of the see of Carlisle when reporting on the names of their chosen proctors. Such an arrangement was common practice for diocesan clergy. Though they were only bound to send two representatives they covered themselves against mischance by naming four, on this occasion.

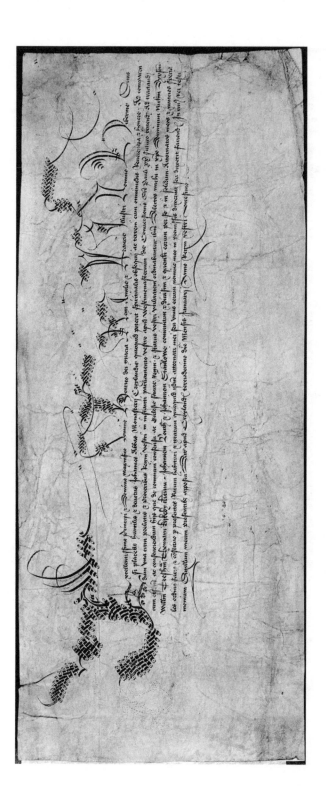

SC 10/50/2452. This letter from the abbot of Crowland, 1442, has by far the most elaborate penwork of any piece in the class. The Crowland scribes had, though, been working up to this elaboration with their decorations to SC 10/49/2411 (1432), and 24/2439 (1432). Increasingly elaborate penwork is a feature of ecclesiastical records of the fifteenth century, from the start of Archbishop Stafford's register (Reg. John Stafford, 1443–52, Lambeth Palace Library, f. 1) and continuing with the registers of York, Salisbury, and Hereford, in particular. The text of this letter is printed in *Proctors*, vol. 1, p. 256.

SC 10/50/2478. 1447. Far too much space was left here, perhaps because of this parliament's unusual location.

THE CALENDAR

PARLIAMENTS OF THE REIGN OF RICHARD II (1377–99)

PARLIAMENT AT WESTMINSTER, 13 OCTOBER 1377

32/1560	[John de Ombersley], abbot of Evesham	Robert Faryngton [Farrington]*, clerk John Cassy*	Evesham, 6 Oct. 1377
32/1561	[Henry of Overton], abbot of Peterborough	Richard de Tretton*, clerk F. Thomas de Bury, monk of abbey John de Harwedon * [Harrowden]	Peterborough, 9 Oct. 1377
32/1562	[Thomas Pethy], abbot of Hyde near Winchester	F. John Eynesham [Eynsham]*, monk of abbey Thomas de Warenn' [Warenne]	Hyde, *[no day or month]* 1377
32/1563	[Richard de Shenington], abbot of Ramsey	Michael de Ravendale*, clerk Robert Muskham*, clerk Robert Waryn*, esquire	Ramsey, 10 Oct. 1377
32/1564	Robert [Stretton], bishop of Coventry and Lichfield	M. Richard de Bermyngham [Birmingham], canon of Lichfield John de Morton, canon of Lichfield M. John de Shillingford*, advocate of the court of Canterbury	Heywode [Haywood], 1 Oct. 1377
32/1565	[William Marreys], abbot of St Mary's, York	F. Richard de Appilton [Appleton], monk of abbey Michael de Ravendale*	York, *[no day]*, Oct. 1377

32/1566	[William Methwold], abbot of St Benet of Hulme	John de Herlyngg [Harling]	Hulme, 4 Oct. 1377
32/1567	[Nicholas Ampney], abbot of Cirencester	M. Richard Zaneworth [Yanworth]*, skilled in law John de Everdon*, clerk John Wardon, clerk	Cirencester, 7 Oct. 1377
32/1568	Chapter of Durham	John de Dent* John de Killyngale [Killinghall] William Lambert Gilbert de Elvett [Elvet]	Durham, 4 Oct. 1377
32/1569	[Thomas de Stapelton], abbot of Bardney	Peter de Barton* Robert Beverage*	Bardney, 29 Sept. 1377
32/1570	[John Dedham], abbot of St John's, Colchester	M. Richard de Pyriton [Pirton]*, archdeacon of Colchester	Colchester, 8 Oct. 1377
32/1571A	[John of Sutton], abbot of Reading	F. John de Spersholt, monk of abbey Peter de Barton*, clerk	Reading, 29 Sept. 1377
32/1571B	[Thomas de la Mare], abbot of St Albans	F. Robert Chestan, monk of abbey	[Illegible]
32/1572	[Walter of Winforton], abbot of Winchcombe	M. John de Appelby [Appleby]*, dean of St Paul's, London Richard de Piryton [Pirton]*, canon of St Paul's	Winchcombe, 27 Sept. 1377

PARLIAMENT AT WESTMINSTER, 20 OCTOBER 1378

32/1573	[Richard Yateley], abbot of Reading	F. John de Spersholt, monk of abbey Peter de Barton*	Reading, 4 Oct. 1378
32/1574	William [Spridlington], bishop of St Asaph	John Fordham*, canon of St Asaph M. Nicholas Philip, canon of St Asaph	Lynedon [Lyndon], 1 Oct. 1378
32/1575	[William de Greneburgh], prior of Coventry	F. Roger de Wentebrigg [Wentbridge], monk of abbey Robert de Melton*, clerk	Coventry, 14 Oct. 1378
32/1576	[Peter de Hanney], abbot of Abingdon	William de Shiltewode [Shiltwood], rector of Chelreye [Childrey]	Abingdon, St Dionysius [9 Oct.] 1378
32/1577	[John de Ashby], abbot of Crowland	Robert Muskham*, clerk John Folkingham*, clerk	Crowland, 3 Oct. 1378
32/1578	Michael [de Pecham], abbot of St Augustine's, Canterbury	Robert Bealknappe [Bealknap]* William Borstalle [Burstall]*	Canterbury, morrow of translation of Edward, king and confessor [14 Oct.] 1378
32/1579	Robert [Stretton], bishop of Coventry and Lichfield	M. Edmund de Stafford*, canon of Lichfield John de Morton, canon of Lichfield	Heywode [Haywood], 3 Oct.1378
32/1580	[William de Gritton], abbot of St John's, Colchester	Robert Faryngton [Farrington]*, clerk and canon of Lincoln	Colchester, 7 Oct. 1378
32/1581	[William Marreys], abbot of St Mary's, York	F. Richard de Appilton [Appleton], monk of abbey Michael de Ravendale*, clerk	York, 13 Oct. 1378

259

32/1582	[Edmund Ellington], abbot of Ramsey	Robert de Muskham* John de Burton*, rector of Grafham	Ramsey, 12 Dec. 1378
32/1583	[John de Ombersley], abbot of Evesham	Thomas de Newenham*, clerk Robert de Faryngton [Farrington]*, clerk	Evesham, 6 Oct. 1378
32/1584	[Thomas de Stapelton], abbot of Bardney [LP]	Peter de Barton* Hugh de Hanworth*	Bardney, 29 Sept. 1378
32/1585	[Robert Berrington of Walworth], prior of Durham [LP]	John de Henlay, rector of Segefeld [Sedgefield] John Poppam	Durham, 3 Oct. 1378
32/1586	William [Reade], bishop of Chichester [LP]	John de Bishoppeston [Bishopstone]*, chancellor of Chichester Cathedral M. John Lydeford [Lydford]*, canon and prebendary of Thorney in Chichester Cathedral	Stratham manor [Streatham], 4 Oct. 1378
32/1587	[Thomas Pethey], abbot of Hyde near Winchester	Peter de Barton*, clerk F. John Chaworth, monk of abbey	Hyde, 17 Nov. 1378
32/1588	[Illegible]	John de Wenlingburgh [Wellingborough]*, canon of London	[Illegible] 1378
32/1589	[Thomas de la Mare], abbot of St Albans	Robert Muskham*, clerk	St Albans, 10 Oct. 1378
32/1590	[John de Sherburn], abbot of Selby	John de Ficton, clerk Robert de Melton*, clerk John de Waltham*, clerk	Selby, 30 Sept. 1378

32/1591	[William Methwold], abbot of St Benet of Hulme	John de Herlyngg [Harling]* George de Felbrigg [Felbridge]*	Hulme, 10 Oct. 1378
32/1592	[Henry of Overton], abbot of Peterborough	F. Thomas de Bury, monk of abbey Thomas Thelewall [Thelwall]*, rector of Polebrok [Polebrook]	Peterborough, 15 Oct. 1378
32/1593	[John Brinkley], abbot of Bury St Edmunds	Peter de Barton* M. Richard de Brinkelee [Brinkley]*, rector of Rougham Edmund Heryng	Bury St Edmunds, feast of St Matthew, apostle and evangelist [21 Sept.], 1378

PARLIAMENT AT WESTMINSTER, 24 APRIL 1379

32/1594	Clergy of Bangor diocese [LP]	Gervaise [ap Madog], archdeacon of Bangor John de Berkyng [Barking], rector of Disse [Disserth] Gruffudd ap Ddu', official of Merionyth	Bangor, 3 April 1379
32/1595	[Thomas de la Mare], abbot of St Albans	F. Robert Chestan, monk of abbey Robert Muskham*, clerk	St Albans, 4 April 1379
32/1596	Chapter of Durham Cathedral [LP]	John Swethorp Thomas de Billingham	Durham, 18 April 1379
32/1597	[William Methwold], abbot of St Benet of Hulme	John de Herlyngg [Harling]*	St Benet of Hulme, 24 April 1379
32/1598	Chapter of York [LP]	M. Walter Skirlaw*, canon of York M. John de Waltham*, canon of York Richard de Ravenser*, canon of York	York, 18 April 1379

32/1599	Robert [Stretton], bishop of Coventry and Lichfield	M. Edmund de Stafford*, canon of Lichfield John de Moreton [Morton], canon of Lichfield	Heywode [Haywood], 19 April 1379
32/1600	Henry [Wakefield], bishop of Worcester	M. Thomas de Stowe*, doctor of laws, bishop's official John Blanchard [Blaunchard]*, archdeacon of Worcester	Hertlebury [Hartlebury], 18 April 1379
33/1601	[John Deeping], abbot of Thorney	Adam de Chesterfield*, rector of Stanground John Harlington*	Thorney, 22 April 1379
33/1602	Dean [Roger Freton] and chapter of Chichester Cathedral [LP]	Robert de Derby, precentor of Chichester Cathedral John de Bisshopeston [Bishopstone]*, chancellor of Chichester Cathedral	Chapter House, 12 April 1379
33/1603	John [Boyfeld], abbot of St Peter's, Gloucester	F.John Stonhous [Stonehouse], monk of abbey Robert Muskham*, clerk	Gloucester, 3 April 1379
33/1604	Walter [Camme], abbot of Malmesbury	Robert Charlton* Laurence Drew* John Collyngbourne [Collingbourne]	Malmesbury, Thursday before feast of St George [21 April] 1379
33/1605	Thomas [Pethy], abbot of Hyde near Winchester	F.John de Eynsham*, monk and prior of abbey Peter de Barton*, clerk	Hyde, 17 April 1379
33/1606	John [de Sherburn], abbot of Selby	Richard de Ravenser*, archdeacon of Lincoln John de Waltham*, clerk	Selby, 20 April 1379
33/1607	William [de Greneburgh], prior of Coventry	F. Roger de Wentebeigg [Wentbridge] Robert de Melton*, clerk	Coventry, 22 April 1379

33/1608	Adam [Houghton], bishop of St Davids	Richard Ravenser*, archdeacon of Lincoln Walter Skirlaw*, dean of St Martin le Grand, London John David*, chancellor of St Davids Cathedral	Our palace at St Davids, 16 April 1379
33/1609	[Edmund Ellington], abbot of Ramsey	F. John de Bedford, monk of abbey Robert Muskham*, clerk Robert Waryn*	Ramsey, 23 April 1379
33/1610	John [de Ashby], abbot of Crowland	F. John de Grantham, monk of abbey John Folkingham*, clerk Robert Muskham*, clerk	Crowland, 22 April 1379
33/1611	[Thomas de Stapelton], abbot of Bardney *[LP]*	Peter de Barton*, clerk Hugh de Hanworth*, clerk	Bardney, Sunday in the octave of Easter [17 April] 1379
33/1612	John [Swaffham], bishop of Bangor *[LP]*	Gervaise [ap Madog], archdeacon of Bangor John de Berkyng [Barking], rector of Disse [Disserth] Gruffudd ap Ddu', official of Merioneth	Coventry, 24 April 1379
33/1613	Robert [Berrington of Walworth], prior of Durham *[LP]*	John de Swethorp, clerk Thomas de Byllyngham [Billingham], clerk	Durham, 18 April 1379
33/1614	John Pagge, proctor of John Martyn, dean of Bangor, who is at the Roman court *[LP]*	Gervaise [ap Madog], archdeacon of Bangor John de Berkyng [Barking], rector of Disse [Disserth] Gruffudd ap Ddu', official of Merioneth	Bangor, 3 April 1379
33/1615	John [Chynnok *alias* Wynchestre], abbot of Glastonbury	M. John Blanchard [Blaunchard]*, clerk Walter Broun, clerk	Glastonbury, 18 April 1379

263

33/1616	Alexander [Neville], archbishop of York	Richard de Ravenser*, archdeacon of Lincoln M. Walter de Skirlagh [Skirlaw]*, archdeacon of the East Riding M. John de Waltham*, official of the court of York	Our manor of Cawode [Cawood], 15 April 1379
33/1617	Henry [Despenser], bishop of Norwich	M. Thomas de Lexham* M. John de Shillingford* M. Thomas de Schurford [Shereford]*	Norwich, 23 April 1379
33/1618	William [Marreys], abbot of St Mary's, York	F. Richard de Appilton [Appleton], monk of abbey Michael de Ravendale*	In the monastery, 21 April 1379
33/1619	Walter [of Winforton], abbot of Winchcombe	M. John de Appelby [Appleby]*, dean of St Paul's, London Richard de Piryton [Pirton]*, archdeacon of Colchester	Winchcombe, 12 April 1379
33/1620	John [de Ombersley], abbot of Evesham	Thomas de Newenham* Robert de Faryngton [Farrington]*	Evesham, 18 April 1379
33/1621	[Nicholas Stevens], abbot of Shrewsbury [LP]	F. William de Nesse, monk of abbey	Shrewsbury, 20 April 1379
33/1622	Richard [Yateley], abbot of Reading	Peter de Barton*, clerk F. John de Wynkefeld [Winkfield], monk of abbey	Reading, 21 April 1379

264

PARLIAMENT AT WESTMINSTER, 16 JANUARY 1380

33/1623	Robert [Stretton], bishop of Coventry and Lichfield [LP]	John de Moreton [Morton], canon of Lichfield M. John de Shillingford*, doctor of laws Thomas de Mildeton [Middleton], canon of St Stephen's, Westminster	Heywode [Haywood], 10 Jan. 1380
33/1624	[John Deeping], abbot of Thorney	F. Geoffrey de Brunne, monk of abbey Adam de Chesterfield*, rector of Stanground	Thorney, feast of St Hilary [13 Jan.] 1380
33/1625	[Hugh Branston], abbot of Bardney [LP]	Richard de Ravenser* Peter de Barton*, clerk Robert Beverage*	Bardney, feast of the Nativity of the Lord [25 Dec.] 1379
33/1626	Roger [Cradock], bishop of Llandaff	M. John de Shillingford*, doctor of laws Thomas de Newenham*, clerk	Lank [Lancarfan], 8 Jan. 1380
33/1627	Roger [Yatton], abbot of Evesham [LP]	M. Thomas de Stowe*, archdeacon of Bedford, doctor of laws Robert de Faryngton [Farrington]*, clerk	Evesham, Tuesday after Epiphany [9 Jan.] 1380
33/1628	John [de Sherburn], abbot of Selby	Richard de Ravenser*, archdeacon of Lincoln John de Waltham*, clerk	Selby, 5 Jan. 1380
33/1629	Henry [of Overton], abbot of Peterborough	Richard de Tretton*, clerk Thomas de Thelewall [Thelwall]*, clerk F. Thomas de Bury, monk of abbey	Peterborough, 13 Jan. 1380
33/1630	Henry [Despenser], bishop of Norwich	M. Thomas de Lexham* M. John de Shillingforde [Shillingford]* M. Thomas de Schirford [Shereford]*	Norwich, 12 Jan. 1380

33/1631	Thomas [Pethy], abbot of Hyde near Winchester	F. John de Eynsham*, monk of abbey Peter de Barton*, clerk	Hyde, Monday after feast of the Epiphany [8 Jan.] 1380
33/1632	Thomas [de la Mare], abbot of St Albans	Robert Muskham*, clerk Thomas Charlton	St Albans, 15 Jan. 1380
33/1633	Walter [Camme], abbot of Malmesbury	Robert Cherlton [Charlton]* Laurence Dru [Drew]* John Colyngbourne [Collingbourne]	Malmesbury, 28 Dec. 1379
33/1634	Peter [de Hanney], abbot of Abingdon	Nicholas Draiton [Drayton], fellow-canon William Shiltewode [Shiltwood], rector of Chelrey [Childrey]	Abingdon, 8 Jan. 1380
33/1635	William [Methwold], abbot of St Benet of Hulme	John de Herlyngg [Harling]* George de Felbrygg [Felbridge]*	St Benet of Hulme, 12 Jan. 1380
33/1636	[Edmund Ellington], abbot of Ramsey	F. John de Bedford, monk of abbey Michael de Ravendale* Robert Muskham*, clerk Robert Waryn*	Ramsey, [Damaged] Jan. 1380
33/1637	Henry [Wakefield], bishop of Worcester	M. John Blanchard [Blaunchard]*, archdeacon of Worcester M. Thomas de Stowe*, archdeacon of Bedford	Hertlebury [Hartlebury], 8 Jan. 1380
33/1638	William [de Greneburgh], prior of Coventry	F. Thomas de Wentebrig [Wentbridge], monk of house Richard Piryton [Pirton]*, clerk Robert de Melton*, clerk	Coventry, 9 Jan. 1380

33/1639	Richard [Yateley], abbot of Reading	F.John de Wynkfeld [Winkfield], monk of abbey Peter de Barton*, clerk	Reading, 12 Jan. 1380
33/1640	Robert [Berrington of Walworth], prior of Durham [LP]	Gilbert de Elvet Thomas Billingham	Durham, 5 Jan. 1380
33/1641	Chapter of Durham [LP]	Gilbert de Elvet Thomas Billingham	Durham Chapter House, 5 Jan. 1380
33/1642	William [Marreys], abbot of St Mary's, York	F. Richard de Appilton [Appleton], monk of abbey Michael de Ravendale*	In the monastery, 10 Jan. 1380
33/1643	[John de Ashby], abbot of Crowland	F.John de Grantham, monk of abbey John Folkyngham [Folkingham]*, clerk Richard Wantynge [Wantage]*, clerk	Crowland, 11 Jan.1380

PARLIAMENT AT NORTHAMPTON, 5 NOVEMBER 1380

33/1644	Richard [Yateley], abbot of Reading	F.John de Wynkfeld [Winkfield], monk of abbey Peter de Barton*, clerk	Reading, 18 Oct. 1380
33/1645	Chapter of York Minster [LP]	Richard de Ravenser*, archdeacon of Lincoln M. Walter Skirlaw*, archdeacon of the East Riding M. Adam de Thorp* William de Gunthorpe*, canon of York Michael de Ravendale*, canon of York	Chapter House, 30 Oct. 1380
33/1646	Peter [de Hanney], abbot of Abingdon	William Schiltwode [Shiltwood], rector of Chelreye [Childrey]	Abingdon, 4 [damaged] 1380

33/1647	Chapter of Durham Cathedral [LP]	John Herle, knight John de Beryngton [Berrington], monk of abbey Hugh Herle, rector of Whikham [Whickham] Richard de Elvet, clerk	Durham Chapter House, 8 Oct. 1380
33/1648	John [Harewell], bishop of Bath and Wells [LP]	John de Fordham*, dean of Wells, clerk of king's privy seal M. Thomas Spert*, doctor of laws and canon of Wells Peter de Barton*, canon of Wells John de Wendlyngburgh [Wellingborough]*, canon of St Paul's, London	Woky [Wookey], 1 Nov. 1380
33/1649	Roger [Yatton], abbot of Evesham [LP]	William de Burstall*, clerk Robert de Faryngdon [Farrington]*, clerk	Evesham, Wednesday after SS Simon and Jude [31 Oct.] 1380
33/1650	[Hugh Branston], abbot of Bardney [LP]	Henry Asty*, knight Peter de Barton* F. John de Haynton [Hainton]*, monk of abbey F. Thomas de Welton, monk of abbey	Bardney, 1 Nov. 1380
34/1651	John [de Appleby], dean, and chapter of [St Paul's] London [LP]	William de Dighton*, canon of St Paul's, London John de Wendlyngburgh [Wellingborough]*, canon of St Paul's, London Thomas Crossey, canon of St Paul's, London	Chapter House, 21 Oct. 1380
34/1652	Robert [Berrington of Walworth], prior of Durham [LP]	John Herle, knight John de Beryngton [Berrington], monk of priory Hugh Herle, rector of Whikham [Whickham], clerk Richard de Elvet, clerk	Durham, 8 Oct. 1380

34/1653	Alexander [Neville], archbishop of York	Robert [Derling], bishop of Dunkeld, our suffragan Walter Skirlaw*, archdeacon of the East Riding John de Sleford [Sleaford]*, canon of Ripon collegiate church John de Armesthorp [Armthorp], canon of Ripon collegiate church	Ripon, our manor, 13 Nov. 1380
34/1654	[Nicholas Morice], abbot of Waltham [LP]	Robert de Muskham*	Waltham, 30 Oct. 1380
34/1655	[Roger Cradock], bishop of Llandaff [LP]	Robert Ley Thomas Egleshare [Eccleshare]	Lank [Lancarfan], 31 Oct. 1380
34/1656	Walter [of Winforton], abbot of Winchcombe	Richard Piryton [Pirton]*, clerk Robert Faryngdon [Farrington]*, clerk	Winchcombe, 3 Nov. 1380
34/1657	Nicholas [Litlington], abbot of Westminster	M. Thomas de Southam*, archdeacon of Oxford John Scarle* [the younger], clerk Robert Cherlton [Charlton]*	Westminster, 31 Oct. 1380
34/1658	Robert [Stretton] bishop of Coventry and Lichfield [LP]	M. Richard de Bermynham [Birmingham], canon of Lichfield Cathedral M. John de Ortheby, canon of Lichfield Cathedral M. John de Moreton [Morton], canon of Lichfield Cathedral William de Neuhagh [Newhay], canon of Lichfield Cathedral	Heywode, [Haywood], 13 Oct. 1380

34/1659	[Walter Camme], abbot of Malmesbury	Robert Cherlton [Charlton]* John Colyngbourne [Collingbourne]	Malmesbury, Monday after SS Simon and Jude [29 Oct.] 1380

PARLIAMENT AT WESTMINSTER, 3 NOVEMBER 1381

34/1660	William [de Greneburgh], prior of Coventry	F. John de Tamworth, monk of priory Robert [sic – recte John?] Rome, chaplain John Orwell]*	Coventry, feast of St Luke, evangelist [18 Oct.] 1381
34/1661	Chapter of Worcester Cathedral	M. John Blanchard [Blaunchard]*, archdeacon of Worcester, doctor of laws Robert More*, archdeacon of Llandaff, doctor of laws	Worcester Chapter House, 27 Oct. 1381
34/1662	Roger [Cradock], bishop of Llandaff	M. Robert de la More* D. Thomas de Newenham*, canon of Llandaff Henry de Fynyngleye [Finningley], canon of Llandaff	Lank [Lancarfan], 27 Oct. 1381
34/1664	Roger [Cradock], bishop of Llandaff [LP]	M. Robert de la More* D. Thomas de Newenham*, canon of Llandaff Henry de Fynyngleye [Finningley], canon of Llandaff	Lank [Lancarfan], 27 Oct. 1381
34/1665	William [de Greneburgh], prior of Coventry	Robert de Melton* John de Gaddesby	Coventry, Friday the feast of All Saints [3 Nov.] 1381
34/1666	Walter [de Legh], prior of Worcester	M. John de Blanchard [Blaunchard]*, archdeacon of Worcester, doctor of laws M. Robert More*, archdeacon of Llandaff, doctor of laws	Worcester, 27 Oct. 1381

34/1667	John [Harewell], bishop of Bath and Wells [LP]	M. John Blanchard [Blaunchard]*, doctor of laws; M. John Schillyngford [Shillingford]*, doctor of laws; M. William Byde*, doctor of laws; Henry de Welwes [Willows], rector of St Nicholas Olof [Olave], London	Evercrich [Evercreech], 31 Oct. 1381
34/1668	Peter [de Hanney], abbot of Abingdon	F. Thomas de Chiltone [Chilton], monk of abbey; M. John Bowland, rector of Warefeld [Warfield]	Abingdon, 1 Nov. 1381
34/1669	William [Methwold], abbot of St Benet of Hulme	John de Freton*, archdeacon of Norfolk; John de Herlyng [Harling]*	St Benet of Hulme, 28 Oct. 1381
34/1670	[John de Ashby], abbot of Crowland	F. John de Grantham, monk of abbey; John de Folkyngham [Folkingham]*, clerk; Richard Wantinge [Wantage]*, clerk	Crowland, 31 Oct.1381
34/1671	William [Reade], bishop of Chichester	John de Bysschoppeston [Bishopstone]*, chancellor of Chichester Cathedral; John Lydeford [Lydford]*, canon of Chichester	Our manor of Aumble, [Amberley], 29 Oct. 1381
34/1672	Robert [Berrington of Walworth], prior, and chapter of Durham [LP]	William Lambard [Lambert]; Gilbert de Elvet; John Kylhinggale [Killinghall]	Durham, 7 Oct. 1381
34/1673	[John Deeping], abbot of Thorney	Adam de Chesterfield*, rector of Stanground; John Herlington [Harlington]*	Thorney, 29 Oct. 1381
34/1674	[Nicholas Stevens], abbot of Shrewsbury	Thomas de Lee*; William Taverner*	Shrewsbury, 26 Oct. 1381

PARLIAMENT AT WESTMINSTER, 24 JANUARY 1382 (PROROGATION OF NOVEMBER 1381 SESSION)

34/1675	Alexander [Neville], archbishop of York	M. Richard de Conyngston [Coniston]*, doctor of laws, official of the court of York Thomas Southam*, archdeacon of Oxford	Cawode [Cawood], 20 Jan. 1382
34/1676	[Edmund Ellington], abbot of Ramsey	Michael de Ravendale*, clerk Robert Muskham*, clerk	Ramsey, morrow of St Hilary [14 Jan.] 1382

PARLIAMENT AT WESTMINSTER, 6 OCTOBER 1382

34/1677	Hugh [Branston], abbot of Bardney	F. Thomas de Tathewell [Tathwell], monk of abbey Peter de Barton* William de Helpringham	Bardney, 30 Sept. 1382
34/1678	Robert [Berrington of Walworth], prior, and chapter of Durham	William Lambard [Lambert] Gilbert de Elvet Thomas de Billyngham [Billingham]	Durham, 28 Sept. 1382
34/1679	[Edmund Ellington], abbot of Ramsey	Richard Treton [Tretton]*, clerk Michael Ravendale*, clerk Robert Muskham*, clerk Robert Waryn*, esquire	Ramsey, 5 Oct. 1382
34/1680	[John Deeping], abbot of Thorney	John Harlington* William de Bemewelle [Barnwell]	Thorney, feast of St Jerome [30 Sept.] 1382
34/1681	[Nicholas Stevens], abbot of Shrewsbury [LP]	William de Prine [Prime], clerk Richard de Oteley [Otley]	Shrewsbury, 30 Sept. 1382

34/1682	Nicholas [Litlington], abbot of Westminster	F. John Canterbury, monk of abbey John Scarle* [the younger], clerk	Denham, 4 Oct. 1382
34/1683	Adam [Houghton], bishop of St Davids	M. Walter Skyrlo [Skirlaw]* , dean of St Martin le Grand, London Richard Ravenser*, archdeacon of Lincoln John Bowland, canon of St Davids	Lantefey [Lamphey], 8 Sept. 1382
34/1685	[Henry of Overton], abbot of Peterborough	Richard de Tretton*, clerk Thomas de Bury, monk of abbey William de Thirnyng [Thirning]*	Peterborough, 24 Sept. 1382
34/1686	William [Methwold], abbot of St Benet of Hulme	John de Freton*, clerk, archdeacon of Norfolk	In your monastery [sic], 2 Oct. 1382
34/1687	John [Eynsham],abbot of Hyde near Winchester	M. Peter de Barton* Thomas Warne, steward	Hyde, 5 Oct. 1382
34/1688	William [Reade], bishop of Chichester	M. and D. John de Bisshopeston [Bishopstone]* , chancellor of Chichester Cathedral M. and D. John Lydeford [Lydford]*, canon of Chichester Cathedral John Walton	Aumble [Amberley], 30 Sept. 1382
34/1689	Henry [Wakefield], bishop of Worcester	M. John Blanchard [Blaunchard]*, archdeacon of Worcester, doctor of laws M. Thomas Stowe*, archdeacon of Bedford, doctor of laws M. Richard Cassy, rector of Kemeseye [Kempsey]	Hartlebury, 1 Oct. 1382

273

34/1690	Alexander [Neville], archbishop of York	M. Richard de Conyngton [Coniston]*, doctor of laws, official of the court of York F. Thomas [recte John] de Shirburn [Sherburn], abbot of Selby M. Robert de Manfeld [Manfield]*, provost of St John's [college], Beverley John de Waltham*, canon of St Mary's [college], Southwell	Cawode [Cawode], 28 Sept. 1382
34/1691	Roger [Yatton], abbot of Evesham	M. Thomas de Stowe*, archdeacon of Bedford, doctor of laws Robert de Faryngton [Farrington]*, clerk	Evesham, 29 Sept. 1382
34/1692	Robert [Berrington of Walworth], prior; and chapter of Durham	William Lambard [Lambert] Gilbert de Elvet Thomas de Billyngham [Billingham]	Durham, 28 Sept. 1382
34/1693	[John de Ashby], abbot of Crowland	John de Folkyngham [Folkingham]*, clerk F. John de Grantham, monk of abbey	Crowland, 28 Sept. 1382
34/1694	Walter [Camme], abbot of Malmesbury	F. William Cherlton [Charlton], monk of abbey Robert Cherlton [Charlton]* John Colyngbourne [Collingbourne] William Camme*	Malmesbury, 25 Sept. 1382
34/1695	John [Harewell], bishop of Bath and Wells	M. John Blanchard [Blaunchard]*, doctor of laws, canon of Wells M. John de Schyllingford [Shillingford]*, doctor of laws, canon of Wells M. Thomas Spert*, doctor of laws, canon of Wells Peter de Barton*, canon of Wells	Woky [Wookey], 3 Oct. 1382

34/1696	Robert [Stretton], bishop of Coventry Lichfield	M. John de Shillingford*, canon of Lichfield Cathedral M. John de Outheby [Oudeby], canon of Lichfield Cathedral D.John de Moreton [Morton], canon of Lichfield Cathedral	Heywode [Haywood], 30 Sept. 1382
34/1697	Thomas [de la Mare], abbot of St Albans	F. Robert Chestan, monk of abbey Robert Muskham*, clerk Thomas Charlton	St Albans, 6 Oct. 1382

PARLIAMENT AT WESTMINSTER, 23 FEBRUARY 1383

30/1482	[Roger Yatton], abbot of Evesham	M. Thomas Stowe*, doctor of laws, archdeacon of Bedford Robert Farynton [Farrington]*, clerk	Friday before St Valentine [6 Feb.] 1373 [sic. – recte 1383]
34/1684	Alexander [Neville], archbishop of York	M. Richard de Conynston [Coniston]*, doctor of laws, official of the archbishop's court of York F. John de Shirburn [Sherburn], abbot of Selby	Our manor of Beverlaci [Beverley], 18 Feb. 1383
34/1698	[Henry of Overton], abbot of Peterborough	Richard de Tretton*, clerk Robert de Holt William Thirnyng [Thirning]* F. Thomas de Bury, monk of abbey	Peterborough, 11 Feb. 1383
34/1699	Walter [Camme], abbot of Malmesbury	Robert de Cherlton [Charlton]* Richard de Bere, clerk Hugh Hemyngton [Hemington]	Malmesbury, 12 Feb. 1383

34/1700	William [Reade], bishop of Chichester	M. John de Bishopeston [Bishopston]*, chancellor of Chichester Cathedral John Lydeford [Lydford]*, canon of Chichester Cathedral	Aumble [Amberley], 19 Feb. 1383
35/1701	Thomas [Brinton], bishop of Rochester [LP]	M. John Mory, bishop's clerk Adam, rector of St Michael iuxta ripam regine [Queenhithe], London	Hallyng [Halling], the bishop's manor, 21 Feb. 1383
35/1702	[Nicholas Stevens], abbot of Shrewsbury [LP]	William de Preone [Prime], clerk Thomas de Lee*	Shrewsbury, 10 Feb. 1383
35/1703	John [Harewell], bishop of Bath and Wells [LP]	M. John de Blaunchard*, doctor of laws M. John de Schillyngforde [Shillingford]*, doctor of laws M. William Byde*, doctor of laws	Banewelle [Banwell], 19 Feb. 1383
35/1704	[Adam Houghton], bishop of St Davids	Richard de Ravenser*, archdeacon of Lincoln John Bouland [Bowland]*, canon of St Davids Cathedral	Lantefey [Lamphey] manor, 11 Feb. 1383
35/1705	Walter [of Winforton], abbot of Winchcombe	Richard Piryton [Pirton]*, archdeacon of Colchester Robert Cherlton [Charlton]* William Clyve	Winchcombe, 18 Feb. 1383
35/1706	Chapter of Chichester Cathedral [LP]	John de Bisshopeston [Bishopstone]*, chancellor of Chichester Cathedral	Chichester Chapter House, 18 Feb. 1383
35/1707	[Richard Yateley], abbot of Reading	F. Nicholas Wynkefeld [Winkfield], monk of abbey Peter de Barton*, clerk	Reading, 16 Feb. 1383

35/1708	John [Fordham], bishop of Durham	John Bacoun [Bacon]*, archdeacon of Richmond John Waltham*, clerk of the rolls of chancery Guy de Rouclyf [Roecliffe], canon of Chichester M. John Burgeys, canon of St Mary's collegiate church, Crediton	Stockton manor, 16 Feb. 1383
35/1709	John [Buckingham], bishop of Lincoln [LP]	M. Walter Skirlowe [Skirlaw]*, treasurer of Lincoln Cathedral Richard Ravenser*, archdeacon of Lincoln	Buckden, 18 Feb. 1383
35/1710	[John Deeping], abbot of Thorney	F. Geoffrey de Brunne, monk of house John de Lincoln*, clerk John de Herlyngton [Harlington]*	Thorney, 19 Feb. 1383
35/1711	[John de Ashby], abbot of Crowland	John Waltham*, clerk John Folkyngham [Folkingham]*, clerk F.John de Grantham, monk of abbey	Crowland, 12 Feb. [no year]
C 146/10468	John [Swaffham], bishop of Bangor [LP]	M. Louis de Ab, doctor of canon law, canon of Bangor D. Roger Wellespryng [Wellspring], rector of Llangian, Bangor diocese	Bangor, 16 Feb. 1383

PARLIAMENT AT WESTMINSTER, 26 OCTOBER 1383

35/1712	Thomas [de la Mare], abbot of St Albans	F. Robert Chestan, monk of house Robert Muskham*, clerk Thomas Charlton	St Albans, 23 Oct. 1383

35/1713	[Henry of Overton], abbot of Peterborough (to king, but made patent at the end)	Richard Tretton*, clerk William de Thirnyng [Thirning]* F. Thomas de Bury, monk of abbey Adam de Horsle [Horsley]*, clerk	Peterburgh abbey, 31 Oct. 1383
35/1714	[Illegible – John Timworth, abbot of Bury St Edmunds]	F. Walter de Totyngton [Tottington], monk of house Thomas Baketon M. Thomas Schalford [Shalford] John Scarle* [the younger]	[Illegible]
35/1715	[John Harewell], bishop of Bath and Wells [LP]	M. John Blanchard [Blaunchard]* M. John Shillingford* M. William Byde*	Woky [Wookey], 22 Oct. 1383
35/1716	[Nicholas Stevens], abbot of Shrewsbury [LP]	William de Prene [Prime], clerk Thomas de Lee*	Shrewsbury abbey, 18 Oct. 1383
35/1717	William prior of [Illegible]	Robert [Illegible]	[Illegible]

PARLIAMENT AT WESTMINSTER, 12 NOVEMBER 1384

35/1718	[Henry of Overton], abbot of Peterborough	Richard de Tretton*, clerk F. Thomas de Bury, monk of abbey John de Lincoln*, clerk	Peterborough, feast of St Leonard [6 Nov.] 1384
35/1719	[John Harewell], bishop of Bath and Wells [LP]	M. John de Schillyngford [Shillingford]*, doctor of laws, canon of Wells Peter de Barton*, canon of Wells	Woky [Wookey], 7 Nov. 1384

278

35/1720	Edmund [Ellington], abbot of Ramsey	D. Michael de Ravendale*, clerk D. Robert Muskham*, clerk D. John Lincoln*, clerk	Ramsey, 5 Nov. 1384
35/1721	Thomas [Brinton], bishop of Rochester [LP]	Robert Farryndon [Farrington]*, rector of Wrotham in the archbishop of Canterbury's immediate jurisdiction Richard Launceston, rector of Kemsyng [Kemsing] ch., Rochester diocese	Trottesclyve [Trottiscliffe] bishop's manor, 8 Nov. 1384
35/1722	John [de Sherburn], abbot of Selby	John de Waltham*, canon of York Thomas de Staneley [Stanley]*, clerk Robert de Melton*, clerk	Selby, 4 Nov. 1384
35/1723	William [Methwold], abbot of St Benet of Hulme	John de Freton*, archdeacon of Norfolk	The abbey, Tuesday after feast of St Leonard [7 Nov.] 1384
35/1724	Robert [Stretton], bishop of Coventry and Lichfield [LP]	Thomas de Middelton [Middleton], precentor of Chichester Cathedral M. William de Neuhagh [Newhay], precentor of Lichfield Cathedral M. William Bryan*, skilled in law	Heywode [Haywood], 8 Nov. 1384
35/1725	Walter [Camme], abbot of Malmesbury (to king, but made patent at the end)	F. Thomas Chelesworth [Chelsworth], monk of abbey John Colyngbourne [Collingbourne], clerk John Sutton, clerk	Malmesbury, 7 Nov. 1384

279

35/1726	Walter [de Legh], prior of Worcester	M. Thomas Stowe*, archdeacon of Bedford, doctor of laws M. Robert de la More*, archdeacon of Llandaff, doctor of laws	Worcester, 29 Oct. 1384
35/1727	[Hugh Branston], abbot of Bardney	William de Skypwyth [Skipwith]*, knight F. John de Haynton [Hainton]*, prior of Bardney Peter de Barton* D. John de Folkyngham [Folkingham]*	Bardney, feast of St Leonard [6 Nov.] 1384
35/1728	Richard [Yateley], abbot of Reading	F. John Braye [Bray], monk of abbey Peter de Barton*, clerk	Reading, 8 Nov. 1384
35/1729	Laurence [Child], bishop of St Asaph [LP]	D. John de Herlaston [Harlaston], rector of Ivychurch, Canterbury diocese D. Thomas Forster, rector of Grefford [Gresford], St Asaph diocese	'Allthm', the bishop's manor, 1 Nov. 1384
35/1730	John [Timworth], abbot of Bury St Edmunds	D. John Waltham*, clerk Peter de Barton*, clerk D. John Scarle* [the younger], clerk	Bury St Edmunds, 1 Nov. 1384
35/1731	Adam [Houghton], bishop of St Davids	John [Gilbert]*, bishop of Hereford D. Richard Ravenser*, archdeacon of Lincoln D. John Bouland [Bowland]*, canon of St Davids	Lantefey [Lamphey], 2 Nov. 1384
35/1732	Thomas [de la Mare], abbot of St Albans	F. Robert Chestan, monk of abbey Robert Muskham*, clerk Robert Charltone [Charlton]*	St Albans, 8 Nov. 1384

35/1733	Walter [Froucestre], abbot of St Peter's, Gloucester	Robert Cheorleton [Charlton]* John Cassy*	Gloucester, 6 Nov. 1384
35/1734	Chapter of Worcester Cathedral priory	M. Thomas Stowe*, archdeacon of Bedford, doctor of laws M. Robert de la More*, archdeacon of Llandaff, doctor of laws	Worcester Chapter House, 29 Oct. 1384
35/1735	Clergy of Colchester archdeaconry, London diocese [LP] [appointment also for meeting of Canterbury convocation]	Richard de Piriton [Pirton]*, archdeacon of Colchester	Colchester, Wednesday after feast of St Leonard [9 Nov.] 1384
35/1736	Walter [of Winforton], abbot of Winchcombe	Richard Pyritone [Pirton]*, archdeacon of Colchester Robert Farindone [Farrington]*, clerk	Winchcombe, 7 Nov. 1384
35/1737	John [de Ashby], abbot of Crowland	D. John Waltham* D. John Folkyngham [Folkingham]* F. John de Grantham, monk of abbey	Crowland, 3 Nov. 1384
35/1738	Roger [Yatton], abbot of Evesham [LP]	M. Thomas Stowe* M. Robert Faryngton [Farrington]*	London, 23 Nov. 1384
35/1739	Chapter of York [LP]	M. Walter de Skyrlawe [Skirlaw]*, archdeacon of the East Riding D. John Bacoun [Bacon]*, archdeacon of Richmond D. John de Waltham*, canon of York D. William de Gunthorp [Gunthorpe]*, canon of York	York, 3 Nov. 1384

281

35/1740	Alexander [Neville], archbishop of York	D. John Bacoun [Bacon]*, archdeacon of Richmond D. John de Waltham*, canon of York M. Richard de Conyngham [Coniston]*, official of the court of York, doctor of laws M. Robert Manfeld [Manfield]*, provost of Beverley collegiate church D. Thomas Stanley*, rector of Lythum [Lytham], York diocese	'Rest', 4 Nov. 1384
35/1741	William [Bridford], abbot of St Mary's, York	D. Michael de Ravendale*, clerk D. John de Lincoln*, clerk Robert de Appilton [Appleton], clerk, rector of Sadyngton [Saddington]	York, 27 Oct. 1384
35/1742	John [Fordham], bishop of Durham	D. John Bacoun [Bacon]*, archdeacon of Richmond D. John de Waltham*, canon of York D. William de Dighton*, canon of St Paul's, London D. John de Freton*, archdeacon of Norwich D. William Beverle [Beverley], canon of Westminster	Aukland [Bishop Auckland] manor, 29 Oct. 1384
35/1743	Henry [Wakefield], bishop of Worcester	M. Thomas Stowe*, doctor of laws M. Robert Faryndon [Farrington]*, clerk M. Robert Muskham*, clerk Richard Thurgryn [Thurgrim]*, esquire	Worcester, 29 Oct. 1384
35/1744	William [Reade], bishop of Chichester [LP]	M. and D. Richard le Scrope*, dean of Chichester M. and D. John Lydeford [Lydford]*, canon of Chichester M. and D. John Waltham*	Aumberle [Amberley] manor, 3 Nov. 1384

35/1746	Robert [Berrington of Walworth], prior of Durham [LP]	William Lambard [Lambert] Gilbert de Elvet John de Killynghall [Killinghall]	Durham, 14 Oct. 1385
35/1747	[John Chynnok alias Wynchestre], abbot of Glastonbury	M. John Shillyngford [Shillingford]*, doctor of laws [Damaged], clerk	Glastonbury, 8 Oct. 1385
35/1748	John [Eynsham], abbot of Hyde near Winchester	M. Peter Barton*, clerk John Sutton	Hyde, 12 Oct. 1385
35/1749	John [de Hainton], abbot of Bardney [LP]	F. Thomas de Tathwell, monk of abbey F. Thomas de Welton, monk of abbey Peter de Barton*, clerk D. John de Folkyngham [Folkingham]*, clerk	Bardenay, feast of St Denys [9 Oct.] 1385
35/1750	[Henry of Overton], abbot of Peterborough	Richard de Tretton*, clerk F. Thomas de Bury, monk of abbey D. John de Lincoln*, clerk	[Damaged], 16 Oct. 1385
36/1751	Thomas [Brinton], bishop of Rochester	Robert Faryndon [Farrington]*, rector of Wrotham in the archbishop of Canterbury's immediate jurisdiction M. John Mory, the bishop's clerk	Trottesclyve [Trottiscliffe] episcopal manor, 8 Oct. 1385
36/1752	[John Deeping], abbot of Thorney	F. Thomas de Charwelton*, monk of abbey John Harlington*	Thorney, 14 Oct. 1385
36/1753	Geoffrey [Sturry alias de Sancta Ositha], abbot of St John's, Colchester	F. Thomas Hadeleye [Hadley], monk of abbey Richard Piryngton [Pirton]*, archdeacon of Colchester John de Lyncolne [Lincoln]*, clerk	Colchester, 18 Oct. 1385

36/1754	John [Swaffham], bishop of Bangor [LP]	Richard, rector of Penmynyth [Penmynydd]	Bangor, 9 Oct. 1385
36/1755	John [de Sherburn], abbot of Selby	John de Waltham*, archdeacon of Richmond John Scarle* [the younger] [CoP] Thomas de Stanelay [Stanley]*	Selby, 28 Sept. 1385
36/1756	[John de Ashby], abbot of Crowland	John de Folkyngham [Folkingham]*, clerk Albin de Endirby [Enderby]* F. John de Grantham, monk of abbey F. Thomas de Overton, monk of abbey	Crowland, octave of Michaelmas [6 Oct.] 1385
36/1757	John [Buckingham], bishop of Lincoln [LP]	John Waltham*, archdeacon of Richmond Richard Ravenser*, archdeacon of Lincoln M. John Barnet* [the younger], official of the court of Canterbury Richard Chesterfield*, canon of Lincoln	Sleaford, 11 Oct. 1385
36/1758	Walter [of Winforton], abbot of Winchcombe	Richard de Piriton [Pirton]*, archdeacon of Colchester Robert Faryndone [Farrington]*, clerk	Winchcombe, 16 Oct. 1385
36/1759	John [Timworth], abbot of Bury St Edmunds	William Bray Walter Toryngton [Torrington] D. John Waltham* D. John Scarle* [the younger] [CoP]	Our manor of Elmeswell [Elmswell], 15 Oct. 1385
36/1760	Richard [Yateley], abbot of Reading	F. Thomas Bray, monk of abbey Peter de Barton*, clerk	Reading, 11 Oct. 1385

36/1761	Thomas [de la Mare], abbot of St Albans	Robert Chestan, monk of abbey Robert Muskham* Thomas Charlton	St Albans, 14 Oct. 1385
36/1762	Walter [Froucestre], abbot of St Peter's, Gloucester	Robert Charleton [Charlton]* John Cassy*	Gloucester, 13 Oct. 1385
36/1763	Roger [Yatton], abbot of Evesham *[LP]*	M. Thomas de Stowe*, clerk Robert de Faryngdon [Farrington]*, clerk	Evesham, Sunday before St Luke [15 Oct.] 1385
36/1765	Edmund [Ellington], abbot of Ramsey	John Waltham*, archdeacon of Richmond Michael Ravendale*, clerk John Lincoln*, clerk	Ramsey, Monday before St Luke [16 Oct.] 1385
36/1766	Chapter of Durham *[LP]*	William Lambard [Lambert] Gilbert de Elvet John de Killynghall [Killinghall]	Durham Chapter House, 14 Oct.1385
36/1767	Clergy of Colchester archdeaconry *[LP]*	Richard de Piriton [Pirton]*, archdeacon of Colchester	Colchester, 13 Oct. 1385
36/1768	Chapter of York	John de Waltham*, archdeacon of Richmond William de Gunthorp [Gunthorpe]*, canon of York William del [de] Ford, canon of York William de Ayrmyn [Airmyn]*, canon of York	York, 8 Oct. 1385
36/1769	William [Methwold], abbot of St Benet of Hulme	James de Billyngford [Billingford]*	In the monastery, Monday after St Edward the Confessor [16 Oct.] 1385

PARLIAMENT AT WESTMINSTER, 1 OCTOBER 1386

36/1770	Walter [Camme], abbot of Malmesbury	F. Thomas Chelesworth [Chelsworth], monk of abbey John Colyngbourne [Collingbourne], clerk Thomas Sutton, clerk	Malmesbury, 20 Sept. 1386
36/1771	[John Deeping], abbot of Thorney	F. Thomas de Charwelton*, monk of abbey John Harlington*	Thorney, 26 Sept. 1386
36/1772	John [de Sherburn], abbot of Selby	John de Waltham*, archdeacon of Richmond Thomas de Stanelay [Stanley]*, canon of Lichfield Thomas de Haxay [Haxey]*, clerk	Selby, 10 Sept. 1386
36/1773	Henry [Wakefield], bishop of Worcester [LP]	M. Thomas Stowe*, doctor of laws Thomas Stanley* Robert Faryndon [Farrington]* John Besford* Richard Wynchecombe [Winchcombe]	Hartlebury, 24 Sept. 1386
36/1774	Chapter of York [LP]	William de Gunthorp [Gunthorpe]*, canon of York William del Ferthe [de Ford], canon of York Thomas de Forde [Ford]*, canon of York	York, 24 Sept. 1386
36/1775	Adam [Houghton], bishop of St Davids	John de Waltham*, archdeacon of Richmond M. Robert Manfeld [Manfield]* D. John de Bouland [Bowland]*	Our manor of Laucefey [Lamphey], 24 Sept. 1386

36/1776	William [Bridford], abbot of St Mary's, York	D. Robert de Faryngton [Farrington]*, clerk D. Michael de Ravendale*, clerk D. John de Lincoln*, clerk William Savage Thomas Dawnay [Daunay] Henry de Preston*	York, 20 Sept. 1386
36/1777	Michael [de Pecham], abbot of St Augustine's, Canterbury	F. Peter de Twytham [Twitham], monk of abbey	Canterbury, 30 Sept. 1386
36/1778	Walter [de Legh], prior of Worcester	M. Thomas Stowe*, archdeacon of Bedford, doctor of laws M. Robert de la More*, archdeacon of Llandaff, doctor of laws	Worcester, 18 Sept. 1386
36/1779	Robert [Berrington of Walworth], prior, and chapter of Durham Cathedral	John de Kyllyngall [Killinghall] John de Kyllerby [Killerby]	Durham Chapter House, 26 Sept.1386
36/1780	Thomas [de la Mare], abbot of St Albans	John Lincoln*, clerk John Hervy* Thomas Charlton	In the monastery, 29 Sept. 1386
36/1781	John [Chynnok alias Wynchestre], abbot of Glastonbury	M. John Shillingford*, doctor of laws, clerk Lambert Mor, clerk	Glastonbury, 20 Sept.1386

36/1782	John de Haynton [Hainton], abbot of Bardney	Peter de Barton*, canon of Salisbury F. Thomas de Welton, prior and monk of abbey John de Folkyngham [Folkingham]*, clerk John Frank*, clerk	Bardney, 25 Sept. 1386
36/1783	[Henry of Overton], abbot of Peterborough	Richard de Tretton*, clerk F. Thomas de Bury, monk of abbey John de Lincoln*, clerk	In the monastery, 25 Sept. 1386
36/1784	[Nicholas Stevens], abbot of Shrewsbury [LP]	William de Prene [Prime], clerk Thomas de Lee* Edward de Acton*	Shrewsbury, 26 Sept. 1386
36/1785	Walter [of Winforton], abbot of Winchcombe	Richard Piriton [Pirton]*, archdeacon of Colchester, clerk Robert Faryndon [Farrington]*, clerk Robert Chiltone [Chilton] F. William Lodelowe [Ludlow], prior of abbey	Winchcombe, 28 Sept. 1386
36/1786	Chapter of Worcester Cathedral	M. Thomas Stowe*, archdeacon of Bedford, doctor of laws M. Robert de la More*, archdeacon of Llandaff, doctor of laws	Worcester Chapter House, Sunday after feast of St Michael [30 Sept.] 1386
36/1787	William [de Greneburgh], prior of Coventry	John Rome*, clerk Thomas Seyvill [Saville]*, gentleman	Coventry, 24 Sept. 1386

Ref.			Place and date
36/1788	Thomas [Brinton], bishop of Rochester	Robert Faryngton [Farrington]*, rector of Wrotham parish church in the archbishop of Canterbury's immediate jurisdiction	Our manor of Trottesclyve [Trottiscliffe], 29 Sept. 1386
36/1789	Robert [Berrington of Walworth], prior, and chapter of Durham	John Conyer Gilbert de Elvet John Killynghall [Killinghall] John de Killerby	Durham, 25 Sept. 1386
36/1790	John [Buckingham], bishop of Lincoln	John Waltham*, archdeacon of Richmond M. John Barnet* [the younger], official of the court of Canterbury	Sleaford, 28 Sept. 1386
36/1791	Richard Yatele [Yateley], abbot of Reading	F. William Henle [Henley], monk of abbey Peter de Barton*, clerk John Scarle* [the younger], clerk [CoP]	Reading, 12 Sept.1386
36/1792	Walter [Froucestre], abbot of St Peter's, Gloucester	Robert Cherleton [Charlton]* William de Horbury*, clerk John Cassy*	Gloucester, 29 Sept. 1386
36/1793	John [Eynsham], abbot of Hyde near Winchester	John de Burton*, clerk John Sutton, clerk	Hyde, 28 Sept.1386
36/1794	John de Tymworth [Timworth], abbot of Bury St Edmunds	John Scarle* [the younger], clerk [CoP] Walter de Totyngton [Tottington], monk of abbey William Bray, monk of abbey	Our manor of Elmeswell [Elmswell], 27 Sept. 1386
36/1795	Roger [Yatton], abbot of Evesham	M. Thomas Stowe*, doctor of laws Robert Faryngton [Farrington]*, clerk	Evesham, 10 Sept. 1386

PARLIAMENT AT WESTMINSTER, 3 FEBRUARY 1388

36/1796	John [Buckingham], bishop of Lincoln [LP]	Peter Dalton*, treasurer of Lincoln Cathedral Thomas la Warre, canon of Lincoln D. John Ravenser*, canon of Lincoln John de Lincoln*, rector of Caverfeld [Caversfield], Lincoln diocese	Sleaford, 20 Jan. 1388
36/1797	Thomas de Sudburia [Sudbury], dean of Wells [LP]	M. Thomas Spert*, chancellor of Wells M. John Shillingford*, canon of Wells M. Arnold Brocas*, canon of Wells Peter de Barton*, canon of Wells	Wells, 15 Jan. 1388
36/1798	Walter [de Legh], prior of Worcester	M. Thomas Stowe*, doctor of laws John Obdon, clerk	Worcester, 18 Jan. 1388
36/1799	Thomas [de la Mare], abbot of St Albans	[Damaged] John Lincolne [Lincoln]*, clerk	[Damaged] 1388
36/1800	Thomas de Sudburia [Sudbury], dean of Wells [LP]	M. John Shillingford* M. Thomas Spert*, chancellor of Wells Cathedral Peter Barton*, canon of Wells Arnold Brocas*, canon of Wells	Wells, 20 Jan. 1388
37/1801	[Walter Camme], abbot of Malmesbury	F. Thomas Chelesworth [Chelsworth], monk of abbey John Chitterne*, clerk John Colyngbourne [Collingbourne], clerk John Sutton, clerk	Malmesbury, 22 Jan. 1388

37/1802	[Peter de Hanney], abbot of Abingdon	F. Thomas Salisbure [Salisbury], monk of abbey M. John Bowland, rector of Skarefeld [Sheffield]	Abingdon, vigil of the Purification [1 Feb.] 1388
37/1803	Laurence [Child], bishop of St Asaph	M. John Trevaur [Trevor]*, doctor of laws, precentor of Wells D. Thomas Forster, rector of Yvicherche [Ivychurch] D. Thomas Newman, vicar of Middleton, Canterbury diocese	Shrewsbury, 18 Jan. 1388
37/1804	[William Methwold], abbot of St Benet of Hulme	James de Billyngford [Billingford]*	The abbey, 30 Jan. 1388
37/1805	[Henry of Overton], abbot of Peterborough [LP]	John Lincoln*, clerk William Thirnyng [Thirning]* F. Thomas de Bury, monk of abbey	Peterborough, 30 Jan. 1388
37/1806	[John de Ashby], abbot of Crowland [LP]	John de Folkyngham [Folkingham]*, clerk Albin de Enderby* John de Wessyngton [Wessington], clerk	Crowland, Monday before Purification of the Blessed Virgin Mary [27 Jan.] 1388
37/1807	Prior [Robert Berrington] of Walworth] and chapter of Durham	John de Killynghall [Killinghall] John de Killyrby [Killerby], the younger	Durham, 18 Jan. 1388
37/1808	Clergy of Cleveland archdeaconry	M. Richard de Conyngeston [Coniston], official of the court of Canterbury Richard de Skypsee [Skipsea], rector of Slaytburn [Slaidburn], incipient in canon law	Gysburn [Guisborough], in Cleveland, 6 Jan. 1388

Ref.	Principal	Proctors/Members	Place, Date
37/1809	[William Bridford], abbot of St Mary's, York	Michael de Ravendale*, clerk; Robert de Wycliffe, clerk; John de Rome*, clerk; M. John de Southwell, clerk	York, 12 Jan. 1388
37/1810	Adam [Houghton], bishop of St Davids	John [Gilbert]*, bishop of Hereford; M. Robert Manfeld [Manfield]*, provost of Beverley; John de Bouland [Bowland]*, clerk, canon of St Davids; John Hyet, clerk, canon of St Davids	Lantefey [Lamphey] manor, 29 Jan. 1388
37/1811	[Walter of Winforton], abbot of Winchcombe	M. Richard Wych [Wyche]*, canon of Salisbury, clerk; Robert Faryndon [Farrington]*, clerk	Winchcombe, 29 Jan. 1388
37/1812	[John Deeping], abbot of Thorney	F. Thomas de Charwelton*, monk of abbey; John Harlynton [Harlington]*	Thorney, 28 Jan. 1388
37/1813	[Roger Yatton], abbot of Evesham [LP]	M. Thomas de Stowe*, archdeacon of Bedford, doctor of laws; Robert de Faryndon [Farrington]*	Evesham, 28 Jan. 1388
37/1814	[Walter Froucestre], abbot of St Peter's, Gloucester	Robert Churlton [Charlton]*; William Horbury*, clerk; John Cassy*	Gloucester, 24 Jan. 1388
37/1815	Clergy of York archdeaconry	M. Richard de Conyngston [Coniston]*, canon of York; Richard de Skypse [Skipsea], rector of Slaytburn [Slaidburn]	York, 28 Jan. 1388
37/1816	[John de Sherburn], abbot of Selby	Thomas de Stanley*, clerk; George de Louthorp [Lowthorpe]*, clerk	Selby, 25 Jan. 1388

PARLIAMENT AT WESTMINSTER, 17 JANUARY 1390

37/1817	[Nicholas Stevens], abbot of Shrewsbury	William de Prime, clerk Thomas Pride* of Salop Richard Oteley [Otley]	[Damaged] 1390
37/1818	F. John Eynesham [Eynsham], abbot of Hyde near Winchester	[Illegible] John Suttone [Sutton], clerk John Cole, clerk	Hyde, 14 Jan. 1390
37/1819	John [Fordham], bishop of Ely	[Illegible] John Burton*, keeper of the rolls of chancery Guy de Rouclif [Roecliffe], clerk William de Fulburn [Fulbourn]*, clerk	Dounham [Downham] manor, 12 Jan. 1390
37/1820	[Walter of Winforton], abbot of Winchcombe	Robert Faryndon [Farrington]*, clerk John Derehurste [Deerhurst]	Winchcombe, 8 Jan. 1390
37/1821	[William Cratfeld], abbot of Bury St Edmunds	F. William Bray, monk of abbey Thomas Skelton*	Bury St Edmunds, 13 Jan. 1390
37/1822	[Walter Froucestre], abbot of St Peter's, Gloucester	M. Richard Wiche [Wyche]*, canon of Salisbury William Horbury*, clerk	Gloucester, 10 Jan. 1390
37/1823	[Peter de Hanney], abbot of Abingdon	F. Thomas Salisbury, monk of abbey John de Roderham [Rotherham]*, clerk John Hertlepole [Hartlepool]*, clerk	Abingdon, 14 Jan. 1390

293

37/1824	[William Methwold], abbot of St Benet of Hulme	James de Billingford* [Illegible]	[Damaged]
37/1825	Thomas [Brantingham], bishop of Exeter	Robert Faryndon [Farrington]*, clerk Thomas de Barton*, clerk	Clist [Bishop's Clyst] manor, 8 Jan. 1390
37/1826	[Roger Yatton], abbot of Evesham	M. Thomas de Stowe*, archdeacon of Bedford Robert de Faryndon [Farrington]*, clerk	Evesham, 10 Jan. 1390
37/1827	[Geoffrey Sturry alias de Sancta Ositha], abbot of St John's, Colchester	John Lincolne [Lincoln]*, clerk F.John Horkeslegh [Horkesley]	Colchester, 14 Jan. 1390
37/1828	[Richard Yateley], abbot of Reading	F: William Henle [Henley], monk of abbey Peter de Barton*, clerk William Ordbury, clerk	Reading, 12 Jan.1390
37/1829	[John Deeping], abbot of Thorney	[Illegible] F: Thomas de Charwelton*, monk of abbey John Harlyngton [Harlington]*	Thorney, 11 Jan. 1390
37/1830	[William de Greneburgh], prior of Coventry	F.John de Tamworth, monk of abbey John Rome*, clerk Thomas Seyville [Saville]*, gentleman	Coventry, 4.Jan.1390
37/1831	[Damaged]	[Damaged] canon of Beverley M. William Cawode [Cawood]*, rector of Warton, York diocese John de Lincoln*, clerk	[Damaged], 9 Jan. 1390

PARLIAMENT AT WESTMINSTER, 3 NOVEMBER 1391

37/1832	[Nicholas Elnestowe], abbot of Peterborough]	M. Hugh Grenham, clerk William Crosfeld [Crossfield] F. [Robert] Blatherwyke [Blatherwycke], monk of abbey	[Illegible], 30 Oct. 1391
37/1833	[Walter Froucestre], abbot of St Peter's, Gloucester	William Horbury*, clerk Richard Nayssh [Nash]*	Gloucester, 20 Oct. 1391
37/1834	[William Cratfeld], abbot of Bury St Edmunds	M. Thomas Baketon*, archdeacon of London John Scarle* [the younger], clerk [CoP] F. William Bray, monk of abbey Thomas Skelton*	In the monastery, 29 Oct. 1391
37/1835	[James de Horton], prior of Coventry	John Rome*, clerk Thomas Seyvill [Saville]*, gentleman	Coventry, 24 Oct. 1391
37/1836	[Walter Camme], abbot of Malmesbury	F. Thomas Chelesworth [Chelsworth], monk of abbey John Chitterne* John Sutton John Thornebury [Thornbury]*	Malmesbury, 26 Oct.1391
37/1837	[William Colchester], abbot of Westminster	John Scarle* [the younger] [CoP] M. Nicholas Stoket*, licenciate in laws F. William Sudbery [Sudbury]*, bachelor in theology, monk of abbey F. Thomas Burwell, archdeacon and monk of monastery [sic]	Westminster, 29 Oct.1391

295

37/1838	[Roger Yatton], abbot of Evesham	M. Thomas de Stowe*, archdeacon of Bedford, doctor of laws Robert de Faryndon [Farrington]*, clerk	Evesham, St Luke's Day [18 Oct.] 1391
37/1839	Chapter of Worcester	M. Thomas Stowe*, archdeacon of Bedford, doctor of laws M. Robert More*, archdeacon of Llandaff, doctor of laws M. John Prophyt [Prophet]*, clerk M. Robert Esbache*, clerk	Worcester, 12 Oct. 1391
37/1840	[Geoffrey Sturry *alias* de Sancta Ositha], abbot of St John's, Colchester	John Browne [Brown], clerk	Colchester, 31 Oct.1391
37/1841	[Richard Yateley], abbot of Reading	F. William Henlee [Henley], monk of abbey Peter de Barton*, clerk James Bylyngforde [Billingford]*, clerk	Reading, 31 Oct. 1391
37/1842	Henry [Wakefield], bishop of Worcester	M. Thomas Stowe*, archdeacon of Bedford, doctor of laws M. John Burbache [Burbage]*, doctor of laws Robert de Farynton [Farrington]* Edmund Warham*, archdeacon of Kermerdyn [Carmarthen], St David's diocese John Haseley*, clerk John Besford*, clerk	Wythyndon [Withington], 28 Oct. 1391

37/1843	[John de Hemingborough], prior of Durham [LP]	John Kyrkley [Kirkley] John Kyllyngale [Killinghall]	Durham, 15 Oct. 1391
37/1844	Chapter of Durham [LP]	John Kyrkley [Kirkley] John Kyllyngale [Killinghall]	Durham, 15 Oct. 1391
37/1845	[John Chynnok alias Wynchestre], abbot of Glastonbury	John Folkyngham [Folkingham]* M. Roger Paym*, bachelor in laws	Glastonbury, 24 Oct. 1391
37/1846	[Thomas de Stayngreve], abbot of St Mary's, York	John de Burton*, clerk of king's rolls M. William de Cawode [Cawood]*, rector of Warton, York diocese M. Alan de Newerk [Newark]*, bachelor in laws	The abbey, 20 Oct. 1391
37/1847	[John de Sherburn], abbot of Selby	Thomas Haxay [Haxey]*, clerk John de Rome*, clerk	Selby, 24 Oct. 1391
37/1848	[Walter of Winforton], abbot of Winchcombe	Robert Faryndon [Farrington]*, clerk John Durhust [Deerhurst], layman	Winchcombe, 28 Oct. 1391
37/1849	Thomas [Brantingham], bishop of Exeter	Robert Faryndon [Farrington]*, canon of York William de Dowebrygge [Dowbridge], canon of Exeter John Barton, canon of Exeter	[Bishop's] Clyst manor, 17 Oct. 1391
37/1850	[Thomas de la Mare], abbot of St Albans	Robert Chestan, monk of abbey John Scarburgh [Scarborough]*, clerk Thomas Thorneburgh [Thornbury]	St Albans, 2 Nov.1391

38/1851	[William Methwold], abbot of St Benet of Hulme	James de Billingford* Alan Heigham Geoffrey de Somerton	Hulme, 31 Oct.1391
38/1852	[John Eynsham], abbot of Hyde, Winchester	M. Peter Barton* John Sutton	Hyde, 15 Oct. 1391
38/1853	[John Deeping], abbot of Thorney	F. Roger de Uffyngton [Uffington], monk of abbey John Harlyngton [Harlington]*	Thorney, 31 Oct. 1391
38/1854	Dean [Thomas de Eure] and chapter of St Paul's, London	Laurence Allerthorp [Allerthorpe]* M. Thomas Stowe* John Wenlyburgh [Wellingborough]*, senior	London, 31 Oct. 1391
38/1855	Edmund [Bromfield], bishop of Llandaff	M. Thomas Newenham*, canon of Llandaff Cathedral M. Roger Crook, canon of Llandaff Cathedral	Our manor of [Lancarfan], 24 Oct. 1391
38/1856	[John Buckingham], bishop of Lincoln [LP]	M. John Barnet* [the younger], official of the court of Canterbury John Burton*, canon of Lincoln John Ravenser*, canon of Lincoln M. John Bottisham, canon of Lincoln	Stow Park, 29 Oct. 1391
38/1857	[John Green], prior of Worcester	M. Thomas Stow [Stowe]*, archdeacon of Bedford, doctor of laws M. Robert More*, archdeacon of Llandaff, doctor of laws M. John Prophyt [Prophet]*, clerk M. Robert Esbache*, clerk	Worcester, 12 Oct. 1391

| 38/1858 | William [Bottlesham], bishop of Rochester | Robert Faryngton [Farrington]*, rector of Wrotham in the immediate jurisdiction of the archbishop of Canterbury
M.John Mory, bishop's official | Our manor of Trottesclyv [Trottiscliffe], 31 Oct. 1391 |

PARLIAMENT AT WESTMINSTER, 20 JANUARY 1393

38/1859	[John de Hemingborough], prior of Durham [LP]	John Galon [Galan] Peter de Mordon	Durham, 11 Jan. 1393
38/1860	[Peter de Hanney], abbot of Abingdon	F.William Bereford [Barford], monk of abbey William Horbury*, clerk	Abingdon, morrow of Epiphany [7 Jan.] 1393
38/1861	[Geoffrey Sturry alias de Sancta Osithia], abbot of St John's, Colchester	John Skarle [Scarle]* [the younger], clerk [CoP] John Lincoln*, clerk	Colchester, morrow of Epiphany [7 Jan.] 1393
38/1862	Walter [Skirlaw], bishop of Durham	John de Burton*, canon of Beverley, keeper of the rolls of chancery John de Wendlyngburgh [Wellinborough]*, canon of London Simon de Gaunsted [Gaunstead]*, clerk Robert de Garton*, clerk Henry Malpas*, clerk	La Welhalle [Wheel Hall], 8 Jan. 1393
38/1863	John [Swaffham], bishop of Bangor	Thomas Ardawne, rector of Llandencolyn [Llanddeiniolen], Bangor diocese	Bangor, 10 Jan. 1393

38/1864	Walter [Skirlaw], bishop of Durham	John de Burton*, canon of Beverley, keeper of the rolls of chancery John de Wendlyngburgh [Wellingborough]*, canon of London Simon de Gaunsted [Gaunstead]*, clerk Robert de Garton*, clerk of the chancery Henry Malpas*, clerk of the chancery Stephen de Fall	Welhalle [Wheel Hall], 8 Jan. 1393
38/1865	John [Sheppey], dean, and chapter of Lincoln	John de Burton*, canon of Lincoln John Ravenser*, canon of Lincoln	Lincoln, 15 Jan. 1393
38/1866	[Roger Yatton], abbot of Evesham	Richard Feld [Field], clerk Robert de Farynton [Farrington]*, clerk John Scarborough*, clerk	Evesham, 12 Jan. 1393
38/1867	[John Deeping], abbot of Thorney	F. Roger de Uffyngton [Uffington], monk of abbey John Overton Stephen Burton	Thorney, 6 Jan. 1393
38/1868	Edmund [Bromfield], bishop of Llandaff	M. Thomas Newenham*, canon of Llandaff Cathedral John Newenham, rector of the parish church of Nova Villa Lupi [Wolvesnewton]	Our manor of [Lancarfan], 20 Jan. 1393
38/1869	[John de Hainton], abbot of Bardney	Peter de Barton*, canon of Salisbury John Marcham [Markham] Albin de Enderby* John Franke [Frank]*, clerk	Bardney, Hilary [13 Jan.] 1393

38/1870	[Thomas de Stayngreve], abbot of St Mary's, York	John de Burton*, clerk of the rolls M. William de Cawode [Cawood]*, rector of Warton, York diocese Simon Gawnstede [Gaunstead]*, clerk	York, 21 Dec. 1392
38/1871	[John Buckingham], bishop of Lincoln	John Burton*, canon of Lincoln John Ravenser*, canon of Lincoln Thomas Haxay [Haxey]*, canon of Lichfield	Stow Park, 10 Jan. 1393
38/1872	[John de Sherburn], abbot of Selby	Thomas Haxey*, clerk John Rome*, clerk Robert de Brayton*, clerk	Selby, 10 Dec. 1392
38/1873	John de Carleton, archdeacon of Colchester	M. William Storteford [Stortford]* William Langham	Colchester, 16 Jan. 1393
38/1874	Thomas [de Eure] dean, and chapter of St Paul's, London	Guy Mone, senior, canon of St Paul's John Wendlyngburgh [Wellingborough]*, senior, canon of St Paul's John Scarle* [the younger], canon of York [CoP]	London, 9 Jan. 1393
38/1875	[Walter Froucestre], abbot of St Peter's, Gloucester	William de Horbury*, clerk John Fekkenham [Feckenham] William Chyngulton	Gloucester, 16 Jan. 1393
38/1876	[William Cratfeld], abbot of Bury St Edmunds	John Scarlee [Scarle]* [the younger], clerk [CoP] F. William Bray, monk of abbey F. Richard Wysebech [Wisbech], monk of abbey	In the abbey, 8 Jan. 1393

38/1877	[Thomas Overton], abbot of Crowland	John Folkyngham [Folkingham]*, clerk M. Hugh Grantham Albin Enderby* Richard Muriell*	Crowland, Thursday before St Hilary [9 Jan.] 1393
38/1878	[Walter of Winforton], abbot of Winchcombe	Robert Faryndon [Farrington]*, clerk John Durhurst [Deerhurst], layman	Winchcombe, Monday in the octaves of Epiphany [13 Jan.] 1393
38/1879	Henry [Wakefield], bishop of Worcester	John Burton* Robert Faryngton [Farrington]*, canon of Lincoln John Chitterne* M. John Chewe	Hartlebury, 15 Jan. 1393
38/1880	Thomas [Brantingham], bishop of Exeter	Roger Walden*, canon of Exeter Robert Faryngton [Farrington]*, canon of Lincoln John Wendlyngburgh [Wellingborough]*, canon of Crediton	Clist [Bishop's Clyst] manor, 13 Jan. 1393
38/1881	John [Green], prior of Worcester	M. John Prophete [Prophet]* William Tangubourn Thomas Belne* [MP]	Worcester, 4 Jan. 1393
38/1882	[William Weld], abbot of St Augustine's, Canterbury	John Scarle* [the younger], clerk [CoP] Thomas Hunden, monk of abbey	Canterbury, 6 Jan. 1393
38/1883	[Richard Yateley], abbot of Reading	F. William Henle [Henley], monk of abbey Peter de Barton*, clerk James Billingford*	Reading, 8 Jan. 1393

302

38/1884	Henry [Despenser], bishop of Norwich	M. John de Derlyngton [Darlington], archdeacon of Norwich Henry Bowet*, archdeacon of Lincoln [M] John de Lydeford [Lydford]*, archdeacon of Totnes, Exeter diocese	Norwich, 14 Jan. 1393
38/1885	John [Fordham], bishop of Ely	Robert de Faryndon [Farrington]*, canon of York John Wendlingburgh [Wellingborough]*, senior; canon of London John Sunderassh [Sundridge], rector of Dodyngton [Doddington], Ely diocese	Our manor of Dodding-ton, 12 Jan. 1393
38/1886	[Edmund Ellington], abbot of Ramsey	John Burton*, clerk John Rome*, clerk	Ramsey, 6 Jan. 1393
38/1887	[Walter Camme], abbot of Malmesbury	F. Thomas Chelesworth [Chelsworth], monk of abbey John Chytterne [Chitterne]*, clerk Richard Parker, clerk	Malmesbury, 18 Jan. 1393
38/1888	William [Bottlesham], bishop of Rochester	Robert Faryngton [Farrington]*, rector of Wrotham in the archbishop of Canterbury's immediate jurisdiction	Our manor of Trottesclyv [Trottiscliffe], 9 Jan. 1393
38/1889	[Thomas de la Mare], abbot of St Albans	F. Robert Chestan, monk of abbey Simon Gaunstede [Gaunstead]*, clerk [Illegible]	St Albans, 27 Dec. 1392
38/1890	James [de Horton], prior of Coventry	Thomas Stanley*, clerk John Rome*, clerk Thomas Sayvill [Saville]* William Pole	Coventry, 6 Jan. 1393

38/1891	[Nicholas Stevens], abbot of Shrewsbury	M. John Scarle* [the younger], clerk [CoP] Thomas Pride* of Salop	Shrewsbury, 16 Jan. 1393
38/1892	Chapter of Worcester	M. John Prophete [Prophet]* William Jangulton Thomas Boby	Worcester, 12 Jan. 1393
38/1893	[William Methwold], abbot of St Benet of Hulme	James de Billingford* Alan Heigham	Hulme, 14 Jan. 1393
38/1894	Clergy of Colchester archdeaconry	M. William Storteford [Stortford]* M. William Langham	Colchester, 16 Jan. 1393
38/1895	[Nicholas Elnestowe], abbot of Peterborough	John Burton*, clerk F. Robert Blatherwyk [Blatherwycke], monk of abbey John Tendale	In the monastery, 11 Jan. 1393
38/1896	John [de Hemingborough], prior of Durham	John Galan Peter de Mordon	Durham, 10 Jan. 1393

PARLIAMENT AT WESTMINSTER, 27 JANUARY 1394

38/1897	John [Fordham], bishop of Ely	John Wendlyngburgh [Wellingborough]*, senior, canon of London M. John Bernard*, rector of Litham [Lytham], York diocese	Dodyngton [Doddington], 14 Jan. 1394

38/1898	[John de Hainton], abbot of Bardney [LP]	Peter de Barton*, canon of Salisbury John Markham John Frank*, clerk Albin de Enderby*	Bardney, 24 Jan. 1394
38/1899	[Nicholas Elnestowe], abbot of Peterborough	John Burton*, clerk F. Robert Blatherwyk [Blatherwycke] John Tyndale*	Peterborough, 22 Jan. 1394
38/1900	[Walter of Winforton], abbot of Winchcombe	Robert Faryndon [Farrington]*, clerk John Durhurst [Deerhurst], layman	Winchcombe, 20 Jan. 1394
39/1901	[Walter Froucestre], abbot of St Peter's, Gloucester	M. John Forstall, clerk John Durhurste [Deerhurst] John Fekkenham [Feckenham]	Gloucester, 20 Jan. 1394
39/1902	Henry [Despenser], bishop of Norwich	M. Michael Cergeaux*, dean of the court of Canterbury M. Thomas Hedersete [Hethersett], archdeacon of Sudbury M. John de Thorp, rector of Erpyngham [Erpingham]	Norwich, 24 Jan. 1394
39/1903	Thomas de la Mare], abbot of St Albans	Robert Chestan, monk of abbey Simon Gaunstede [Gaunstead]*, clerk Thomas Thornburgh [Thornbury]	St Albans, 20 Jan. 1394
39/1904	Thomas [Brantingham], bishop of Exeter	William Ermyn [Airmyn]*, clerk Robert Faryngton [Farrington]*, clerk Thomas Barton*, clerk	Our manor of Clyst [Bishop's Clyst], 1 Jan. 1394

39/1905	[Nicholas Stevens], abbot of Shrewsbury	William Prene [Prime], clerk Thomas Neuport [Newport]	Shrewsbury, 13 Jan. 1394
39/1906	William [Bottlesham], bishop of Rochester	Robert Faryngton [Farrington]*, rector of Wrotham in the archbishop of Canterbury's immediate jurisdiction	Our manor of Trottesclyv [Trottiscliffe], 20 Jan. 1394
39/1907	[John Deeping], abbot of Thorney	F. Roger de Uffyngton [Uffington], monk of abbey Hugh Hanworth*, clerk John Harlyngton [Harlington]*	Thorney, 24 Jan. 1394
39/1908	[William Colchester], abbot of Westminster	John Scarle* [the younger], clerk [CoP] Richard Holme*, clerk F. Peter Coumbe, monk of abbey F. John Burwell, monk of abbey	Westminster, 26 Jan. 1394
39/1909	[Roger Yatton], abbot of Evesham	M. Thomas Stowe*, doctor of laws Robert Farynton [Farrington]*, clerk	Evesham, 21 Jan. 1394
39/1910	[Thomas de Stayngreve], abbot of St Mary's, York	John de Burton*, canon of York, clerk of the king's rolls M. William de Cawode [Cawood]*, licenciate in laws, canon of Ripon Simon Gawnstede [Gaunstead]*, clerk F. Richard de Newland, monk of abbey	In the monastery, 28 Jan. 1394
39/1911	Clergy of Northumberland archdeaconry	John Killynghall [Killinghall] William Halywell [Holywell]	Newcastle-on-Tyne, 17 Jan. 1394
39/1912	Clergy of Durham archdeaconry	John de Kylynghale [Killinghall] Thomas de Brauncepath [Brancepath]	Durham, 3 Jan. 1394

39/1913	Chapter of Worcester	M. Thomas Stowe*, archdeacon of Bedford, doctor of laws M. John Elmere [Elmer]*, doctor of laws M. Robert Esbache*	Worcester, 14 Dec. 1393
39/1914	W[alter Skirlaw], bishop of Durham	John de Burton*, canon of Beverley, keeper of the rolls of chancery John de Wendelyngburgh [Wellingborough]*, canon of London *Unnamed others* ('ac alios per *alias* meas litteras patentes constitui')	Welhalle [Wheel Hall], 8 Jan. 1394
39/1915	W[alter Skirlaw], bishop of Durham	John de Burton*, canon of Beverley, keeper of the rolls of chancery John de Wendelyngburgh [Wellingborough]*, canon of London *[Illegible]* *[Illegible]*	*[Illegible]*
39/1916	[John de Sherburn], abbot of Selby	Thomas Haxay [Haxey]*, clerk John de Rome*, clerk Robert de Brayton*, clerk	Selby, 7 Jan. 1394
39/1917	[Walter Camme], abbot of Malmesbury	F. Thomas Chelesworth [Chelsworth], monk of abbey John Chytterne [Chitterne]* Robert Say John Aldurley [Alderley]	Malmesbury, 24 Jan. 1394

39/1918	Prior [John de Hemingborough] and chapter of Durham	Gilbert de Elvett [Elvet] John de Killinghall	Durham, 12 Jan. 1394
39/1919	Chapter of York *[LP]*	Robert de Farynton [Farrington]*, canon of York John Skaryll [Scarle]* [the younger], canon of York [CoP]	York, 14 Jan. 1394
39/1920	[William Methwold], abbot of St Benet of Hulme	James de Billyngford [Billingford]* Alan Heigham Geoffrey de Somerton	In the monastery, 24 Jan. 1394
39/1921	[William Cratfeld], abbot of Bury St Edmunds	John Scarlee [Scarle]* [the younger], clerk [CoP] Thomas Skelton* M. Thomas Baketon* F. William Bray, monk of abbey	Our manor of Elmeswell [Elmswell], 17 Jan. 1394
39/1922	[Peter de Hanney], abbot of Abingdon	F. William Bereford [Barford], monk of abbey John Hertilpole [Hartlepool]*, clerk	Abingdon, 24 Jan. 1394
39/1923	[Richard Yateley], abbot of Reading	Peter de Barton*, clerk James Byllyngford [Billingford]*, clerk	Reading, 4 Jan. 1394
39/1924	[James de Horton], prior of Coventry	John Rome*, clerk Thomas Sayvill [Saville]*, gentleman	Coventry, 16 Jan. 1394
39/1925	[John Chynnok *alias* Wynchestre], abbot of Glastonbury	John Folkyngham [Folkingham]*, clerk M. Roger Payn*, inceptor in law, clerk	Glastonbury, 20 Jan. 1394
39/1926	[Thomas Overton], abbot of Crowland	John de Folkyngham [Folkingham]*, clerk F. William de Walden, monk of abbey Albin de Enderby*	Crowland, Monday after St Hilary [19 Jan.] 1394

39/1927	[John Eynsham], abbot of Hyde near Winchester	M. Peter Barton*, clerk John Sutton	Hyde, 23 Jan. 1394
39/1928	[John Green], prior of Worcester	M. Thomas Stowe*, archdeacon of Bedford, doctor of laws M. John Elmere [Elmer]*, doctor of laws	Worcester, 14 Dec. 1393
39/1929	[Edmund Ellington], abbot of Ramsey	John Burton*, clerk John Rome*, clerk Robert Waryn*	Ramsey, 16 Jan. 1394
39/1930	Clergy of York diocese [LP]	John de Burton*, canon of [Damaged] M. William de Cawode [Cawood]*, residentiary canon of Ripon collegiate church	York, 3 Jan. 1394

PARLIAMENT AT WESTMINSTER, 27 JANUARY 1395

39/1931	[John de Hainton], abbot of Bardney	Peter de Barton*, canon of Salisbury John Frank*, clerk William de Frisknay [Friskney] Albin de Enderby*	Bardney, 24 Jan. 1395
39/1932	Prior [John de Hemingborough] and chapter of Durham Cathedral	John Kylhinghale [Killinghall] John de Burne [Burn]	Durham, 8 Jan. 1395
39/1933	[William Methwold], abbot of St Benet of Hulme	James de Billingford* Geoffrey de Somerton	Hulme, Saturday before the Conversion of Paul [23 Jan.] 1395

309

39/1934	[John Chynnok alias Wynchestre], abbot of Glastonbury	M. Thomas Stowe*, doctor of laws John Folkyngham [Folkingham]* M. Roger Payn*, bachelor in laws	Glastonbury, 20 Jan. 1395
39/1935	[Peter de Hanney], abbot of Abingdon	F. William Bereford [Barford], monk of abbey John Hertelpole [Hartlepool]*	Abingdon, 22 Jan. 1395
39/1936	[Walter Froucestre], abbot of St Peter's, Gloucester	John Forstall, clerk Thomas Durhurst [Deerhurst] William Bruyse [Bruce]	Gloucester, 12 Jan. 1395
39/1937	[James de Horton], prior of Coventry	Thomas Stanley*, clerk John Rome*, clerk William Pole, clerk	Coventry, 8 Jan. 1395
39/1938	[Thomas de la Mare], abbot of St Albans	Robert Botheby [Boothby], monk of abbey [Damaged]	In the monastery, 20 Jan.1395
39/1939	Henry [Despenser], bishop of Norwich	M. Thomas Hedersete [Hethersett], archdeacon of Sudbury Michael Cergeaux* John Thorp Henry Well	Our manor of Southelm-ham [South Elmham], 11 Jan. 1395
39/1940	[Walter Camme], abbot of Malmesbury	F. Thomas Chelesworth [Chelsworth], monk of abbey John Chitterne*, clerk Robert Say, clerk	Malmesbury, [Damaged]

39/1941	[William Cratfeld], abbot of Bury St Edmunds	John Scarlee [Scarle]* [the younger] M. Thomas Baketon*, archdeacon of London Thomas Skelton*, knight F. William Bray, monk of abbey	Elmeswell [Elmswell] manor, 17 Jan. 1395
39/1942	[Walter of Winforton], abbot of Winchcombe	Robert More*, clerk John Durhurst [Deerhurst], layman	Winchcombe, 15 Jan. 1395
39/1943	[Nicholas Elnestowe], abbot of Peterborough	John Scyh' F. Robert Blatherwyk [Blatherwycke], monk of abbey John Tyndale*	In the monastery 23 Jan. 1395
39/1944	Richard [Scrope], bishop of Coventry and Lichfield	Thomas Stanley*, canon of Lichfield Thomas Hexx' [Haxey]*, canon of Lichfield Thomas Hilton, canon of Lichfield	Eccleshall, 20 Jan. 1395
39/1945	[John Deeping], abbot of Thorney	John Harlyngton [Harlington]* William Wakefield	Thorney, 20 Jan. 1395
39/1946	J[ohn Swaffham], bishop of Bangor	M. William Hundon, rector of Aber, Bangor diocese M. John Neuborgh [Newborough]	Bangor, 16 Jan. 1395
39/1947	[Thomas de Stayngreve], abbot of St Mary's, York	John Scarle* [the younger], clerk, master of the rolls of chancery M. William Cawode [Cawood]*, rector of Warton Simon Gaunsted [Gaunstead]*, clerk	In the monastery, 4 Jan. 1395
39/1948	[Nicholas Stevens], abbot of Shrewsbury	Roger Westwode [Westwood], clerk William Prene [Prime], clerk	Shrewsbury, 18 Jan. 1395

39/1949	[John Letcombe], abbot of Hyde near Winchester	M. Peter Barton* / F. John London, monk of abbey	Hyde, 24 Jan. 1395
39/1950	[William Weld], abbot of St Augustine's, Canterbury	John Scarlee [Scarle] * [the younger], clerk / F. Peter Twytham [Twitham], monk of abbey / F. Thomas Hunden, monk of abbey	In the monastery, 21 Jan.1395
40/1951	Chapter of Worcester Cathedral	M. John Prophet*, dean of Hereford / Robert Esebache [Esbache]*, canon of Lichfield	Worcester Chapter House, 18 Jan. 1395
40/1952	John [de Sherburn], abbot of Selby	Thomas Haxey*, clerk / John de Rome*, clerk / Robert de Brayton*, clerk	Selby, 10 Jan. 1395
40/1953	John [Crane], abbot of Battle	John Scarle* [the younger], clerk of the rolls of chancery / Robert Oxenbregg [Oxenbridge]	In the monastery, 16 Jan. 1395

PARLIAMENT AT WESTMINSTER, 22 JANUARY 1397

40/1954	John [Chynnok alias Wynchestre], abbot of Glastonbury	M. Thomas Stowe*, doctor of laws / William Souday [Sounday], doctor of laws	Glastonbury, 13 Jan. 1397
40/1955	Richard [Yateley], abbot of Reading	Peter de Barton*, clerk / John Frank*, clerk / John Scharle [Scarle]* [the younger], clerk / F. John Chynele [Chinley], monk of abbey	Reading, 15 Jan. 1397
40/1956	Peter [de Hanney], abbot of Abingdon	William Bereford [Barford], monk of abbey / John Hertilpole [Hartlepool]*, clerk	Abingdon, 20 Jan. 1397

40/1957	John [Letcombe], abbot of Hyde near Winchester	John Chittern [Chitterne]* John Sutton	Hyde, 18 Jan. 1397
40/1958	Walter [Skirlaw], bishop of Durham	John Scarle* [the younger], canon of York, keeper of the rolls of chancery Simon de Gaunsted [Gaunstead]*, canon of Lincoln Robert de Garton*, clerk Henry Malpas*, clerk of chancery	Our manor of Aukland [Bishop Auckland], 7 Jan. 1397
40/1959	[Nicholas Stevens], abbot of Shrewsbury [LP]	William Prene [Prime], clerk	Shrewsbury, 14 Jan. 1397
40/1960	Walter [Skirlaw], bishop of Durham	John Scarle* [the younger], canon of York, keeper of the rolls of chancery Simon de Gaunsted [Gaunstead]*, canon of Lincoln Robert de Garton*, clerk Henry Malpas*, clerk of chancery Stephen de Falle [Fall]	Our manor of Aukland [Bishop Auckland], 7 Jan. 1397
40/1961	[Thomas Overton], abbot of Crowland	F. William Walden, monk of abbey Albin de Enderby* John de Wessyngton [Wessington]	Crowland, 8 Jan. 1397
40/1962	Subdean and chapter of Lincoln, in the dean's absence [LP]	M. Thomas Stowe*, archdeacon of Bedford John de Neuport [Newport], precentor of Lincoln D. Robert de Whitteby [Whitby], prebendary of Keten [Ketton], Lincoln Cathedral	Lincoln Chapter House, 10 Jan. 1397

40/1963	William [Weld], abbot of St Augustine's, Canterbury	John Scarle* [the younger], clerk; Peter Twytham [Twitham], monk of abbey	Canterbury, 20 Jan. 1397
40/1964	John [de Sherburn], abbot of Selby	Thomas Haxey*, clerk; John Rome*, clerk	Selby, 8 Jan. 1397
40/1965	[Nicholas Elnestowe], abbot of Peterborough	John Scarle* [the younger], clerk; F. Thomas de Suthorp, monk of abbey; John Tyndale*	In the monastery, 19 Jan. 1397
40/1966	William [Bottlesham], bishop of Rochester [LP]	Robert Faryngton [Farrington]*, clerk; M. John Launce', bishop's official	Our manor of Trottesclyve [Trottisclffe], 20 Jan. 1397
40/1967	Thomas [de Stayngreve], abbot of St Mary's, York	John Scarlee [Scarle]* [the younger], canon of York and clerk of the rolls; M. Alan de Newerk [Newark]*; Simon Gaunstede [Gaunstead]*, clerk	In the monastery, 12 Jan. 1397
40/1968	[John de Deeping], abbot of Thorney	Robert Whytteby [Whitby], clerk; John Roderham [Rotherham]*, lerk; John Herlyngton [Harlington]*	Thorney, 10 Jan. 1397
40/1969	John [de Malvern], prior of Worcester Cathedral	M. Robert Esebache [Esbache]*	Worcester, 4 Jan. 1397
40/1970	Ralph [Erghum], bishop of Bath and Wells	John Scarle* [the younger], canon of Lincoln; M. William Waltham*, canon of Salisbury; Gilbert de Stone, canon of Wells; John Fytelton [Fittleton], steward of the bishop's lands	Our manor of Banewell [Banwell], 12 Jan. 1397

40/1971	William [Cratfeld], abbot of Bury St Edmunds	John Scarlee [Scarle]* [the younger], clerk Thomas Skelton*, knight M. Richard Brynklee [Brinkley]* F: Thomas Plumpton, monk of abbey	In the monastery, 18 Jan. 1397
40/1972	[Walter Froucestre], abbot of St Peter's, Gloucester	Nicholas [*Illegible*], monk of abbey John Durhurst [Deerhurst] William Bruyse [Bruce]	Gloucester, 14 Jan. 1397
40/1973	Chapter of Worcester Cathedral	M. Robert Esebache [Esbache]*, canon of Lichfield John Obdon, clerk	Worcester Chapter House, 4 Jan. 1397
40/1974	John [de Hainton], abbot of Bardney	John de Roderham [Rotherham]*, clerk John Frank* William de Fryskenay [Friskney] Albin de Enderby* F: William atte See, monk of abbey	Bardney, 15 Jan. 1397
40/1975	Simon [Brigham], abbot of St Benet of Hulme	James Billingford* John Gilberd	St Benet of Hulme, 18 Jan. 1397
40/1976	John [de Hemingborough], prior, and chapter of Durham	Gilbert Elvett [Elvet] John Killynghall [Killinghall] John Burn	Durham Chapter House, 6 Jan. 1397
40/1977	Thomas [Butturwyk], abbot of Ramsey	John Rome*, clerk Henry Maupas [Malpas]*, clerk	Ramsey, 17 Jan. 1397

315

PARLIAMENT AT WESTMINSTER, 17 SEPTEMBER 1397

| 40/1978 | John [de Malvern], prior of Worcester Cathedral | M. Robert [*Damaged*] [*Damaged*]abbe, rector of Hambury near Wych [Hambury near Droitwich] | Worcester, 2 Sept. 1397 |

PARLIAMENT AT SHREWSBURY, 27 JANUARY 1398

| 40/1979 | John [Chynnok *alias* Wynchestre], abbot of Glastonbury | D. John Lyncoln [Lincoln] M. William Sanday | Glastonbury, 22 Jan. 1398 |

PARLIAMENTS OF THE REIGN OF HENRY IV (1399–1413)

PARLIAMENT AT WESTMINSTER, 6 OCTOBER 1399

40/1980	John [de Hainton], abbot of Bardney	John de Roderham [Rotherham]*, clerk [Illegible]	Bardney, [Illegible]
40/1981	[Illegible]	F. John [Illegible]	[Illegible]
40/1982	Roger [Yatton], abbot of Evesham	Thomas de Stowe*, archdeacon of London and Bedford, doctor of laws; M. William Stewkele [Stewkley]	Evesham, 4 Oct. 1399
40/1983	Chapter of Worcester Cathedral [LP]	M. Thomas Stow [Stowe]*, doctor of laws, archdeacon of London [Illegible]; M. Robert Esebach [Esbache]*, canon of Lichfield	Worcester Chapter House, 3 Oct. 1399

PARLIAMENT AT WESTMINSTER, 20 JANUARY 1401 (INITIALLY SUMMONED FOR YORK)

40/1984	John [Chynnok alias Wynchestre], abbot of Glastonbury	M. William Sanday; M. Simon Sydenham*, doctor of laws; John Frank*, clerk	Glastonbury, 15 Jan. 1401
40/1985	William [Walpole], prior, and convent of Ely [LP]	M. John Judde*, doctor of canon law; D. John Rome*, perpetual rector [sic] of Over, Ely diocese	Ely Chapter House, 10 Jan. 1401

40/1986	John [Burghill], bishop of Coventry and Lichfield [LP]	Thomas Stanley*, clerk Nicholas Bubbewyth [Bubwith]*, clerk Walter Bullock [Bullock]*, clerk John Abyndon [Abingdon]*, clerk Thomas Tykhill [Tickhill]*, literate Richard Lugge, literate	Our manor of Heywode [Haywood], 12 Jan. 1401
40/1987	Subdean [John Carleton] and chapter of Lincoln Cathedral [LP]	M. John Newport, precentor of Lincoln M. Thomas Bekyngham [Beckingham]*, canon of Lincoln D. Robert Whitteby [Whitby], canon of Lincoln M. John Kyngton [Kington]*, canon of Lincoln	Lincoln Chapter House, 12 Jan. 1401
40/1988	William [of Wykeham], bishop of Winchester	Thomas Stanle [Stanley]*, clerk M. John Campeden [Campden]*, clerk D. Robert Faryngton [Farrington]*, clerk Thomas Aylward, clerk Henry Shelford*, clerk	Farnham, 17 Jan. 1401
40/1989	[Nicholas Islip], abbot of Thorney	F. John Skillyngton [Skillington], monk of abbey M. John Rotheram [Rotherham]* Thomas Harlyngton [Harlington]	Thorney, 14 Jan. 1401
40/1990	Geoffrey [Sturry *alias* de Sancta Ositha], abbot of St John's, Colchester	F. John Herst, monk of abbey John Pygot*, junior	Colchester, the feast of St Hilary [13 Jan.] 1401
40/1991	John [Letcombe], abbot of Hyde near Winchester	John Chitterne*, clerk John Sutton, literate	Hyde, 3 Jan. 1401

318

40/1992	John [Fordham], bishop of Ely	Thomas Stanle [Stanley]*, dean of St Martin le Grand, London Robert Faryndon [Farrington]*, canon of York John Rome*, rector of Over M. John Bernard*, dean of Tamworth royal free chapel D. Thomas Patesle [Pattesley], rector of Walpool [Wal-pole] Robert de Wetheryngsete [Wetheringsett]*, rector of Northwold	Our manor of Downham, 14 Jan. 1401
40/1993	John [Lidbury], abbot of Battle	Thomas Stanle [Stanley]*, clerk of the rolls Simon Gaunstede [Gaunstead]*	Battle, 16 Jan. 1401
40/1994	Thomas [Pygot], abbot of St Mary's, York	Thomas Stanley*, clerk of the rolls Simon Gaunstede [Gaunstead]*, clerk Robert de Malton*, clerk John de Kyrkeby [Kirkby], monk of abbey	In the monastery, 12 Jan. 1401
40/1995	Chapter of York [LP]	John Scarle* [the younger], canon of York Robert Faryngton [Farrington]*, canon of York William de Forth, canon of York Laurence Allerthorp [Allerthorpe]*, canon of York M. Richard Conyngston [Coniston]*, canon of York M. Thomas Weston*, canon of York	Chapter House, 18 Jan. 1401
40/1996	Thomas Stowe, doctor of laws, dean, and chapter of London [LP]	D. John Wyke, canon of St Paul's, London M. John Skyftelyng, canon of St Paul's, London	London Chapter House, 15 Jan. 1401

319

40/1997	Hebdomdarius [duty officer for the week] and chapter of Hereford [LP]	M. John Prophet*, dean of Hereford Richard Kyngeston [Kingston], archdeacon of Hereford Reginald Wolston [Wollaston], canon of Hereford	Chapter House, 11 Jan. 1401
40/1998	Thomas [Chellesworth], abbot of Malmesbury	John Chitterne* John Thornbury*	Malmesbury, 20 Jan. 1401
40/1999	William [Bradley], abbot of Winchcombe	M. Nicholas Bubbewyth [Bubwith]*, clerk M. John Rome*, clerk	Winchcombe, 1 Jan. 1401
40/2000	Roger [Yatton], abbot of Evesham [LP]	M. Thomas Stowe*, doctor of laws Robert Faryngton [Farrington]* M. John Barel*, clerk	Evesham, Tuesday after Epiphany [11 Jan.] 1401

CONVOCATION AT ST PAUL'S, 26 JANUARY 1401

41/2001	[Robert Reed], bishop of Chichester [LP]	M. Robert Hallum*, archdeacon of Canterbury	Bishop's Manor of Duringewyk [Duringwick], 20 Jan. 1401

PARLIAMENT AT WESTMINSTER, 30 SEPTEMBER 1402

41/2002	Richard [Salford], abbot of Abingdon	John Blokley [Blockley], monk of abbey John Wakeryng [Wakering]*, clerk John Hertilpole [Hartlepool]*, clerk	[No place], 1 Sept. 1402

41/2003	William [of Wykeham], bishop of Winchester	M. John Prophete [Prophet]*, clerk M. Thomas Stanle [Stanley]*, clerk M. Robert Feryngton [Farrington]*, clerk M. John Elmer*, clerk M. John Campeden [Campden]*, clerk M. Robert Keten [Ketton]*, clerk	Suthwaltham [Bishop's Waltham], 27 Sept. 1402
41/2004	Subdean [John Carleton] and chapter of Lincoln [LP]	M. Thomas Bekyngham [Beckingham]*, archdeacon of Northampton M. John Southam*, prebendary of Dunham, canon of Lincoln M. John Kyngton [Kington]*, prebendary of Clifton, canon of Lincoln M. Simon Gaunstede [Gaunstead]*, prebendary of Crakepole [Crackpole], canon of Lincoln	Lincoln, 12 Sept. 1402
41/2005	William [Weld], abbot of St Augustine's, Canterbury	F. Thomas Hunden, monk of abbey John Clerk* Thomas Offewelle [Offwell]	Canterbury, 25 Sept. 1402
41/2006	Simon [Brigham], abbot of St Benet of Hulme	James Billyngford [Billingford]* John Burgh	[No place], 26 Sept. 1402
41/2007	[Roger Yatton], abbot of Evesham [LP]	M. Thomas Stowe*, doctor of laws Robert Faryngton[Farrington]*	Evesham, Monday after feast of the Exaltation of the Holy Cross [18 Sept.] 1402

41/2008	[Thomas Overton], abbot of Crowland	John Rotherham*, clerk Albin de Endirby* Thomas de Endirby [Enderby]*	Crowland, Tuesday before Michaelmas [26 Sept.] 1402
41/2009	[Nicholas Islip], abbot of Thorney	John Rotheram* F. Richard de Berndon, monk of abbey John Bloghwy*	Thorney, 27 Sept. 1402
41/2010	John [de Malvern], prior of Worcester	M. Thomas Stowe*, doctor of laws, dean of London M. Robert Esebach [Esbache]*, canon of Lichfield	Worcester, 24 Sept. 1402
41/2011	Chapter of Worcester	M. Thomas Stowe*, doctor of laws, dean of London M. Robert Esebach [Esbache]*, canon of Lichfield	Worcester, 24 Sept.1402
41/2012	Walter [Skirlaw], bishop of Durham	[Thomas Langley]*, dean of York, keeper of the privy seal Simon Gaunsted [Gaunstead]*, canon of Lincoln Robert Malton*, clerk William Lasyngby [Lasingby]* Robert Cave	'Welehalle' [Wheel Hall], the bishop of Durham's manor, York diocese, 20 Sept. 1402
41/2013	Prior [John de Hemingborough] and chapter of Durham [LP]	Walter Tesedale [Teesdale], monk of priory John Belassys [Belasis]*	Durham, 21 Sept. 1402
41/2014	[John de Sherburn], abbot of Selby	John de Rome*, clerk Peter de Crulle [Crowle], clerk John Pygot*, junior, clerk	Selby, 24 Sept. 1402

322

41/2015	Thomas Stowe, dean, and chapter of London *[LP]*	M. William Storteford [Stortford]*, residentiary canon of St Paul's M. William Styuecle [Stukeley]*, canon of St Paul's M. John Skyftelyng, canon of St Paul's	Chapter House, London, 29 Sept. 1402
41/2016	Chapter of Hereford *[LP]*	M. Reginald Walastone [Wollaston], canon of Hereford M. Reginald Kentwode [Kentwood]*, canon of Hereford M. Thomas More, canon of Hereford M. Thomas Pikton, canon of Hereford	Hereford, feast of St Matthew, apostle [21 Sept.] 1402
41/2017	John Dalton, archdeacon of Northumberland and official of Durham *[LP]*	Walter Tesedale [Teesdale], monk of Durham, by permission of his prior John Belasys [Belasis]*, esquire	Durham, 8 Sept. 1402
41/2018	[Thomas Pygot], abbot of St Mary's, York	M. William de Waltham*, canon residentiary of York F. William Dalton, prior of our cell of Romeburgh [Rumburgh], monk of abbey Simon Gaunsted [Gaunstead]*, clerk of the petty bag Robert de Malton*, clerk of the pipe Robert Gare*	York, morrow of St Matthew, apostle [22 Sept.] 1402
41/2019	[William Genge], abbot of Peterborough	*[Illegible]*	Peterborough, 26 Sept. 1402
41/2020	[John Chynnok *alias* Wynchestre], abbot of Glastonbury	John Chitterne* M. Simon Sydenham*, doctor of laws, clerk M. William Sanday, doctor of laws, clerk	Glastonbury, 25 Sept. 1402

41/2021	[John Letcombe], abbot of Hyde near Winchester	John Chytterne [Chitterne]*, clerk John Cole, clerk John Dutton, literate	Hyde, 28 Sept. 1402
41/2022	John [de Hainton], abbot of Bardney [LP]	John de Roder[ham] [Rotherham]*, clerk Richard de Bolton* Thomas de Enderby* Thomas Wace* Nicholas Horne	[No place], 23 Sept. 1402
41/2023	[Thomas Prestbury alias Shrewsbury], abbot of Shrewsbury	Roger Westwode [Westwood], rector of Hodenet [Hodnet] Richard Celle, rector of 'Keeston'	Shrewsbury, 27 Sept. 1402
41/2024	[John Lidbury], abbot of Battle	John Pelham*, knight Simon Gaunstede [Gaunstead]*, clerk F: Thomas Beche, monk of abbey [One name erased]	Battle, 26 Sept. 1402
41/2025	Walter [Froucestre], abbot of St Peter's, Gloucester	M. Robert Halome [Hallum]* M. William Mylton [Milton]* F: William Brut, monk of abbey	Gloucester, 29 Sept. 1402
41/2026	Richard [Crosby], prior of Coventry	Ralph Rocheford [Rochford]*, knight John Wakeryng [Wakering]*, clerk	Coventry, Exaltation of the Holy Cross [14 Sept.] 1402
41/2027	Richard [Yateley], abbot of Reading	F. John Chevele [Chieveley], monk of abbey, our clerk John Frank* James Billyngford [Billingford]* Roger de Sheffeld [Sheffield]	Reading, 24 Sept. 1402

324

41/2028	John [Burghill], bishop of Coventry and Lichfield [LP]	Edmund [Stafford], earl of Stafford M. John Prophete [Prophet]*, dean of Hereford M. Walter Bullok [Bullock]*, chancellor of Lichfield Cathedral Peter de [la] Pole* John Fynderne [Findern]*	Eccleshale [Eccleshall] castle, 20 Sept. 1402
41/2029	Thomas [Butturwyk], abbot of Ramsey	D. John Rome*, clerk Henry Malpas*, clerk	Ramsey, 29 Sept. 1402

PARLIAMENT AT WESTMINSTER, 14 JANUARY 1404 (ORIGINALLY SUMMONED TO COVENTRY FOR 3 DECEMBER 1403)

41/2030	Edmund [Stafford], bishop of Exeter [LP] [Response to original summonss]	Nicholas Bubbewyth [Bubwith]*, keeper of the rolls of chancery John Chytterne [Chitterne]*, master in chancery John Rome*, master in chancery	Our manor of Chuddelegh [Chudleigh], 13 Nov. 1403
41/2031	Prior [sic] of St Augustine's, Canterbury	M. Robert Halum [Hallum]*, doctor of canon law Thomas Hunden, monk of abbey Thomas Eswell [Eastwell]	London, in our house at Suthward [Southwark], 20 Jan. 1404
41/2032	[John Carleton], subdean of Lincoln [LP]	M. Thomas Bekyngham [Beckingham]*, archdeacon of Lincoln M. William Milton*, archdeacon of Buckingham D. Nicholas Bubbewith [Bubwith]*, canon of Lincoln M. John Southam*, canon of Lincoln M. John Kyngton [Kington]*, canon of Lincoln	Lincoln, 5 Jan. 1404

41/2033	Chapter of Durham Cathedral [LP]	Richard Ulston*, clerk William [Damaged] Joseph Haryngton [Harrington]	Durham, 4 Jan. 1404
41/2034	Richard [Crosby], prior of Coventry	John Wakeryng [Wakering]*, clerk William Mirfeld [Mirfield], clerk	Coventry Chapter House, 1 Jan. 1404
41/2035	John [Burghill], bishop of Coventry and Lichfield [LP]	M. Thomas Felde [Field]*, dean of Hereford Cathedral John Wakeryng [Wakering]*, canon of Wells Cathedral William Neuhagh [Newhay], canon of Lichfield Cathedral John Oudeby*, canon of Lichfield Cathedral William Brynkelowe [Brinklow], canon of Lichfield Cathedral John Abyndon [Abingdon]*, rector of Grendon, Lichfield diocese Thomas Remston [Rempston]*, knight Nicholas Bradshawe [Bradshaw]*, esquire John Fyndern [Findern]*, esquire	Eccleshale [Eccleshall] castle, 7 Jan. 1404
41/2036	Thomas [Butturwyk], abbot of Ramsey	John Rome*, clerk Simon Gaunstede [Gaunstead]*, clerk	Ramsey, 10 Jan. 1404
41/2037	[Thomas Charwelton], abbot of Thorney	F. Richard Berwden, monk of abbey John Rotherham* John Herlyngton [Harlington]*	Thorney, 8 Jan. 1404
41/2038	Richard [Yateley], abbot of Reading	F. John Grundone [Grendon], monk of abbey John Frank* James Billyngforde [Billingford]*	Reading, 8 Jan. 1404

41/2039	John [Chynnok *alias* Wynchestre], abbot of Glastonbury	M. Simon Sydenham*, doctor of laws, clerk M. William Sanday, doctor of laws, clerk	Glastonbury, 15 Jan. 1404
41/2040	William [Genge], abbot of Peterborough	M. John Keynton, clerk F. Thomas Fannell, monk of abbey	Peterborough, 11 Jan. 1404
41/2041	William [Powcher], prior, and chapter of Ely *[LP]*	M. John Metefeld [Metfield], inceptor in both laws M. Robert Flat	Ely Chapter House, 10 Jan. 1404
41/2042	Walter [Froucestre], abbot of St Peter's, Gloucester	M. William Mylton [Milton]*, archdeacon of Buckingham Richard Riall' [Ruyhale]* John Cole*	Gloucester, 1 Jan. 1404
41/2043	Robert [Braybooke], bishop of London *[LP]*	Thomas Longeley [Langley]*, dean of York and keeper of the privy seal D. Nicholas Bubbewith [Bubwith]*, canon of London and keeper of the rolls of chancery M. William Styuecle [Stukeley]*, canon of London, bishop's official	Our manor of Hadham, 11 Jan. 1404
41/2044	Roger [Yatton], abbot of Evesham *[LP]*	M. Thomas Stowe*, doctor of laws D. Robert Farndon, clerk John Scarburgh [Scarborough]*	Evesham, 6 Jan. 1404
41/2045	John [de Malvern], prior of Worcester	M. William Milton*, archdeacon of Buckingham Robert Esbach [Esbache]*, canon of Lichfield Cathedral	Worcester, 24 Dec. 1403
41/2046	Chapter of Exeter Cathedral	M. Robert Hallum* D. Laurence Hadly or Haucyn	Exeter, Chapter House, vigil of Epiphany [5 Jan.] 1404

Ref.	Grantee	Witnesses	Place and date
41/2047	John [Letcombe], abbot of Hyde near Winchester	M. John Chyterne [Chitterne]*, clerk John Schelford [Shelford], clerk John Cole, clerk Thomas Hornby*, skilled in law William Cheyny [Cheney]*, skilled in law	Hyde abbey, 9 Jan. 1404
41/2048	Thomas Stowe, doctor of laws, dean, and chapter of London [LP]	D. Nicholas Bubbewyth [Bubwith]*, canon of London D. Thomas More*, canon of London D. John Edenham, canon of London Thomas Horston, clerk Simon Gaunstede [Gaunstead]*, clerk	London Chapter House, 1 Jan. 1404
41/2049	John [de Sherburn], abbot of Selby	D. John de Rome*, clerk Peter de Crulle [Crowle], king's esquire John Pygot*, junior, clerk John de Birne, clerk	Selby, 5 Jan. 1404
41/2050	John [Lidbury], abbot of Battle	Nicholas Bubbewyth [Bubwith]*, clerk Simon Gaunstede [Gaunstead]*, clerk John Rome*, clerk	Battle, 18 Dec. 1403
42/2051	Edmund [Stafford], bishop of Exeter	D. Nicholas Bubbewyth [Bubwith]*, clerk of the rolls John Rome*, master in chancery	[Damaged]
42/2052	Thomas [Pygot], abbot of St Mary's, York	D. John Rome*, master in chancery Simon Gaunstede [Gaunstead]*, master in chancery M. Antony de Sancto Quintino [St Quentin], rector of Hornsee [Hornsea] John de Carlton, clerk Robert de Gare*	The abbey, the morrow of Epiphany [7 Jan.] 1404

42/2053	Walter [Skirlaw], bishop of Durham	Thomas de Longley [Langley]*, dean of York, keeper of the privy seal Nicholas de Bubbewyth [Bubwith]*, canon of York Simon Gaunstede [Gaunstead]*, canon of Lincoln John Carlton	Aukland manor [Bishop's Auckland], 27 Dec. 1403
42/2054	John [de Hainton], abbot of Bardney	D. John de Roderham [Rotherham]*, clerk Richard de Malton, clerk Thomas de Enderby*	Bardney, 5 Jan. 1404
42/2055	[Richard Medford], bishop of Salisbury [LP]	John Chitterne*, canon of Salisbury William Denys, canon of Salisbury M. Simon Sydenham*, doctor of laws	Potterne, 1 Jan. 1404
42/2056	[Thomas Overton], abbot of Crowland	F. John Boston, monk of abbey D. John Roderham [Rotherham]* Thomas Enderby*	Crowland, Friday before Hilary [11 Jan.] 1404
42/2057	William [of Wykeham], bishop of Winchester	M. Nicholas Wykeham* M. Robert Faryngton[Farrington]* M. John Elmer* M. John Campeden [Campden]* M. Robert Keten [Ketton]* Simon Gaunstede [Gaunstead]*, clerk D. Thomas Aileward, clerk D. Henry Shelford*, clerk	South Waltham [Bishop's Waltham], 10 Jan. 1404

42/2058	William [Cratfeld], abbot of Bury St Edmunds	D. Thomas Skelton*, knight D. John Rome*, clerk D. James Byllyngforth [Billingford]* F. Thomas Plumpton, monk of abbey	Elmeswelle [Elmswell] manor, 10 Jan. 1404
42/2059	Thomas [Chellesworth], abbot of Malmesbury	D. John Chitterne*, clerk William Westbury*	Malmesbury, 10 Jan. 1404
42/2060	Simon [Brigham], abbot of St Benet of Hulme	James de Billyngford [Billingford]* William Champeneys [Champneys]* John Alderford*	Hulme, 11 Jan. 1404
42/2061	Chapter of Worcester	M. William Milton*, archdeacon of Buckingham M. Robert Esbache*, canon of Lichfield	Worcester Chapter House, 24 Dec. 1403

PARLIAMENT AT COVENTRY, 6 OCTOBER 1404

42/2062	Prior and convent of Carlisle	Thomas de Scausby, clerk Hugh Burgh	Carlisle Chapter House, Michaelmas [29 Sept.] 1404
42/2063	Thomas [Butturwyk], abbot of Ramsey	John Rome*, clerk Richard Stoughton	Ramsey, 29 Sept. 1404
42/2064	John [Letcombe], abbot of Hyde near Winchester	John Chytterne [Chitterne]*, clerk Henry Schelford [Shelford]*, clerk [Henry] Popham*, esquire John Waterton, esquire William Wygge*, citizen of Winchester	Hyde, 23 Sept. 1404

42/2065	Richard [Yateley], abbot of Reading	John Frank*, clerk James Billyngford [Billingford]*, clerk	Reading, 26 Sept. 1404
42/2066	John [Lekhampton], abbot of Cirencester	John Chitterne*, clerk William Milton*, clerk Thomas Wybbe, clerk	The abbey, 4 Oct. 1404
42/2067	William Norton, abbot of Torre [LP]	Laurence Hawkyn, chaplain of Exeter diocese John Barel*, chaplain of Exeter diocese John Hethene, chaplain of Exeter diocese	Torre, 28 Sept. 1404
42/2068	John [de Sherburn], abbot of Selby	John Rome*, clerk Thomas Haxhey [Haxey]*, clerk	Selby, 2 Oct. 1404
42/2069	Thomas Stowe, doctor of laws, dean of London [LP]	D. Nicholas Bubbwyth [Bubwith]*, canon of London Simon Gaunstede [Gaunstead]*	London, 1 Oct. 1404
42/2070	William [Weld], abbot of St Augustine's, Canterbury	Roger Paternoster, clerk Thomas Estwell [Eastwell], clerk	Canterbury, 12 Sept. 1404
42/2071	Roger [Yatton], abbot of Evesham	D. Robert Farynghton [Farrington]*, clerk John Scarborough*, clerk William Grace, clerk	Evesham, Sunday before Michaelmas 28 Sept.] 1404
42/2072	Thomas [Chellesworth], abbot of Malmesbury	John Chitterne*, clerk Robert Frye*, clerk	The abbey, 4 Oct. 1404
42/2073	John [de Hainton], abbot of Bardney	D John de Roderham [Rotherham]*, clerk Robert Tirwyht [Tirwhite]* John de Wodeburn [Woodburn]*, gentleman	Bardney, 25 Sept. 1404

42/2074	Thomas [Pygot], abbot of St Mary's, York	M. Richard Conyngston [Coniston]*, canon of York Robert Wolden, canon of York D. John Rome*, master in chancery D. Simon Gaunstede [Gaunstead]*, master in chancery Robert de Appilton [Appleton], rector of Stretton Robert Malton*, clerk	The abbey, 1 Oct. 1404
42/2075	[Thomas Field], dean, and chapter of Hereford	M. Richard Kyngeston [Kingston], archdeacon of Hereford M. John Prophet*, canon of Hereford M. Nicholas Hereford*, treasurer of Hereford M. John Kyngton [Kington]*, canon of Hereford	Hereford, 28 Sept. 1404
42/2076	Subdean [John Carleton] and chapter of Lincoln	D. Hugh Hanneworth [Hanworth]*, archdeacon of Stow Thomas Haxay [Haxey]*, canon of Lincoln Robert Trays, canon of Lincoln Matthew Edenham, canon of Lincoln	Lincoln, 30 Sept.1404
42/2077	Chapter of Worcester Cathedral	M. William Mylton [Milton]*, archdeacon of Buckingham M. John Pavy*, batchelor of laws	Worcester Chapter House, 28 Sept. 1404
42/2078	Prior [John de Hemingborough] and chapter of Durham	John Rome*, clerk Robert Sores of Newcastle on Tyne, monk of priory William Appleby, monk of priory Thomas Rome, monk of priory	Durham, 27 Sept. 1404

42/2079	John [de Hainton], abbot of Bardney	D. John de Roderham [Rotherham]*, clerk F. Robert de Thornton, monk of abbey Richard de Bolton*, clerk John de Wodeburn [Woodburn]*	Bardney, 3 Oct. 1404
42/2080	William Storeford, archdeacon of Middlesex, official of London and keeper of the spiritualities of the bishopric of London *sede vacante*	Simon de Gaunsted [Gaunstead]*, clerk	London, 24 Sept. 1404
42/2081	Thomas Stowe, doctor of laws, dean of London and the chapter	D. Nicholas Bubbwyth [Bubwith]*, canon of London Simon Gaunstede [Gaunstead]*, clerk	London Chapter House, 1 Oct. 1404
42/2082	[Thomas Charwelton], abbot of Thorney	[*Illegible*], clerk F. Roger Uffyngton [Uffington], monk of abbey F. Alan de Kirketon, monk of abbey Thomas Mapilton [Mapleton], clerk	Thorney, 2 Oct. 1404
42/2083	William [Cratfeld], abbot of Bury St Edmunds	D. Thomas Skelton*, knight D. Thomas Moor [More]*, archdeacon of Colchester D. John Rome*, clerk	Elmeswelle [Elmswell] manor, 27 Sept. 1404
42/2084	Clergy of Carlisle diocese	M. Thomas Stanceby, rector of Hoton [Hutton], Carlisle diocese Hugh Burgh, clerk	Carlisle, 26 Sept. 1404
42/2085	John [de Malvern], prior of Worcester Cathedral	M. William Mylton [Milton]*, archdeacon of Buckingham M. John Pavy*, bachelor of laws	Worcester, 28 Sept. 1404

333

42/2086	Thomas Beckingham, archdeacon of Lincoln	M. John Hauberk [Hawberk]*, doctor of canon law and rector of Eketan [Ecton], Lincoln diocese Thomas Haxay [Haxey]*, canon of Lincoln	Lincoln, 2 Oct. 1404
42/2087	Thomas Stirkeland [Strickland], archdeacon of Carlisle	Thomas Stanceby, clerk John Ebor [York], chaplain	Carlisle, 4 Oct. 1404
42/2088	Walter [Skirlaw], bishop of Durham	[Thomas Langley]*, dean of York, keeper of the privy seal Simon Gaunstede [Gaunstead]*, canon of Lincoln Robert Malton*, clerk Robert Gare*	Welehalle [Wheel Hall] manor, 18 Sept. 1404
42/2089	John [Chynnok *alias* Wynchestre], abbot of Glastonbury	D. John Chitterne*, clerk M. John Parys*, clerk M. Thomas Barton*, clerk	Glastonbury, 1 Oct. 1404
42/2090	Henry [Despenser], bishop of Norwich	M. Thomas Langley*, archdeacon of Norfolk M. Eudo le Souch [Zouche], archdeacon of Huntingdon John Rome*, clerk	Northelmham [North Elmham] manor, 1 Oct. 1404
42/2091	Richard [Clifford], bishop of Worcester	D. Thomas Langeley [Langley]*, dean of York, keeper of the privy seal M. John Prophete [Prophet]*, king's secretary	Alvechurch manor, 9 Oct. 1404
42/2092	William [Strickland], bishop of Carlisle	M. Richard Conyngeston [Coniston]*, clerk M. Robert Woldene [Wolden], clerk M. Thomas Carnyca, clerk M. Thomas de Stanceby, clerk M. Hugh Burgh, clerk	Rosa [Rose Castle] manor, 26 Sept. 1404

334

42/2093	William [Harleton], abbot of Waltham	M. William Brynglowe [Brinklow] M.John Wysebech [Wisbech]*	Waltham, 6 Oct. 1404
42/2094	John [Burghill], bishop of Coventry and Lichfield	D. Nicholas Bubbewyth [Bubwith]*, archdeacon of Dorset D. John Wakering*, canon of Wells Cathedral D. Walter Bullok [Bullock]*, canon of Lichfield Cathedral D. Thomas de Aston*, knight D. William Neuport [Newport]*, knight D. Roger Leche*, knight Nicholas Bradeschawe [Bradshaw]*, gentleman	Eccleshale [Eccleshall] castle, 28 Sept. 1404
42/2095	John [Lidbury], abbot of Battle	M. John Kyngton [Kington]*, clerk D.John Rome*, clerk D.John Roderham [Rotherham]*, clerk John Frank*, clerk Richard Bolton* clerk	Battle, 28 Sept. 1404
42/2096	[Thomas Overton], abbot of Crowland	M.John Roderham [Rotherham]* William Flete [Fleet]* John Wodeburn [Woodburn]* John Hardyng [Harding]	Crowland, Thursday after Michaelmas [2 Oct.] 1404
45/2236	Richard [Medford], bishop of Salisbury	M. John Phrophete [Prophet]*, canon of Salisbury John Chitterne*, canon of Salisbury Richard Prentys*, canon of Salisbury	Shirburn [Sherborne], 20 Sept. 1404

335

PARLIAMENT AT WESTMINSTER, 1 MARCH 1406

42/2097	Chapter of Exeter Cathedral	M. William Langton, canon of Exeter D. Laurence Hawkyn, canon of Exeter	Exeter, 3 Jan. 1406
42/2098	Prior [John de Hemingborough] and chapter of Durham	Robert Lyle [Lisle]* Thomas Rokeby* John Claveryng [Clavering]*	Durham, 6 Feb. 1406
42/2099	Walter [Skirlaw], bishop of Durham	D. Nicholas Bubbewyth [Bubwith]*, keeper of the privy seal Robert Wolden, canon of York Simon Gaunstede [Gaunstead]*, canon of York	Houedon [Howden] manor, York diocese, 6 Feb. 1406
42/2100	Ralph Tregrisiow, dean of Exeter	Laurence Hawkyn, canon of Exeter William Wymmok	Exeter, 31 Jan. 1406
43/2101	William [Heyworth], abbot of St Albans	D. John Rome*, clerk D. Simon Gaunstede [Gaunstead]*, clerk William Wyche, clerk	St Albans, 10 Feb. 1406
43/2102	Chapter of York, and dean being absent and the archbishopric vacant [LP]	Nicholas Bubwith*, canon of York M. John Profet [Prophet]*, canon of York M. Roger Corringham*, canon of York	York, Chapter House, 6 Feb. 1406
43/2103	Thomas [Butturwyk], abbot of Ramsey	John Roome [Rome]*, clerk John Wissyngsted [Whissonsett]*	Ramsey, 10 Feb. 1406

43/2104	Prior [Thomas de Hoton] and chapter of Carlisle [LP]	John Rome*, clerk Thomas Scanceby [Stanceby], clerk	In the Chapter House, morrow of the Purification of the Blessed Mary [3 Feb.] 1406
43/2105	[John de Malvern], prior of Worcester	M. William Milton*, archdeacon of Buckingham M. Robert Esbach [Esbache]*, canon of Lichfield	Worcester, 21 Feb. 1406
43/2106	Simon [Brigham], abbot of St Benet of Hulme	[Illegible] James Billyngford [Billingford]* John Champneys	Hulme, 25 Feb. 1406
43/2107	John [Letcombe], abbot of Hyde near Winchester	D. John Chytterne [Chitterne]*, clerk D. Henry Schelforde [Shelford]*, clerk D. John Cole, clerk William Overton, esquire John Bullok [Bullock], esquire	Hyde, 20 Feb. 1406
43/2108	Roger [Best], abbot of St John's, Colchester	D. John Rome*, clerk D. John Pygot*, clerk	Colchester, 18 Feb. 1406
43/2109	President and chapter of Lincoln, in the dean's absence [LP]	M. John Hauberk [Hawberk]*, doctor of canon law Thomas Haxey*, canon of Lincoln Simon Gaunstede [Gaunstead]*, canon of Lincoln Matthew Edenham, canon of Lincoln	Lincoln Chapter House, 20 Feb. 1406
43/2110	Thomas [Prestbury alias Shrewsbury], abbot of Shrewsbury [LP]	F. Richard Hull, monk of abbey	Shrewsbury, 24 Feb. 1406

43/2111	Chapter of Worcester	M. William Milton*, archdeacon of Buckingham M. Robert Esbach [Esbache]*, canon of Lichfield	Worcester, 21 Feb. 1406
43/2112	William [Bradley] , abbot of Winchcombe	Thomas Schelford [Shelford], clerk	Winchcombe, 26 Feb. 1406
43/2113	Thomas [Chellesworth], abbot of Malmesbury	John Chitterne* William Westbury* William Wydecombe [Widdecombe]	Malmesbury, 2[0] Feb. 1406
43/2114	[Thomas Overton], abbot of Crowland	Sir John Lytulbery [Littlebury]*, knight D.John Rotherham*, clerk Thomas Enderby*	Crowland, feast of St Mat- thias, apostle [24 Feb.] 1406
43/2115	Walter [Froucestre], abbot of St Peter's, Gloucester	M. William Mylton [Milton]*, archdeacon of Bucking- ham William Kyngescote [Kingscote]	Gloucester, 20 Feb. 1406
43/2116	[John Woxbrigge], abbot of Bard- ney [LP]	John Roderham [Rotherham]*, clerk William Ewen*, clerk F. Robert Thornton, monk of abbey	Bardney, 24 Feb. 1406
43/2117	Richard [Yateley], abbot of Reading	F.John Abendon [Abingdon], monk of abbey M.John Bathe [Bath]*, clerk John Frank*, clerk	Reading, 24 Feb. 1406
43/2118	Richard [Medford], bishop of Salisbury [LP]	M.John Prophete [Prophet]* M. Henry Chichele*, chancellor [sic] M. Walter Medeford [Medford]*, canon of Salisbury M.John Frank*, canon of Salisbury	Poterne [Potterne], 24 Feb. 1406

338

43/2119	Thomas [Butturwyk], abbot of Ramsey	John Roome [Rome]*, clerk John Wissyngsed [Whissonsett]*	Ramsey, 25 Feb. 1406
43/2120	[Thomas Charwelton], abbot of Thorney	D. John Rotheram [Rotherham]*, chancery clerk John Clerk*, chancery clerk F. Roger de Uffyngton [Uffington], monk of abbey	Thorney, 20 Feb. 1406
43/2121	John [de Sherburn], abbot of Selby	D. John de Rome*, clerk D. Thomas de Haxay [Haxey]*, clerk D. Robert de Selby, clerk D. John Pygot*, clerk John de Birne	Selby, 20 Feb. 1406
43/2122	Thomas [Spofforth], abbot of St Mary's, York	D. John Wakeryng [Wakering]*, master or keeper of the rolls of chancery D. John Rome*, master in chancery D. Simon Gaunstede [Gaunstead]*, master in chancery	In the monastery, vigil of St Matthias, apostle [23 Feb.] 1406
43/2123	John [Burghill], bishop of Coventry and Lichfield [LP]	D. Thomas Langeley [Langley]*, chancellor of England D. Nicholas Bubbewyth [Bubwith]*, keeper of the privy seal D. Thomas de Aston*, knight D. Nicholas Bradeschawe [Bradshaw]*, esquire	Eccleshale [Eccleshall] castle, 20 Feb. 1406
43/2124	Roger [Yatton], abbot of Evesham [LP]	M. William Miltone [Milton]*, clerk M. John Westone [Weston]*, clerk John Scarborugh [Scarborough]*, clerk	Evesham, 25 Feb. 1406

43/2125	John [Chynnok alias Wynchestre], abbot of Glastonbury	D. John Chytterne [Chitterne]*, clerk M. William Sanday, doctor of laws, clerk M. John Steorthwayte [Storthwaite]*, rector of Corymalet, [Curry Mallet] clerk	Glastonbury, 22 Feb. 1406
43/2126	Simon [Brigham], abbot of St Benet of Hulme	James Billyngford [Billingford]* William Champeneys [Champneys]*	Hulme, 20 Feb. 1406
43/2127	Keeper of the spiritualities of York sede vacante	Nicholas Bubwith* John Profit [Prophet]* John Rome*	[No place], 18 Feb. 1406
43/2128	John [Lekhampton], abbot of Cirencester	M. William Milton*, clerk M. John Chitterne*, clerk	Cirencester, 18 Feb. 1406
43/2129	William [Cratfeld], abbot of Bury St Edmunds	D. Thomas Skelton*, knight D. John Rome*, clerk D. James Billyngford [Billingford]*	Our manor of Elmeswell, 22 Feb. 1406
43/2130	William [Strickland], bishop of Carlisle	John Rome*, clerk Robert Walden, clerk Simon Gawnested [Gaunstead]*, clerk Thomas de Scanceby [Stanceby], clerk	Rose manor, 4 Feb. 1406

PARLIAMENT AT GLOUCESTER, 20 OCTOBER 1407

| 43/2131 | John Loveney, archdeacon of Hereford
[LP] | M. John Catesby, canon of Hereford
John Stretton, rector of Ovybury [Overbury]
John Stanewell [Stanwell], clerk, archdeacon's official | Hereford, 16 Oct. 1407 |

43/2132	Simon [Brigham], abbot of St Benet of Hulme	James Billyngford [Billingford]* William Champneys*	Hulme, 12 Oct. 1407
43/2133	John [Letcombe] abbot of Hyde near Winchester	John Chitterne* M. Thomas Hurslee [Hursley]	Hyde, 16 Oct. 1407
43/2134	Richard [Yateley], abbot of Reading	F. John Abendon [Abingdon], monk of abbey D. John Frank*, clerk John Golafre* James Billyngford [Billingford]*	Reading, 10 Oct. 1407
43/2135	Chapter of York, in the dean's absence [LP]	M. John Prophet*, dean of York M. Roger Coryngham [Corringham]*, archdeacon of York M. Robert Wolveden, canon of York M. Simon Gaunstede [Gaunstead]*, canon of York	York Chapter House, 10 Oct. 1407
43/2136	Roger [Yatton], abbot of Evesham [LP]	M. Nicholas Ryxston [Rishton]* John Mylton [Milton] John Weston* John Scarborth [Scarborough]*	Evesham, feast of St Luke, evangelist, [18 Oct.] 1407
43/2137	William [Merssh], abbot of Battle	D. John Wakeryng [Wakering]*, clerk D. John Pelham*, knight	Battle abbey, 8 Oct. 1407
43/2138	Edmund [Stafford], bishop of Exeter [LP]	D. John Wakeryng [Wakering]*, keeper of the king's rolls John Rome*, master in the king's chancery John Hertelpole [Hartlepool]*, master of the king's chancery	Our manor of Crediton, 28 Sept. 1407

341

43/2139	Chapter of York [LP]	M. John Prophet*, dean and keeper of the privy seal M. Roger Coryngham [Corringham]*, archdeacon of York M. John Wakeryng [Wakering]* John Rome*, master in chancery Robert Wolveden, canon of York Simon Gaunstede [Gaunstead]*, canon of York	York, 10 Oct. 1407
43/2140	[John de Malvern], prior of Worcester	M. William Pylton [Pilton]*, [king's] secretary M. Thomas Feld [Field]*, doctor of laws M. Richard Grafton*, bachelor of laws	Worcester, 16 Oct. 1407
43/2141	Thomas [Spofforth], abbot of St Mary's, York	D. John Wakeryng [Wakering]*, master or keeper of the rolls of chancery D. John Rome*, master in chancery Simon Gaunstede [Gaunstead]*, master in chancery	York, 3 Oct. 1407

PARLIAMENT AT WESTMINSTER, 27 JANUARY 1410

43/2142	Simon [de Brigham], abbot of St Benet Hulme	William Chaumpeneys [Champneys]* John Alderforth [Alderford]*	Hulme, 24 Jan. 1410
43/2143	William [Strickland], bishop of Carlisle	M. Robert Wolden, canon of York M. John Wyghtman [Wightman], clerk M. Thomas Stanceby, clerk William Overton, clerk	Our manor of Rose, 12 Jan. 1410
43/2144	Prior [Thomas de Hoton] and chapter of Carlisle [LP]	Thomas Carnyca, clerk Thomas Stanceby, clerk	Chapter House, 14 January 1410

342

43/2145	William [Pigot], abbot of Selby	D. John de Rome*, clerk D. John Pygot*, clerk Robert de Babthorp [Babthorpe]*, king's esquire William de Babthorp [Babthorpe]*, his brother	Selby, the morrow of St Hilary [14 Jan.] 1410
43/2146	Thomas [Hunden], abbot of St Augustine's, Canterbury	D. John Rome*, clerk D. John Spryngthorp [Springthorpe]*, clerk Thomas Brown, esquire	[No place], 19 Feb. 1410
43/2147	John [Woxbrigge], abbot of Bardney [LP]	D. John Roderam [Rotherham]*, clerk John Kyeme [Kyme]* F. William de Friskenay [Friskney], monk of abbey	Bardney, 16 Jan. 1410
43/2148	[Thomas Charwelton], abbot of Thorney	D. John Rotheram [Rotherham]*, clerk William Ewen*, clerk F. Alan de Kirketon, monk of abbey	Thorney, 24 Jan. 1410
43/2149	Thomas [Erle], abbot of Reading	M. John Bathe [Bath]*, clerk John Frank*, clerk	Reading, 25 Jan. 1410
43/2150	Thomas Stirkeland [Strickland], archdeacon of Carlisle [LP]	M. John Wightmann [Wightman], clerk Thomas Stanceby, clerk	[No place], 14 Jan. 1410
44/2151	Richard Elvet, archdeacon of Leicester [LP]	John Rome*, clerk John Leybourn, clerk Thomas Southwell, clerk	Leicester, 16 Jan. 1410
44/2152	President and chapter of Hereford [LP]	M. John Cateby [Catesby], canon of Hereford M. John Kyngton [Kington]*, canon of Hereford M. John Pavy*, canon of Hereford	Hereford, 21 Jan. 1410

343

44/2153	Walter [Froucestre], abbot of St Peter's Gloucester	John Russell [III]* M. William Milton*, archdeacon of Buckingham	'La Wynyward iuxta Gloucester' [The Vineyard next to Gloucester – Hignam Manor], 12 Jan. 1410
44/2154	Dean [John Sheppey] and chapter of Lincoln [LP]	John Wakeryng [Wakering]*, canon of Lincoln John Rome*, canon of Lincoln M. John Kyngton [Kington]*, canon of Lincoln M. John Southam*, archdeacon of Oxford, canon of Lincoln M. Richard Hethe, subdean of Lincoln M. Robert Grays, canon of Lincoln	Lincoln Chapter House, 12 Jan. 1410
44/2155	John de Paciencia [Deeping], abbot of Peterborough	John Rome*, clerk Thomas Pykwell [Pickwell], gentleman	Peterborough, 5 Jan. 1410
44/2156	Richard [Salford], abbot of Abingdon	Robert [Hallum]*, bishop of Salisbury John Whitchurche [Whitchurch], monk of abbey Geoffrey Crucadam, clerk Thomas Haseley*, clerk	Abingdon, 6 Jan. 1410
44/2157	Philip [Repingdon], bishop of Lincoln [LP]	William Aghton*, archdeacon of Bedford in Lincoln Cathedral M. John Rome*, canon of Lincoln M. John Kyngton [Kington]*, canon of Lincoln M. John Hauberk [Hawberk]*, canon of Lincoln	Sleford [Sleaford], 22 Jan. 1410
44/2158	Clergy of Carlisle diocese [LP]	M. John Wightmann [Wightman], clerk Thomas Stanceby, rector of Lowthur [Lowther], Carlisle diocese	Carlisle, 14 Jan. 1410

44/2159	John [de Heminborough], prior, and chapter of Durham [LP]	John Thoralby*, rector of Lokyngton [Lockington]	Durham, 10 Jan. 1410
44/2160	John [Burghill], bishop of Coventry and Lichfield [LP]	John Stanley*, senior, knight of the lord king's household M. John Prophete [Prophet]*, clerk of the king's privy seal John Rome*, canon of Lichfield Nicholas Bradeschawe [Bradshaw]*, *scutiferus* [esquire]	Ecleshale [Eccleshall], 12 Jan. 1410
44/2161	William [Cratfeld], abbot of Bury St Edmunds	William Pylton [Pilton]*, clerk John Rome*, clerk William Barwe, monk of abbey	Elmeswell [Elmswell] our manor, 22 Jan. 1410
44/2162	Thomas [Peverel], bishop of Worcester [LP]	Lord Henry lord of Bello Monte [Beaumont] [William Bradley], abbot of Winchcombe M. William Mylton [Milton]*, archdeacon of Buckingham Thomas Burdet*, knight John Emond*, gentleman John Felyp*, gentleman John Holbache, gentleman John Grevell*, gentleman	Alvechurch our manor, 12 Jan. 1410
44/2163	Chapter of Exeter [LP]	M. William Hundene [Hundon], canon of Exeter	Exeter Chapter House, 17 Jan. 1410
44/2164	John [Chymnok *alias* Wynchestre], abbot of Glastonbury	M. John Bathe [Bath]* John Chitterne* M. Nicholas Wilton, bachelor in laws	Glastonbury, 20 Jan. 1410

345

44/2165	Roger [Yatton], abbot of Evesham [LP]	M. Thomas Feld [Field]*, doctor of laws, clerk John Scarburgh [Scarborough]*, clerk	Evesham, Tuesday after Epiphany [7 Jan.] 1410
44/2166	John [Fordham], prior of Worcester	M. William Milton*, archdeacon of Buckingham M. Robert Essbach [Esbache]*, canon of Lichfield	Worcester, 12 Jan. 1410
44/2167	Thomas [Butturwyk], abbot of Ramsey	John Roome [Rome]*, clerk M. James Cole*	Ramsey, 6 Jan. 1410
44/2168	Thomas [Chellesworth], abbot of Malmesbury	John Chitterne*, clerk William Wydecoumbe [Widdecombe], clerk John Brystowe [Bristowe], monk of abbey	In the monastery, 10 Jan. 1410
44/2169	Chapter of Worcester	M. William Milton*, archdeacon of Buckingham M. Robert Essbach [Esbache]*, canon of Lichfield	Worcester Chapter House, 12 Jan. 1410
44/2170	[Thomas Overton], abbot of Crowland	John Rotheram [Rotherham]*, clerk William Flete [Fleet]* Thomas Endirby [Enderby]*	Tuesday after Epiphany [7 Jan.] 1410
44/2171	John [London], abbot of Hyde near Winchester	[Illegible] Henry Schelford [Shelford]*, clerk	Hyde, 25 Jan. 1410

PARLIAMENT AT WESTMINSTER, 6 APRIL 1410 (PROROGATION OF JANUARY 1410 SESSION)

44/2172	Thomas [Spofforth], abbot of St. Mary's York	John Rome*, master in the king's chancery Simon Gaunstede [Gaunstead]*, master in the king's chancery	In the monastery, 31 March 1410

22/1056	[Damaged – Thomas Charwelton, abbot of Thorney]	D. John Rotherham*, clerk D. William Bolton, clerk F. Alan de Kyrketon [Kirketon], monk of abbey	Thorney, 28 Oct. 1411
44/2173	Thomas [Butturwyk], abbot of Ramsey	John Rome*, clerk	Ramsey, 20 Oct. 1411
44/2174	Richard [Crosby], prior of Coventry	John Wakering*, clerk Henry Malpas*, clerk F. William Haloughton [Halloughton], monk of priory Richard Friday, literate William Donyngton [Donnington]*, literate	Coventry, 21 Oct. 1411
44/2175	Walter [Froucestre], abbot of St Peter's, Gloucester	M. William Mylton [Milton]*, archdeacon of Buckingham John Russell [III]*	Gloucester, 15 Oct. 1411
44/2176	Richard [Young], bishop of Rochester [LP]	[Richard Clifford], bishop of London [Robert Hallum]*, bishop of Salisbury [Thomas Langley]*, bishop of Durham [Nicholas Bubwith]*, bishop of Bath and Wells	Our manor of Trottesclive [Trottiscliffe], 24 Oct. 1411
44/2177	Prior [John Wodnesbergh] and chapter of Christ Church, Canterbury [LP]	M. Philip Morgan*	Canterbury, 23 Oct. 1411
44/2178	[John Lekhampton], abbot of Cirencester	M. John Chittern [Chitterne]*, clerk M. William Mylton [Milton]*, clerk M. John Stevens [Stevens], clerk	[Hagbourne] our manor, 30 Oct. 1411

44/2179	John [Chynnok *alias* Wynchestre], abbot of Glastonbury	John Chitterne*, clerk M. William Sanday, doctor of laws, clerk M. John Bathe [Bath]*, clerk	Glastonbury, 30 Oct. 1411
44/2180	[Richard de South Walsham], abbot of St Benet of Hulme	William Chaumpeneys [Champneys]* [*Illegible* – John] Aldeforth [Alderford]*	St Benet Hulme, 28 Oct. 1411
44/2181	[Roger Best], abbot of St John's, Colchester	F. John Herst, monk of abbey Thomas Smith [Smyth]*	Colchester 26 Oct. 1411
44/2182A	John [Woxbrigge], abbot of Bardney [*LP*]	John de Roderam [Rotherham]*, clerk John Rome*, clerk Robert Godebow F. Richard de Ponte Fracto [Pontefract], monk of the abbey Thomas Pykworth [Pickworth]*	[*Illegible*], feast of SS Simon and Jude [28 Oct.] 1411
44/2182B	[*Damaged*] – Alexander Tottington, bishop of Norwich]	[*Damaged*]	Thorp iuxta Norwich [Thorpe next Norwich], 2[6] Oct. 1411
44/2183	John [London], abbot of Hyde near Winchester	John Chitterne*, clerk Henry Schelfforde [Shelford]*, clerk	Hyde, 31 Oct. [*Damaged*]

PARLIAMENTS OF THE REIGN OF HENRY V (1413–22)

PARLIAMENT AT WESTMINSTER, 14 MAY 1413

44/2184	[Roger Yatton], abbot of Evesham	[*Illegible*], doctor of laws John Scarborough* W[illiam] Stokes*	Evesham, 6 May 1413

CONVOCATION AT ST PAUL'S, 20 NOVEMBER 1413

44/2185	*President and chapter of Hereford Cathedral*	M. Thomas Felde [Field]*, *dean of Hereford* M. Richard Talbot*, *dean of Chichester* M. Edmund Lacy* M. Robert Felton, *precentor of Hereford* M. John Hereford, *canon of Hereford*	*Hereford Chapter House, 9 Nov. 1413*
44/2186	*John Hereford, archdeacon of Salop [LP]*	M. Philip Morgan*, *doctor of laws* M. Richard Talbot*, *dean of Chichester* M. Edmund Lacy*, *canon of Hereford* M. Robert Felton, *precentor of Hereford* William Stowe, *clerk*	[No place], *9 Nov. 1413*

PARLIAMENT AT LEICESTER, 29 JANUARY 1414 (PROROGUED TO 30 APRIL 1414)

44/2187	Hugh Hanneworth [Hanworth], archdeacon of Stow, Lincoln diocese *[LP]*	M. Robert Gilbert*, precentor of Lincoln Richard Elvet, archdeacon of Leicester John Rome*, canon of Lincoln	Lincoln, 27 Jan. 1414

| 44/2188 | Subdean [Richard Hethe] and chapter of Lincoln [LP] | M. Robert Gilbert*, precentor of Lincoln Richard Elvet, archdeacon of Leicester John Rome*, canon of Lincoln | Lincoln Chapter House, 27 Jan. 1414 |

PARLIAMENT AT LEICESTER, 30 APRIL 1414

44/2189	John [Lekhampton], abbot of Cirencester	M. Walter Medford*, dean of Wells M. William Milton* John Wilkotus [Wilcotes]*, gentleman F. Nicholas Lekhampton [Leckhampton], monk of abbey	Cirencester, 26 April 1414
44/2190	John [London], abbot of Hyde near Winchester	M. Walter Medeford [Medford]*, clerk John Chitterne*, clerk John Rome*, clerk	Hyde, 20 April 1414
44/2191	John Fordam [Fordham], prior of Worcester	M. Thomas Rudbourn [Rodbourne]*, archdeacon of Sudbury M. Nicholas Colnet*	Worcester, 26 April 1414
44/2192	William [Strickland], bishop of Carlisle	M. Robert Wolden, clerk M. Richard Holme*, clerk M. William Broune, clerk M. John Wodeham [Woodham]*, clerk M. Thomas de Barton*, clerk M. Roger de Dokwra*, clerk M. Thomas de Stanceby, clerk M. Thomas Clogh [Clough], clerk	Rose our manor, 20 April 1414

44/2193	[Geoffrey Hemingby], abbot of Bardney [LP]	John Rome*, clerk F. Richard de Ponte Fracto [Pontefract], monk of abbey Thomas Pycworth [Pickworth]*	Bardney, 24 April 1414
44/2194	Richard [de South Walsham], abbot of St Benet of Hulme	William Chaumpeneys [Champneys]*	St Benet of Hulme, 27 April 1414
44/2195	John de Kirkeby, archdeacon of Carlisle [LP]	M. Robert Wolden, clerk M. Richard Holme*, clerk M. William Broune, clerk M. John Wodhame [Woodham]*, clerk M. Thomas de Barton*, clerk M. Roger de Dokwra*, clerk M. Thomas de Stanceby, clerk M. Thomas Clugh [Clough], clerk	Carlisle, 16 April 1414
44/2196	John Kirkeby, archdeacon of Carlisle [LP]	M. Robert Wolden, clerk M. Richard Holme*, clerk M. William Broune, clerk M. John Wodham [Woodham]*, clerk M. Thomas de Barton*, clerk M. Roger de Dokwra*, clerk M. Thomas de Stanceby, clerk M. Thomas Clogh [Clough], clerk	Carlisle, 16 April 1414
44/2197	John [Chynnok alias Wynchestre], abbot of Glastonbury	M. John Shirforde [Sherford], canon of Wells M. Thomas Mordon*, bachelor in laws	Glastonbury, 24 April 1414
44/2198	Roger [Yatton], abbot of Evesham [LP]	M. Thomas Felde [Field]*, doctor of laws M. John Weston*, bachelor in laws John Scharborouh [Scarborough]*	Evesham abbey, 23 April 1414

44/2199	John [Deeping], abbot of Peterborough	John Rome*, clerk F: Richard Harlton, canon [sic] of the abbey	Peterborough, 1 May 1414
44/2200	Thomas [Butterwyk], abbot of Ramsey	M. William Lassell, clerk M. James Cole*, clerk	Ramsey, 26 April 1414
45/2201	William [Powcher], prior of Ely Cathedral	John Rome*, rector of Over Henry Shelford*, rector of Wyk [Wyke] Regis, Salisbury diocese	Ely Chapter House, 24 April 1414
45/2202	John [Burghill], bishop of Coventry and Lichfield [LP]	Edmund de Ferrers, lord of Chartelay [Chartley] Roger Leche*, knight D. John Wakeryng [Wakering]*, archdeacon of Canterbury John Rome*, canon of Lichfield	Our manor of Heywode [Haywood], 27 April 1414
45/2203	[Thomas Charwelton], abbot of Thorney	John Rotherham*, clerk M. David Pryce [David ap Rees]*, licentiate in laws John Rodborn [Rodbourne]	Thorney, 26 April 1414
45/2204	Richard [Crosby], prior of Coventry Cathedral	John Wakeryng [Wakering]*, archdeacon of Canterbury John Rome* Henry Malpas* Robert Castell*, gentleman John Weston* F: William Halughton, monk of priory F: Thomas Pakynton [Packington], monk of priory F.John Wolvey, monk of priory	Coventry, feast of St George, martyr [23 April] 1414

45/2205	Robert [Reed], bishop of Chichester [LP]	M. John Hovyngham [Hovingham]*, archdeacon of [Durham] John Blounham [Blunham], precentor of Chichester	Our manor of Aldyngborne [Aldingbourne], 28 April 1414
45/2206	William [Merssh], abbot of Battle	D. John Wakeryng [Wakering]*, clerk Simon Gaunstede [Gaunstead]*, clerk William Prestwyk [Prestwick]*, clerk	Battle, 21 April 1414
45/2207	Thomas [Spofforth], abbot of St Mary's, York	M. John Prophete [Prophet]*, keeper of the privy seal, dean of York M. Richard Holme*, bachelor in laws, canon of York M. John Frank*, master in chancery	In the monastery, 12 April 1414
45/2208	William [Cratfeld], abbot of Bury St Edmunds	John Stone*, secretary John Rome*, clerk of parliament William Champeneys [Champneys]*	Our manor of Elmeswell [Elmswell], 18 April 1414
45/2209	Thomas [Prestbury alias Shrewsbury], abbot of Shrewsbury [LP]	David Holbach [Holbache]*	In the monastery, 27 April 1414
45/2210	Clergy of the city and diocese of Carlisle	M. Robert Wolden, clerk M. Richard Holme*, clerk M. William Broune, clerk M. John Wodham [Woodham]*, clerk M. Thomas de Barton*, clerk M. Roger Dokwra*, clerk M. Thomas Stanceby, clerk M. Thomas Clogh [Clough], clerk	Carlisle, 20 April 1414

45/2211	[Thomas Overton], abbot of Crowland	John Rome*, clerk John Rotheram [Rotherham]* William Flete [Fleet]*	Crowland, feast of SS Philip and James [1 May] 1414
45/2213	Prior [Thomas de Hoton] and chapter of Carlisle	M. Robert Wolden, clerk M. Richard Holme*, clerk M. William Broune, clerk M. John Wodham [Woodham]*, clerk M. Thomas de Barton*, clerk M. Roger Dokwra*, clerk M. Thomas Stanceby, clerk M. Thomas Clogh [Clough], clerk	Carlisle Chapter House, 16 April 1414
45/2214	William [Pigot], abbot of Selby	John de Rome*, clerk Henry Malpas*, clerk Robert de Babthorp [Babthorpe]*, gentleman William de Babthorp [Babthorpe]*, gentleman John de Wissingshet [Whissonsett]* John Totty	Selby, 22 April 1414
45/2215	William [Bradley], abbot of Winchcombe	M. Walter Medeford [Medford]*, dean of Wells John Rome*, clerk Thomas Bekyngham [Beckingham]*, gentleman	Winchcombe, 25 April 1414
45/2216	Chapter of Worcester	M. Thomas Radborn [Rodbourne]*, archdeacon of Sudbury M. Nicholas Colnet*	Worcester Chapter House, 26 April 1414

45/2217	Thomas [Erle], abbot of Reading	John Frank*, canon of Salisbury John Mapleton*, clerk John Wyssyngsete [Whissonsett]*, clerk Richard Sowrworth, clerk	Reading, 26 April 1414

PARLIAMENT AT WESTMINSTER, 19 NOVEMBER 1414

45/2201A	Richard Hethe, archdeacon of Huntingdon [*Notarial instrument. Witnesses: 1 illegible; Henry Hughwassh; John Pyrt, chaplain of Lincoln diocese. Notarial sign and attestation of John Hoggesthorp.*]	M. Robert Gilbert*, precentor of Lincoln John Bray	[*Illegible*] Nov. 1414
45/2218	William [Strickland], bishop of Carlisle	Richard Holme*, clerk John Wodhame [Woodham]*, clerk Thomas Stanceby, clerk William de Overton, clerk William Keldesyk [Kelsick], clerk	Rosa [Rose] manor, 4 Nov. 1414
45/2219	John [London], abbot of Hyde near Winchester	M. Walter Medforde [Medford]*, clerk John Chittern [Chitterne]*, clerk Henry Shelford*, clerk	Hyde, 14 Nov. 1414
45/2220A	William [Powcher], prior of Ely Cathedral [*LP*]	M. Richard Derham*, dean of St Martin's, London John Rome*, clerk, rector of Overe [Over], Ely diocese	Ely, 24 Oct. 1414

355

45/2220B	Ralph Derham, subprior of Ely and the chapter	M. Richard Derham*, dean of St Martin's, London John Rome*, clerk, rector of Overe [Over], Ely diocese	Ely Chapter House, Monday after octave of Michaelmas [22 Oct.] 1414
45/2221	Richard [Salford], abbot of Abingdon	Ralph Hamm, monk of abbey Thomas Hasele [Haseley]*, clerk	Abingdon, 9 Nov. 1414
45/2222	[Roger Best], abbot of St John's, Colchester	F. Robert Gryttone [Gritton], prior and monk of abbey William Prestwyk [Prestwick]*, clerk	Colchester, 15 Nov. 1414
45/2223	Hugh Hameweth [Hanworth], archdeacon of Stow	John Macworth [Mackworth]*, dean of Lincoln M. Thomas Brouns*, canon and subdeacon of Lincoln Nicholas Calton [Carlton]*, canon of collegiate church of Southwellen [Southwell]	Lincoln, 8 Nov. 1414
45/2224	Thomas [Chellesworth], abbot of Malmesbury	John Chitterne*, clerk John Morpath [Morpeth]*, clerk	In the monastery, 8 Nov. 1414
45/2225	John [Chynnok alias Wynchestre], abbot of Glastonbury	F. John Gloucestre [Gloucester], monk of abbey M. Thomas Mordon*, bachelor of laws	Glastonbury, 14 Nov. 1414
45/2226	Prior [Thomas de Hoton] and chapter of Carlisle Cathedral [LP]	M. Richard Holme*, canon of York M. John Wodhame [Woodham]*, canon of Lincoln M. Thomas Sanceby [Stanceby], rector of Louthir [Lowther] M. William Keldesyke [Kelsick], vicar of Artureth [Arthuret], Carlisle diocese M. William Overton, clerk	Chapter House, 9 Nov. 1414

45/2227	Clergy of the city and diocese of Carlisle [LP]	William de Keldsyk [Kelsick], clerk John de Birkrig, clerk	Carlisle, 4 Nov. 1414
45/2228	President and chapter of Lincoln Cathedral	M. Robert Gilbert*, precentor of Lincoln M. Thomas Brouns*, subdean of Lincoln M. John Southam*, archdeacon of Oxford M. William Aghton*, archdeacon of Bedford	Lincoln Chapter House, 2 Nov. 1414
45/2229	Geoffrey [Hemingby], abbot of Bardney	[Illegible], clerk John Frank*, clerk Richard de Pountfreit [Pontefract], monk of abbey John Kyme* Richard Duffeld [Duffield]*	[Illegible], 2 Henry V
45/2230	[Thomas Charwelton], abbot of Thorney	William Bolton, clerk John Rodeborn [Rodbourne], clerk F. Alan de Kyrton [Kirketon], monk of abbey	Thorney, 9 Nov. 1414

PARLIAMENT AT WESTMINSTER, 16 MARCH 1416

45/2231	Edmund [Stafford], bishop of Exeter	John Wakeryng [Wakering]*, keeper of the privy seal	[Bishop's] Clyst manor, 7 March 1416
45/2232	Thomas [Erle], abbot of Reading	M. Walter Medford*, dean of Wells D. John Frank*, canon of Salisbury	Reading, 13 March 1416

45/2233	Geoffrey [Hemingby], abbot of Bardney [LP]	John Sp[damaged]thorp [Springthorpe]*, clerk John Frank*, clerk F. William de Burgh, monk of abbey Robert de Welton Thomas Pykeworth [Pickworth]*	Bardney, 9 March 1416
45/2234	John [Fordham], prior of Worcester Cathedral	M. Robert Esebach [Esbache]*, bachelor of civil law M. Walter London*, bachelor of laws, canon of Prestbury collegiate church	Worcester, 10 March 1416
45/2235	John [Lekhampton], abbot of Cirencester	M. Walter Metforde [Medford]*, dean of Wells M. Adam Usk*, clerk Roger Hurne, clerk	In the monastery, 12 March 1416
45/2237	Roger [Yatton], abbot of Evesham	M. John Westone [Weston]*, bachelor of law J[ohn] Scarborough*, clerk W[illiam] Stoke [Stokes]*	Evesham, feast of St Gregory, pope [12 March] 1414
45/2238	[Thomas Overton], abbot of Crowland	John Thoralby*, clerk Richard Petworth*, clerk	Crowland, 8 March 1416
45/2239	Roger [Best], abbot of St John's, Colchester	F. John London, monk of abbey William Prestwyk [Prestwick]*, clerk	Colchester, 9 March 1416
45/2240	Thomas [Chellesworth], abbot of Malmesbury	John Frank*, clerk William Wydecombe [Widdecombe]	In the monastery, 29 Feb. 1416
45/2241	Chapter of Worcester	M. Robert Esebach [Esbache]*, bachelor of civil law M. Walter London*, bachelor of both laws	Worcester Chapter House, 10 March 1416

45/2242	[Thomas Charwelton], abbot of Thorney	D. John Rodeburne [Rodbourne] John Marshall [Marshall] F. Alan de Kyrketon [Kirketon], monk of abbey	Thorney, 8 March 1416
45/2243	Hugh Hanworth, archdeacon of Stow [LP]	M. Thomas Duffeld [Duffield]*, doctor of theology, chancellor of Lincoln M. Thomas Brounes [Brouns]*, doctor of both laws, subdean of Lincoln D. John Teleby, residentiary canon of Lincoln	My residence in Lincoln Cathedral close, 12 March 1416
45/2244	Thomas [Butturwyk], abbot of Ramsey	William Aghton*, clerk M. Robert Hethlode	Ramsey, 12 March 1416
45/2245	William [Bradley], abbot of Winchcombe	John Willicotes [Wilcotes]*, gentleman	Winchcombe, 4 March 1416
45/2246	President and chapter of Lincoln Cathedral	M. Robert Gilbert*, precentor of Lincoln M. Thomas Brouns*, subdean of Lincoln M. Philip Morgan*, canon of Lincoln M. David Price [ap Rees]*, canon of Lincoln	Lincoln Chapter House, 2 March 1416
45/2247	[Robert Lancaster], bishop of St Asaph	M. Adam Uske [Usk]*, doctor of laws, canon of St Asaph John Escourt [Estcourt]* of 'Llanduelos', rector in the diocese Richard Mountain of Llanarmion [Llanarmon], rector in the diocese	Valle Crucis Abbey, 9 March 1416
45/2248	John [Prophet], dean, and the chapter of York Cathedral [LP]	M. Richard de Holme*, canon of York Simon Gaunstede [Gaunstead]*, canon of York Henry Merston*, canon of York	York Chapter House, 9 March 1416

PARLIAMENT AT WESTMINSTER, 19 OCTOBER 1416

45/2249	Chapter of Worcester Cathedral [LP]	M. Walter London*, bachelor of both laws M. Robert Esebach [Esbache]*, bachelor of civil law	Worcester Chapter House, 11 Oct. 1416
45/2250A	[Thomas Overton], abbot of Crowland	John Springthorp [Springthorpe]*, clerk John Thoralby*, clerk Richard Petworth*, clerk	Crowland, Thursday before the [translation] of St Etheldreda [15 Oct.] 1416
46/2251	Hugh Hanworth, archdeacon of Stow [LP]	M. David Pryce [David ap Rees]*, bachelor of laws Nicholas Calton [Carlton]*, archdeacon of Taunton William Aghton*, archdeacon of Bedford	My residence in the close of Lincoln, 15 Oct.1416
46/2252	Edmund [Stafford], bishop of Exeter [LP]	Simon Gaunstede [Gaunstead]*, keeper of the rolls Richard Gabryell [Gabriel]*, canon of Exeter	Clist [Bishop's Clyst] manor , 3 Oct. 1416
46/2253	Hugh [Morton], abbot of St Peter's, Gloucester	M. John Fraunk [Frank]* Thomas Hasley [Haseley]* William Wydecombe [Widdecombe] Robert Gilbert*	[No place], 7 Oct. 1416
46/2254	Roger [Yatton], abbot of Evesham [LP]	M. Thomas Feolde [Field]*, doctor of laws, dean of Hereford M.John Westone [Weston]* John Scarborough*	Evesham, 16 Oct. 1416

46/2255	[Thomas Charwelton], abbot of Thorney	John Rodeborn [Rodbourne], clerk William Yslep [Islip], clerk F. Alan de Kyrton [Kirketon], monk of abbey	Thorney, 12 Oct. 1416
46/2256	Geoffrey [Hemingby], abbot of Bardney [LP]	John Fraunk [Frank]*, clerk Alan Humerston [Humberston]*, clerk Richard Duffeld [Duffield]*	Bardney, feast of St Luke, evangelist [18 Oct.] 1416
46/2257	Thomas [Butturwyk], abbot of Ramsey	William Aghton*, clerk M. Robert Northlode	Ramsey, 17 Oct. 1416
46/2258	Nicholas [Strode], abbot of Hyde near Winchester	John Chitterne*, clerk John Forest*, clerk Henry Shelford*, clerk	Hyde, 4 Oct. 1416
46/2259	Thomas [Erle], abbot of Reading	M. Walter Medeford [Medford]*, dean of Wells John Frank*, canon of Salisbury Thomas Hasele [Haseley]*, clerk	Reading, 16 Oct. 1416
46/2260	Robert [Lancaster], bishop of St Asaph [LP]	Benedict [Nicolls]*, bishop of Bangor John [de la Zouche]*, bishop of Llandaff David Holbach [Holbache]*, gentleman M. Adam Usk*, doctor of laws, canon of St Asaph John Estcourt*, bachelor in laws Richard Mountayn [Mountain], rector of Llanarmon in Yale [Llanarmon Dyffryn Ceiriog], St Asaph diocese William Lee [II]*, literate	St Asaph, 10 Oct. 1416
46/2261	Thomas [Chellesworth], abbot of Malmesbury	John Frank*, clerk William Wydecombe [Widdecombe]	In the monastery, 12 Oct. 1416

361

| 46/2262 | John [Deeping], abbot of Peterborough | M. Thomas Brounis [Brouns]*, clerk
M. David Prise [ap Rees]*, clerk
F. Thomas Fannell, monk of abbey | Peterborough, 16 Oct. 1416 |
| 46/2263 | John [Chynnok alias Wynchestre], abbot of Glastonbury | John Frank*
John Chitterne*
F. Richard Froome, monk of abbey | Glastonbury, 14 Oct. 1416 |

PARLIAMENT AT WESTMINSTER, 16 NOVEMBER 1417

45/2250B	Edmund [Stafford], bishop of Exeter	[Illegible] John Rome*, clerk	[Bishop's] Clyst manor, 24 Oct. 1417[7]
46/2264	Prior [Thomas de Hoton] and chapter of Carlisle Cathedral [LP]	M. Roger Docwra [Dokwra]*, clerk William Wall, clerk William Louther John Birkrig	Chapter House, 28 Oct. 1417
46/2265	Thomas [Chellesworth], abbot of Malmesbury	Thomas Evesham, monk of abbey William Wydecumbe [Widdecombe], clerk	In the monastery, feast of St Martin [11 Nov.] 1417
46/2266	Nicholas [Strode], abbot of Hyde near Winchester	John Chittern [Chitterne]*, clerk Henry Shelford*, clerk	Hyde, 10 Nov. 1417
46/2267	[Thomas Charwelton], abbot of Thorney	John Rodebourn [Rodbourne], clerk William Islep [Islip]*, clerk F. Alan de Kirketon, monk of abbey	Thorney, 4 Nov. 1417

46/2268	[Hugh Morton], abbot of St Peter's, Gloucester	M. William Mylton [Milton]*, archdeacon of Buckingham John Russell [III]* John Wydecombe [Widdecombe]	Gloucester, 12 Nov. 1417
46/2269	William [Best], abbot of Cirencester	M. John Frank* F. Thomas Sturmey, monk of abbey	In the monastery, 13 Nov. 1417
46/2270	Edmund [Stafford], bishop of Exeter [LP]	M. Henry Ware*, keeper of the privy seal Richard Gabryell [Gabriel]*, canon of Exeter	[Bishop's] Clyst our manor, 16 Oct. 1417
46/2271	Thomas de Grysedale, archdeacon of Carlisle [LP]	Roger Dokwra*, clerk William del Wall, clerk William de Loughre [Louther], clerk John Byrkerig [Birkrig], clerk	Carlisle, 5 Nov. 1417
46/2272	[Robert Lancaster], bishop of St Asaph [LP]	[Benedict Nicolls]*, bishop of Bangor David Holbach [Holbache]*, gentleman M. Adam Usk*, bachelor in both laws, canon of St Asaph M. John Estcourt*, bachelor in laws M. Richard Mountryn [Mountain], rector of 'Gethien in Yerle'	[Illegible], 9 Nov. 1417
46/2273	President and chapter of Lincoln Cathedral [LP]	M. John Southam*, archdeacon of Oxford M. William Aghton*, archdeacon of Bedford William Kynwelmersche [Killamarsh], prebendary of Thame John Legburn*, prebendary of Sexaginta Solidorum M. David Pryce [ap Rees]*, prebendary of Clyfton [Clifton]	Lincoln Chapter House, 26 Oct. 1417

46/2274	Clergy of the city and diocese of Carlisle [LP]	Roger de Dokwra*, clerk William del Wall, clerk William de Louthre [Louther], clerk John de Brikrygg [Birkrig], clerk	Carlisle, 28 Oct. 1417
46/2275	Richard [de South Walsham], abbot of St Benet of Hulme	William Paston * John Alderforth [Alderford]*	St Benet of Hulme, 13 Nov. 1417
46/2276	Hugh de Hanworth, archdeacon of Stow [LP]	Nicholas Calton [Carlton]*, archdeacon of Taunton William Aghton*, archdeacon of Bedford Thomas Grove de Messyngham, clerk of Lincoln diocese	My residence in Lincoln Cathedral close, 25 Oct. 1417
46/2277	Henry [Bowet], archbishop of York	Thomas [Langley]*, bishop of Durham M. Simon Gaunsted [Gaunstead]*, canon of York Richard Holme*, canon of York	Cawode [Cawood] our manor, 4 Nov. 1417
46/2278	William [Pigot], abbot of Selby	Thomas Haseley* William Babthorp [Babthorpe]* John Cotty	Selby, 20 Oct. 1417
46/2279	Richard [Young], bishop of Rochester	[Thomas Langley]*, bishop of Durham [John Fordham], bishop of Ely [Benedict Nicolls]*, bishop of Bangor	Our manor of Hallyng [Halling], [Illegible] Sept.1417
46/2280	William [Strickland], bishop of [Carlisle]	[Damaged] William de Wall, clerk William de Louthre [Louther], clerk John Birkerig [Birkrig], clerk	Rose our manor, 5 Nov. 1417

46/2281	Roger [Yatton], abbot of Evesham [LP]	John [Illegible], clerk William Stokes*	Evesham, 10 Nov. 1417
46/2282	John [Deeping], abbot of Peterborough	D. William Actan [Aghton]*, archdeacon of Bedford F. Thomas Fannell, monk of abbey	Peterborough, 13 Nov. 1417
46/2283	Thomas [Butterwyk], abbot of Ramsey	F. Thomas Pylton [Pilton], monk of abbey William Aghton*, clerk	Ramsey, 10 Nov. 1417

PARLIAMENT AT WESTMINSTER, 16 OCTOBER 1419

46/2284	[Thomas Charwelton], abbot of Thorney	William Islep [Islip]*, clerk F. Alan de Kirketon, monk of abbey	Thorney, 12 Oct.1419
46/2285	Thomas [Erle], abbot of Reading	John Frank*, clerk Thomas Hasele [Haseley]*, clerk F. Thomas Staunton, monk of abbey	Reading, 14 Oct. 1419
46/2286	John de Paciencia [Deeping], abbot of Peterborough	William [Aghton]*, attorney, archdeacon of Bedford M. Robert Keten [Ketton]* M. David Prys [ap Rees]*	Peterborough, 12 Oct. 1419
46/2287	Robert [Lancaster], bishop of St Asaph [LP]	Benedict [Nicolls]*, bishop of St Davids Richard [recte William] Barrow, bishop of Bangor M. Richard Leyot, dean of St Asaph M. Howel Kyffin [Hywel Cyffin]*, canon of St Asaph M. Adam Uske [Usk]*, canon of St Asaph M. Thomas Gyles [Giles], canon of St Asaph John Estcourt*, examiner of the court of [Arches], London	St Asaph, 5 Oct. 1419

365

46/2288	Prior [John de Washington] and chapter of Durham Cathedral [LP]	John Thoralby*, rector of Whitbern [Whitburn] Christopher Beynt, gentleman Robert Lampton, gentleman	Durham, 4 Oct. 1419
46/2289	William [Bradley], abbot of Winchcombe	John Wilcotes*, gentleman	Winchcombe, 10 Oct. 1419
46/2290	Philip [Repingdon], bishop of Lincoln [LP]	Simon Gaunstede [Gaunstead]*, clerk, keeper of the rolls John Fraunk [Frank]*, clerk of parliament M. Thomas Brunne [Brouns]*	Sleaford, 8 Oct. 1419
46/2291	Henry [Bowet], archbishop of York [LP]	Henry [Beaufort]*, bishop of Winchester Thomas [Langley]*, bishop of Durham William Kynwolmerssh [Killamarsh], provost of Beverlaci [Beverley] Simon Gaunsted [Gaunstead]* canon of York M. Richard Holme*, canon of York	Cawood, 2 Oct. 1419
46/2292	Thomas [Chellesworth], abbot of Malmesbury	John Fraunk [Frank]*, clerk Alexander Sparowe [Sparrow]*, clerk	In the monastery, 8 Sept. 1419
46/2293	Geoffrey [Hemingby], abbot of Bardney [LP]	John Spryngthorp [Springthorpe]*, clerk John Franke [Frank]*, clerk F.John Newcastell [Newcastle], monk of abbey Richard Duffeld [Duffield]* Thomas Pikworth [Pickworth]*	Bardney, 8 Oct. 1419

46/2295	Richard Heth [Hethe], archdeacon of Huntingdon [LP]	John Southam*, archdeacon of Oxford Thomas Broune [Brouns]*, archdeacon of Stow David Pryce [David ap Rees]*, canon of Lincoln John Legburn*, canon of Lincoln	Lincoln, 1 Oct. 1419
46/2296	Nicholas [Strode], abbot of Hyde near Winchester	John Forest*, archdeacon of Surrey Henry Shelford*, clerk M. John Cole, clerk	Hyde, 9 Oct. 1419
46/2297	John [Chynnok alias Wynchestre], abbot of Glastonbury	John Franke [Frank]* M. David Pryce [David ap Rees]*, doctor of laws, advocate of the court of Arches in London F. Nicholas Frome, monk of abbey	Glastonbury, 2 Oct. 1419
46/2298	William [Best], abbot of Cirencester	M. John Frank*, clerk F. William Wotton*, monk of abbey	In the monastery, 11 Oct. 1419
46/2299	Richard Elvet, archdeacon of Leicester [LP] [Also commissions proctors for convocation of southern province on 30 Oct. at St Paul's, London]	M. John Southam*, archdeacon of Oxford Thomas Broune [Brouns]*, archdeacon of Stow William Acton [Aghton]*, archdeacon of Bedford	Leicester, 29 Sept. 1419
46/2300	President and chapter of Lincoln [LP]	M. John Southam*, archdeacon of Oxford M. Thomas Brouns*, archdeacon of Stow Richard Layot, canon of Lincoln John Legburn*, canon of Lincoln	Lincoln Chapter House, 7 Sept. 1419

PARLIAMENT AT WESTMINSTER, 2 DECEMBER 1420

47/2301	Richard [de South Walsham], abbot of St Benet of Hulme	William Paston* John Mannyng John Alderforthe [Alderford]*	St Benet of Hulme, 29 Nov. 1420
47/2302	Richard [Bromsgrove], abbot of Evesham [LP]	Thomas Hasle [Haseley]* John Waget William Stokes*	Evesham, feast of St Katherine, virgin [25 Nov.] 1420
47/2303	Thomas [Spofforth], abbot of St Mary's, York	Simon Gaunstede [Gaunstead]*, keeper of the rolls of chancery Richard Norton*, chief justice of common pleas John Thoralby*, master in chancery Richard Malton, clerk Thomas Hasley [Haseley]*	In the monastery, 10 Nov. 1420
47/2304	Thomas [Chellesworth], abbot of Malmesbury	John Frank*, clerk Alexander Sparowe [Sparrow]*, clerk	In the monastery, 11 Nov. 1420
47/2305	William [Excetre], abbot of Bury St Edmunds	William Kynwolmersshe [Killamarsh] Nicholas Wymbyssh [Wymbush]* F. Robert Wesenham [Weasenham], monk of abbey	Our manor of Elmswell, 26 Nov. 1420
47/2306	Robert [Gritton], abbot of St John's, Colchester	F. John Horkisleye [Horkesley], monk of abbey William Prestwyk [Prestwick]*	[No place], 10 Nov. 1420

47/2307	Henry [Bowet], archbishop of York [LP]	Henry [Beaufort]*, bishop of Winchester Thomas [Langley]*, bishop of Durham William Kynwolmerssh [Killamarsh], provost of St John's, Beverley Simon Gaunsted [Gaunstead]*, canon of York M. Richard Holme*, canon of York	Cawod [Cawood], 12 Nov. 1420
47/2308	[Thomas Charwelton], abbot of Thorney	William Islep [Islip]*, clerk Thomas Morton*, clerk	Thorney, 26 Nov. 1420
47/2309	John [Deeping], abbot of Peterborough	William Aghton*, archdeacon of Bedford M. David Prys [ap Rees]*, clerk F. Walter Fryney [Friskney], monk of abbey	Peterborough, 15 Dec. 1420
47/2310	Robert [Lancaster], bishop of St Asaph [LP]	Benedict [Nicolls]*, bishop of St Davids John [de la Zouche]*, bishop of Llandaff William [Barrow]*, bishop of Bangor M. Walter Bullok [Bullock]*, dean of St Asaph M. Howel Kyffin [Hywel Cyffin]*, canon of St Asaph M. Adam Usk*, canon of St Asaph M. John Estcourt*, examiner-general of the court of Canterbury William Ryman*, literate gentleman William Lee [II]*, literate gentleman	St Asaph, 14 Nov. 1420

369

47/2311	William [Bradley], abbot of Winchcombe	John Willycotes [Wilcotes]*, gentleman	Winchcombe, Monday the feast of St Katherine, virgin [25 Nov.] 1420
47/2312	William [Best], abbot of Cirencester	M. John Fraunk [Frank]*, clerk F. William Wotton*, monk of abbey	In the monastery, 22 Nov. 1420
47/2313	Nicholas [Frome], abbot of Glastonbury	John Franke [Frank]* M. David ap Rys [ap Rees]*, advocate in the court of Arches	Glastonbury, 16 Nov. 1420

PARLIAMENT AT WESTMINSTER, 1 DECEMBER 1421

47/2314	John [Chaundler], bishop of Salisbury [LP]	John Frank*, canon of Salisbury	Our London house, [Illegible] Dec. 1421
47/2316	Henry [Bowet], archbishop of York [LP]	Henry [Beaufort]*, bishop of Winchester William Kynwolmerssh [Killamarsh], provost of Beverley Simon Gaunstede [Gaunstead]*, canon of York M. Richard Holme*, canon of York	Bishopthorpe, 10 Nov. 1421
47/2317	Richard Elvet, archdeacon of Leicester [LP]	M William Aghton*, archdeacon of Bedford M. David Pryce [David ap Rees]*, canon and prebendary of Lincoln	Leicester, 24 Nov. 1421

47/2318	Lewis Coychurch, archdeacon of Lewes [LP]	M. William Mylton [Milton]*, dean of Chichester M. David Pryce [David ap Rees]*, advocate of the court of Arches M. William Bray*, advocate of the court of Arches M. James Cole*, proctor-general of the court of Arches M. Simon Kempston*, proctor-general of the court of Arches M. Robert Rosomonde, proctor-general of the court of Arches M. John Ratsey, proctor-general of the court of Arches	Chichester, 8 Nov. 1421
47/2319	John [Marwent], abbot of St Peter's, Gloucester	M. William Mylton [Milton]*, archdeacon of Buckingham Thomas Hasseley [Haseley]*	[No place], 21 Nov. 1421
47/2320	Robert [Gritton], abbot of St John's, Colchester	F. John Horkisle [Horkesley], monk of abbey William Perstwyk [Prestwick]*	Colchester, 7 Nov. 1421
47/2321	[Thomas Charwelton], abbot of Thorney	Thomas Morton* William Yslep [Islip] F. Alan de Kirketon, monk of abbey	Thorney, 13 Nov. 1421
47/2322	Richard [de South Walsham], abbot of St Benet of Hulme	William Paston* John Alderforth [Alderford]*	St Benet of Hulme, 26 Nov. 1421
47/2323	Geoffrey [Hemingby], abbot of Bardney	John Spryngthorp [Springthorpe]*, clerk John Frank*, clerk	Bardney, 23 Nov. 1421
47/2324	Thomas [Erle], abbot of Reading	John Frank*, clerk Thomas Haselee [Haseley]*, clerk	Reading, 28 Nov. 1421

47/2325	William [Excetre], abbot of Bury St Edmunds	Nicholas Wymbyssh [Wymbush]*, clerk William Bonard F. Robert Wesenham [Weasenham], monk of abbey	Manor of Elmswell, 25 Nov. 1421
47/2326	Richard [Bromsgrove], abbot of Evesham [LP]	John Wyleapes, gentleman John Derby William Stokes*	Evesham, 10 Nov. 1421
47/2327	Robert [Lancaster], bishop of St Asaph [LP]	Benedict [Nicholls]*, bishop of St David's William [Barrow]*, bishop of Bangor M. Walter Bullok [Bullock]*, dean of St Asaph M. John Estcourt*, bachelor of laws M. Richard Monteyn [Mountain] M. John Forster Thomas Gyles [Giles], canon of St Asaph	St Asaph, 22 Nov. 1421
47/2328	Chapter of St Asaph [LP]	M. John Escourt [Estcourt]*, bachelor in laws M. Richard Monteyn [Mountain] M. John Forster Thomas Exley, canon of St Asaph	St Asaph, 20 Nov. 1421
47/2329	[Damaged – William Best, abbot of Cirencester]	M. John Frank*, clerk M. David ap Res [ap Rees]*, clerk* F. William Wotton*, monk of abbey	In the monastery, 24 Nov. 1421
47/2330	Nicholas [Strode], abbot of Hyde near Winchester	M. Walter Medeford [Medford]*, dean of Wells John Frank*, master in chancery, clerk Henry Shelford*, master in chancery, clerk	Hyde, 31 Nov. 1421

47/2331	John [Deeping], abbot of Peterborough	M. Bartholomew Leek, doctor of laws William Atton [Aghton]*, archdeacon of Bedford William Islep [Islip]*, clerk	Peterborough, 4 Nov. 1421
47/2332	Thomas [Chellesworth], abbot of Malmesbury	John Franke [Frank]*, clerk Nicholas Wotton*	In the monastery, 24 Nov. 1421
47/2333	Thomas [Chellesworth], abbot of Malmesbury [LP]	M. Alexander Sparowe [Sparrow]*, bachelor of laws John Frank*, clerk	Malmesbury, 24 Nov. 1421
47/2334	[Richard Upton], abbot of Crowland	William Babyngton [Babington]*, chief baron of the exchequer William Ward*	Crowland, 13 Nov. 1421

PARLIAMENTS OF THE FIRST REIGN OF HENRY VI (1422–61)

PARLIAMENT AT WESTMINSTER, 9 NOVEMBER 1422

47/2335	John [Deeping], abbot of Peterborough	M. Thomas Whiston* William Acton [Aghton]*, archdeacon of Bedford F. Walter Frisney [Friskney], monk of abbey	Peterborough, 6 Nov. 1422
47/2336	[Thomas Charwelton], abbot of Thorney	Thomas Morton*, clerk D. William Iselep [Islip], clerk F. Alan Kirketon, monk of abbey	Thorney, 4 Nov. 1422
47/2337	Thomas [Chellesworth], abbot of Malmesbury	John Franke [Frank]*, clerk Nicholas Wotton*	In the monastery, 3 Nov. 1422
47/2338	Thomas Wollaston, precentor of St Davids Cathedral and the chapter [LP]	M. David Pryce [David ap Rees]*, chancellor of St Davids M. William Neuport [Newport], archdeacon of Carmarthen M. Philip ap David, canon of St Davids D. Thomas Staundon [Staunton]*, canon of St Davids	St Davids Chapter House, 22 Oct. 1422
47/2339	William [Best], abbot of Cirencester	M. John Frank*, clerk F. William Wotton*, monk of abbey	In the monastery, 2 Nov. 1422

47/2340	Robert [Lancaster], bishop of St Asaph	Benedict [Nicolls]*, bishop of St Davids William [Barrow]*, bishop of Bangor M. Walter Bullok [Bullock]*, dean of St Asaph M. Howel Kiffyn [Hywel Cyffin]*, doctor of both laws, canon of St Asaph M. John Estcourt*, examiner-general of the court of Canterbury	St Asaph, 31 Oct. 1422
47/2341	John [Chaundler], bishop of Salisbury	M. Walter Medeford [Medford]*, canon of Salisbury M. John Franke [Frank]*, canon of Salisbury John Symondesburgh [Symondsbury]*, treasurer of St Paul's, London	Ramsbury, 30 Oct. 1422
47/2342	Robert [Gritton], abbot of St John's, Colchester	F. John Horkyssey [Horkesley], monk of abbey William Prestwyk [Prestwick]*	Colchester, 6 Nov. 1422

PARLIAMENT AT WESTMINSTER, 20 OCTOBER 1423

47/2343	John [Fordham], bishop of Ely	Richard Weynyflete [Wetheringsett]*, archdeacon of Ely M. John Bernard*, licenciate in laws Henry Skelford [Shelford]*, master in chancery William Derby*, rector of Tyryngton [Terrington], Norwich diocese Henry Sharyngton [Sharrington], bachelor of laws	Our manor of Dounham [Downham], 10 Oct. 1423
47/2344	Nicholas [Strode], abbot of Hyde near Winchester	John Forest*, archdeacon of Surrey John Frank*, clerk John Mapleton*, clerk Henry Shilforde [Shelford]*, clerk	Hyde, 15 Oct. 1423

375

47/2345	Geoffrey [Hemingby], abbot of Bardney [LP]	John Frank*, clerk John Spryngthorp [Springthorpe]*, clerk	Bardney, 6 Oct. 1423
47/2346	[Thomas Charwelton], abbot of Thorney	Thomas Morton*, clerk William Islep [Islip]*, clerk F. Alan Kirketon [Kirkton], monk of abbey	Thorney, 14 Oct. 1423
47/2347	William [Excetre], abbot of Bury St Edmunds	John Wodehous [Woodhouse]*, gentleman Nicholas Wymbyssh [Wymbush]*, clerk F. Robert Wesenham [Weasenham], monk of abbey	Our manor of Elmesewell [Elmswell], 12 Oct. 1423
47/2348	Henry [Bowet], archbishop of York [LP]	Henry [Beaufort]*, bishop of Winchester Thomas [Langley]*, bishop of Durham M. William Alnewyk [Alnwick]*, doctor of laws, canon of York Simon Gaunstede [Gaunstead]*, canon of York	Cawode [Cawood], 29 Sept. 1423
47/2349	Robert [Lancaster], bishop of St Asaph [LP]	[Benedict Nicolls]*, bishop of St Davids Edmund [Lacy]*, bishop of Exeter M. Walter Bullok [Bullock]*, doctor of laws M. Adam Usk*, doctor of laws, canon of St Asaph M. John Estcourt*, examiner-general in the court of Canterbury M. Peter Thomas, bachelor of laws M. John Forster	Our manor of Vallecrucis [Valle Crucis], 10 Oct. 1423
47/2350	William [Heyworth], bishop of Coventry and Lichfield	M. John Stafford*, dean of St Martin-le-Grand, London John Fraunk [Frank]*, archdeacon of Suffolk David Pryse [ap Rees]*, archdeacon of Chester	Our manor of Heywode [Haywood], 22 Oct. 1423

48/2351	John [Chaundler], bishop of Salisbury	M. John Stafford*, canon of Salisbury John Frank*, canon of Salisbury M. John Symondesburgh [Symondsbury]*, treasurer of St Paul's, London	Poterne [Potterne] our manor, 12 Oct. 1423
48/2352	John [Deeping], abbot of Peterborough	M. Thomas Brouns*, clerk M. David appe Rys [David [ap Rees]*, clerk Walter Frysney [Friskney], monk of abbey	Peterborough, 16 Oct. 1423
48/2353	Robert [Gritton], abbot of St John's, Colchester	F. John London, monk of abbey William Prestwick*	Colchester, 16 Oct. 1423
48/2354	Subdean [John Percy] and chapter of Lincoln Cathedral [LP]	M. John Southam*, archdeacon of Oxford M. Thomas Brouns*, archdeacon of Stow M. Richard Caudrey, archdeacon of Bedford David Pryce [David ap Rees]*, canon of Lincoln	Lincoln Chapter House, 1 Oct. 1423
48/2355	Thomas [Chellesworth], abbot of Malmesbury	John Franke [Frank]*, clerk Nicholas Wotton*	In the monastery, 1 Oct. 1423
48/2356	John [Tychemersh], abbot of Ramsey	Thomas Smyth*, rector of Ripton Robert Poleyn	Ramsey, 18 Oct. 1423
48/2357	William [Best], abbot of Cirencester	M. John Franke [Frank]*, clerk M. David Apris [ap Rees]*, clerk	In the monastery, 16 Oct. 1423

PARLIAMENT AT WESTMINSTER, 30 APRIL 1425

48/2358	Robert [Gritton], abbot of St John's, Colchester	[Illegible] F. John Horkesleye [Horkesley], monk of abbey	Colchester, 20 April 1425
48/2359	John [Chaundler], bishop of Salisbury	M. John Stafford*, treasurer of England, bishop of Bath and Wells John Frank*, canon of Salisbury	Our manor of Ramsbury, [Damaged]
48/2360	Edmund [Lacy], bishop of Exeter [LP]	Philip [Morgan]*, bishop of Worcester Benedict [Nicolls]*, bishop of St Davids M. Richard Betty, canon of St Paul's Cathedral	Lawhuton [Llawhitton], 8 April 1425
48/2361	John [Fordham], prior of Worcester Cathedral	M. David Price [ap Rees]*, licentiate in canon law, canon of Lincoln, advocate of the court of Arches M. Walter London*, preceptor of the hospital of St Wulfstan, Worcester, bachelor of civil law	Worcester, 26 April 1425
48/2362	Thomas [Prestbury alias Shrewsbury], abbot of Shrewsbury [LP]	F. William Pole, monk of abbey	In the monastery, 22 April 1425
48/2363	Roger [Pershore], abbot of Malmesbury	Robert Andrewe [Andrew]* Nicholas Wotton*	In the monastery, 26 April 1425
48/2364	[Thomas Charwelton], abbot of Thorney	Thomas Morton*, clerk D. William Islep [Islip]*, clerk F. Alan Kirketon, monk of abbey	Thorney, 23 April 1425
48/2365	Chapter of Worcester Cathedral	M. David Price [ap Rees]* M. Walter London*	Worcester Chapter House, 26 April 1425

48/2366	Nicholas [Strode], abbot of Hyde near Winchester	John Frank* Henry Shelford*	Hyde, 25 April 1425
48/2367	[Illegible]	William Prestwyk [Prestwick]* [Illegible]	[Illegible]
48/2368	Robert [Lancaster], bishop of St Asaph [LP]	M. John Stafford* [Illegible]	St Asaph, 22 April 1425
48/2369	John [Deeping], abbot of Peterborough	M. David appe Rys [ap Rees]*, clerk Thomas Smyth*, clerk	Peterborough, 20 April 1425
48/2370	Peter [de Ely], prior, and chapter of Ely Cathedral [LP]	Richard Wetheryngflete [Wetheringsett]*, archdeacon of Ely John Hals*, king's justice Richard Grethararp	Ely Chapter House, 11 April 1425
48/2371	Marcellus [Daundelyon], abbot of St Augustine's, Canterbury [LP]	F. William Kenyngton [Kennington], monk of abbey, bachelor of canon law M. David Price [ap Rees]*, inceptor in canon law	In the monastery, 20 April 1425
48/2372	John [Tychemersh], abbot of Ramsey	Thomas Smyth*, clerk F. Richard Croweland [Crowland], monk of abbey	Ramsey, 1 April 1425
48/2390	Richard [Upton], abbot of Crowland	William Babyngton [Babington]*, chief justice of the common bench William Warde [Ward]*, clerk John Thoraldby [Thoralby]*, clerk James Strangwise [Strangeways]* Roger Flore* of Okeham [Oakham]	Crowland, 20 April, 6 [sic] Henry VI [1428 – recte 1425] [The parliament referred to in the the text is that 'at Westminster on the last day of April'.]

PARLIAMENT AT LEICESTER, 18 FEBRUARY 1426

48/2374	Robert [Gritton], abbot of St John's, Colchester	F. John Horkysleye [Horkesley], monk of abbey William Prestwyk [Prestwick]*	Colchester, 5 Feb. 1426
48/2375	William [Best], abbot of Cirencester	William Prestwyk [Prestwick]*, clerk M. William Henton*	In the monastery, [no date]
48/2376	Roger [Pershore], abbot of Malmesbury [LP]	John Franke [Frank]*, clerk Robert Andrew*	In the monastery, 10 Feb. 1426
48/2377	Dean [John Mackworth] and chapter of Lincoln [LP]	M. Thomas Brouns*, archdeacon of Stow M. Richard Caudrey, archdeacon of Bedford Nicholas Dixon*, canon of Lincoln Richard Selby*, canon of Lincoln	Lincoln Chapter House, 10 Feb. 1426
48/2378	William [sic – recte Thomas Prestbury alias Shrewsbury], abbot of Shrewsbury [LP]	F. William Pole, monk of abbey	In the monastery, 16 Feb. 1426
48/2379	John [Tychemersh], abbot of Ramsey	William Prestwyk [Prestwick]*, clerk Roger Hunte [Hunt]* Thomas Brygge [Bridge]	Ramsey, 10 Feb. 1426
48/2380	William [Heyworth], bishop of Coventry and Lichfield [LP]	Nicholas Wymyssh [Wymbush]*, clerk Thomas Hal', clerk	Heywode [Haywood] manor, 16 Feb. 1426
48/2381	Richard [de South Walsham], abbot of St Benet of Hulme	M. John Repynghale [Rippingale], doctor of theology	St Benet of Hulme, 7 Feb. 1426

48/2382	William [Excetre], abbot of Bury St Edmunds	F. Robert Wesenham [Weasenham], monk of abbey Nicholas Wymbyssh [Wymbush]*, clerk Robert Wyot*, clerk	Elmeswell [Elmswell] manor, 6 Feb. 1426
48/2383	Richard [Upton], abbot of Crowland	Thomas Brouns*, doctor of laws James Strangwys [Strangeways]* Roger Flore* of Okeham [Oakham] John Langholm* of Conyngsholm [Conisholme]	Crowland, feast of St Valentine, martyr [14 Feb.] 1426
48/2384	Nicholas [Strode], abbot of Hyde near Winchester	John Frank*, clerk, master in chancery Henry Shelford*, clerk, master in chancery Richard Turnaunt*, citizen of the city of Winchester	Hyde, 7 Jan. 1426
48/2386	[John Deeping], abbot of Peterborough	M. Thomas Brouns* Thomas Smyth* Thomas [Illegible] [Illegible – Thomas] Brigge [Bridge], clerk	Peterborough, 14 Feb. 1426
48/2387	Edmund [Lacy], bishop of Exeter [LP]	Philip [Morgan]*, bishop of Worcester M. William Prestwyke [Prestwick]*, chaplain	In our house in London, 2 Feb. 1426
48/2388	Robert [Lancaster], bishop of St Asaph [LP]	John Stafford*, bishop of Bath and Wells, treasurer of England M. Thomas Brouns*, archdeacon [sic] of Canterbury M. Walter Bullok [Bullock]*, archdeacon of Derby M. John Forster	Valle Crucis abbey, 12 Feb. 1426
48/2389	Nicholas [Frome], abbot of Glastonbury	William Prestwyk [Prestwick]*, clerk Thomas Haseley*	Glastonbury, 11 Feb. 1426

PARLIAMENT AT WESTMINSTER, 22 SEPTEMBER 1429

The following seventeen documents, all damaged to some extent, are filed between 48/2390 and 48/2391 and do not have a Record Office number stamped on the back. Instead, there are only numbers written in pencil. Confusingly, one incomplete series of non-sequential numbers has been written along the bottom of these letters, while another (presumably later) sequence of sequential numbers has been written along the top. Here, the sequential (top) order is given first, with the non-sequential (bottom) numbers noted in parentheses.

1 (1)	John [Wells], bishop of Llandaff	M. John Blodewell [Blodwell]*, doctor of canon law / John Langton, bachelor of canon law	[*Illegible*] 8 Sept. 1429
2 (7)	[Thomas Langley], bishop of Durham	John Frank*, keeper of the rolls of chancery / William Prestwyk [Prestwick]*	Howden our manor, 12 Sept. 1429
3 (10)	Clergy of the diocese of St Asaph [*LP*]	M. John [*Illegible*] / David Prys [ap Rees]*, canon of St Paul's, London	St Asaph, 13 Sept. 1429
4 (9)	Chapter of St Asaph [*LP*]	[M. John Blodwell]*, doctor of [civil] law, dean of St Asaph / David Prys [ap Rees]*, canon of St Paul's	St Asaph Chapter House, 15 Sept. 1429
5 (4)	Chapter of Worcester Cathedral	M. John Hody* / [*Damaged*]	Worcester; 16 Sept. 1429
6 (5)	John, [*Damaged* – Fordham, Prior of Worcester]	[*Damaged* – John Hody]*, chancellor of Wells Cathedral	Worcester Chapter House, 16 [*Damaged*] 1429
7 (8)	[John Litlington], abbot of [*Damaged* – Crowland]	D. Nicholas Dikson [Dixon]*, clerk / D. Nicholas Wymbissh [Wymbush]*, clerk / D. John Thoraleby [Thoralby], clerk	Crowland, 16 [*Damaged*]

8 (11)	[Damaged – Robert Lancaster], bishop of St Asaph	[Damaged] Philip [Morgan]*, bishop of Ely John [Cliderow]*, bishop of Bangor	Valle Crucis abbey, 16 Sept. 1429
9 (–)	[Damaged – William Best, abbot of] Cirencester	D. William Prestwyk [Prestwick]* [Damaged]	In the monastery, 16 Sept. 1429
10 (7)	John Hampton, abbot of [Damaged – Shrewsbury]	John Blodewell [Blodwell]*, professor of laws William Borley [Burley]*, gentleman	In the monastery, 17 Sept. [damaged]
11 (12)	[Damaged – Chapter of] Lincoln, the dean being absent [LP]	David Price [ap Rees]*, canon of Lincoln Richard de Caudrey, canon of Lincoln	Lincoln Chapter House, 7 Sept. [damaged]
12 (–)	[Damaged – Nicholas Strode, abbot of] Hyde near Winchester	John Frank*	[Damaged], 10 Sept. [damaged]
13 (16)	[Damaged – John Deeping, abbot of Peterborough]	[Damaged – at least one name lost] Thomas Brigge [Bridge] Ralph Jolyff	Peterborough, 17 Sept. [damaged]
14 (6)	John [Tychemersh], abbot of Ramsey	D. William Prestwyk [Prestwick]* [Damaged] William Babthorp [Babthorpe]*	Ramsey, 18 Sept. 1429
15 (3)	Thomas [Langley], bishop of Durham	[Damaged] Nicholas Dixon*, clerk	Houden [Howden] manor, [Damaged] 1429

16 (15)	Richard [de South Walsham], abbot of [*Damaged* – St Benet of Hulme]	William Paston* Christopher Meducroft [Meadowcroft]	St Benet of Hulme, [*Damaged*] Sept. 1429
17 (2)	Geoffrey [Hemingby], abbot of Bardney	F. Thomas de Barton, monk of abbey Thomas Basley William Stanlowe [Stanlow] Richard Duffeld [Duffield]*	Bardney, 12 Sept. 1429

PARLIAMENT AT WESTMINSTER, 12 JANUARY 1431

48/2391	John [Tychemersh], abbot of Ramsey	William Prestwik [Prestwick]* Thomas Smyth*	Ramsey, 10 Jan. 1431
48/2392	William [Wotton], abbot of Cirencester	D. William Prestwyk [Prestwick]* William Henton*	In the monastery, 6 Jan. 1431
48/2393	Thomas [Langley], bishop of Durham	John Frank*, keeper of the rolls of chancery John Thoralby*, clerk William Prestwyk [Prestwick]*, clerk Nicholas Dixson [Dixon]*, clerk	Aukland [Bishop Auckland], 2 Jan. 1431
48/2394	Thomas [Ludlowe], abbot of Battle	William Prestwik [Prestwick]*, clerk	Battle, 5 Jan. 1431
48/2395	Robert [Gritton], abbot of St John's, Colchester	M. William Prestwyk [Prestwick]* F. John Horkyslegh [Horkesley], monk of abbey	Colchester, 10 Jan. 1431
48/2396	John [Hampton], abbot of Shrewsbury [*LP*]	M. John Blodewell [Blodwell]*, doctor of canon law William Boerley [Burley]*, gentleman	Shrewsbury, Monday after feast of the Epiphany [8 Jan.] 1431

48/2397	Dean [John Mackworth] and chapter of Lincoln Cathedral [LP]	M. Thomas Brouns*, canon of Lincoln M. David Price [ap Rees]*, canon of Lincoln M. Nicholas Wymbush [Wymbysh]*, canon of Lincoln	Lincoln Chapter House, 31 Dec. 1430
48/2398	John [Cliderow], bishop of Bangor [LP]	John [Langdon]*, bishop of Rochester Thomas Banastre, archdeacon of Bangor John Elslak [Elslack]	Bangor, 3 Jan. 1431
48/2399	[Thomas Barnby], prior, and chapter of Carlisle Cathedral [LP]	M. John Pinkney*, clerk John [Damaged], clerk	Chapter House, 2 Jan. 1431
48/2400	Geoffrey [Hemingby], abbot of Bardney [LP]	Nicholas Wymbys [Wymbush]*, clerk William Prestwyk [Prestwick]*, clerk F. John Bray, monk of abbey Richard Duffelde [Duffield]* Thomas Folkyngham [Folkingham]	Bardney, 10 Jan. 1431
49/2401	John [Litlington], abbot of Crowland	Nicholas Dykson [Dixon]*, baron of the exchequer John Ellerker [Ellerker], sergeant-at-law William Tressham [Tresham]*	Crowland, 7 Jan. 1431
49/2402	Richard [de South Walsham], abbot of St Benet of Hulme	William Paston* Christopher Meducroft [Meadowcroft]	St Benet of Hulme, 10 Jan. 1431
49/2403	John [Deeping], abbot of Peterborough	William Tresseham [Tresham]* F. Richard Staunford [Stanford], monk of abbey Thomas Brygg [Bridge] Ralph Jolyff	Peterborough, 9 Jan. 1431
49/2404	Edmund [Lacy], bishop of Exeter [LP]	[Philip Morgan]*, bishop of Ely [John Stafford]*, bishop of Bath and Wells	[Damaged] Jan. 1431

PARLIAMENT AT WESTMINSTER, 12 MAY 1432

49/2405	[Alexander Cok], archdeacon of Carlisle [LP]	M. John Pynkney [Pinkney]* D. John Langton, chaplain	Carlisle, feast of St Mark, evangelist [25 April] 1432
49/2406	Robert [Lancaster], bishop of St Asaph [LP]	Philip [Morgan]*, bishop of Ely Benedict [Nicolls]*, bishop of St Davids M. John Blodewell [Blodwell]*, doctor of canon law, dean of St Asaph Richard Cordon*, doctor of laws, canon of St Asaph	Monastery of Valle Crucis, 25 April 1432
49/2407	John [Cave], abbot of Selby	Richard Selby*, clerk Roger Byrne, clerk	Selby, 19 April 1432
49/2408	[Robert Gritton], abbot of St John's, Colchester	M. William Prestwyk [Prestwick]* John Horkyslegh [Horkesley], monk of abbey	Colchester, 6 May 1432
49/2409	John [Deeping], abbot of Peterborough	Nicholas Dykson [Dixon]*, clerk William Prestewyk [Prestwick]*, clerk William Tresseham [Tresham]* Ralph Jolyff	Peterborough, 8 May 1432
49/2410	Clergy of Carlisle diocese	M. John Pynkney [Pinkney]* D. John Langton, chaplain	Carlisle, feast of St Mark, evangelist [25 April] 1432
49/2411	John [Litlington], abbot of Crowland	Nicholas Dykson [Dixon]*, baron of the exchequer John Ellerkerr [Ellerker], sergeant at law William Tressham [Tresham]*	Crowland, 3 May 1432

386

49/2412	Richard [Bromsgrove], abbot of Evesham	William Prestwyk [Prestwick]*, clerk William Stokes* John Andrewe [Andrew]*	Evesham, 10 May 1432
49/2413	John [Tychemersh], abbot of Ramsey	D. William Prestwik [Prestwick]* D. Thomas Smyth*	Ramsey, 10 May 1432
49/2414	Roger [Pershore], abbot of Malmesbury	Robert Andrewe [Andrew]*, gentleman Nicholas Wotton*	Malmesbury, 7 May 1432
49/2415	Thomas [Ludlowe], abbot of Battle	William Prestwik [Prestwick]*, clerk	Battle, 8 May 1432
49/2416	Prior [Thomas Barnby] and chapter of Carlisle Cathedral [LP]	M. John Pynkney [Pinkney]* John Langton, chaplain	Chapter House, feast of St Mark, evangelist [25 April] 1432
49/2417	Richard [de South Walsham], abbot of St Benet of Hulme	William Paston* D. William Prestwyk [Prestwick] * John Hamond	St Benet of Hulme, 9 May 1432
49/2418	John [Cheltenham], abbot of Winchcombe	William Prestwyk [Prestwick]*, clerk F. John London, prior and monk of abbey	Winchcombe, 10 May 1432
49/2419	Geoffrey [Hemingby], abbot of Bardney [LP]	Nicholas Wymbysch [Wymbush]*, clerk Richard Caudray [Caudrey], clerk John Prestwyk [Prestwick], clerk	Bardney, 8 May 1432

PARLIAMENT AT WESTMINSTER, 8 JULY 1433

49/2420	Richard [Crosby], prior of Coventry Cathedral	M. Richard Leyott [Leyot] D. William Prestewyk [Prestwick]* Thomas Haseley* William Donyngton [Donnington]* John Northwode [Northwood]	Coventry, 20 June 1433

PARLIAMENT AT WESTMINSTER, 10 OCTOBER 1435

49/2421	John [Marwent], abbot of St Peter's, Gloucester	F. Reginald Boulers*, monk of abbey, doctor of theology Richard Neuton [Newton]*	Gloucester, 4 Oct. 1435
49/2422	John [Litlington], abbot of Crowland	D. Nicholas Dixon* John Ellerkare [Ellerker], sergeant at law [L] William Tressham [Tresham]* [MP]	Crowland, 7 Oct. 1435
49/2423	John [Deeping], abbot of Peterborough	William Treseham [Tresham]* William Prestewyke [Prestwick]* Ralph Jolyff	Peterborough, [Illegible] Oct. 1435
49/2424	John [Cave], abbot of Selby	William Prestwyk [Prestwick]*, master in chancery Thomas Morton*, master in chancery Richard Selby*, clerk John Seirf Roger Birne [Byrne]	Selby, 20 Sept. 1435
49/2425	Richard [de South Walsham], abbot of St Benet of Hulme	William Paston* Christopher Medwecroft [Meadowcroft]	St Benet of Hulme, 7 Oct. 1435

49/2426	John [Wells], bishop of Llandaff	M. Lewis Coychurch*, archdeacon of Lewes, canon of Llandaff John Salyngton [Salvington], canon of Llandaff	Our manor of [Lancarfan], 10 Oct. 1435
49/2427	John [Wykewan], abbot of Evesham	M. Peter Styuecle [Stukeley]* John Throkmarton [Throckmorton]* John Vampage William Stokes* John Bate*	Evesham, 4 Oct. 1435
49/2428	Richard [Crosby], prior of Coventry	William Prestewyk [Prestwick]*, clerk John Everdon*, clerk Thomas Hugeford*, gentleman Nicholas Metteley, gentleman	Coventry, 6 Oct. 1435
49/2429	John [Croyland], abbot of Ramsey	William Prestewyk [Prestwick]*, clerk Nicholas Dixon*, clerk Walter Tayllard	Ramsey, 29 Oct. 1435
49/2430	John [Cheltenham], abbot of Winchcombe	William Prestwyk [Prestwick]* F. William Wynchecomb [Winchcombe], monk of abbey	Winchcombe, feast of St Denys [9 Oct.] 1435
49/2431	[Alan Kirketon], abbot of Thorney	[Illegible]	[Illegible] 1435

PARLIAMENT AT WESTMINSTER, 12 NOVEMBER 1439

49/2432	John [Wykewan], abbot of Evesham	John Bate*, clerk John Throgmarton [Throckmorton]* John Andrewes [Andrew]* Roger Wynter [Winter]*	Evesham, 20 Oct. 1439
49/2433	Nicholas [Frome], abbot of Glastonbury	M. Thomas Bekyngton [Beckington]*, canon of Wells M. John Storthwayt [Storthwaite]*, precentor of Wells M. Adam Moleyns*, canon of Wells M. Thomas Kyrkeby [Kirkby]*, clerk of parliament F. John Ledbury, monk of abbey	Glastonbury, 15 Nov. 1439
49/2434	Nicholas [Strode], abbot of Hyde near Winchester	M. Stephen Wilton*, doctor of canon law William Coly William Chamberlayn [Chamberlain]*	Hyde, [Illegible] 1439
49/2435	Richard [Nottingham], prior of Coventry	M. John Bate*, clerk M. John de la Ber', clerk William Donyngton [Donnington]* John Norwode [Northwood]	Coventry, 5 Nov. 1439
49/2436	William Southbroke [Southbrook], prior of Bath [LP]	F. William Salforde [Salford], monk of priory	Bath, 10 Nov. 1439
49/2437	William [Wotton], abbot of Cirencester	Thomas de Kirkeby [Kirkby]*	In the monastery, 8 Nov. 1439

Reference		Witnesses	Place and date
49/2438	John [Stowe], abbot of Ramsey	Roger Hunte [Hunt]* Nicholas Dixon* Thomas Kirkeby [Kirkby]*	Ramsey, Monday before feast of St Martin [9 Nov.] 1439
49/2439	John [Litlington], abbot of Crowland	D. Nicholas Dyxson [Dixon]* William Tresshame [Tresham]* Thomas Kirkeby [Kirkby]*, clerk John Staunelowe [Stanlow]* John Louthe [Louth]*	Crowland, 7 Nov. 1439
49/2440	Thomas Bubewyth [Bubwith], archdeacon of Wells [LP]	M. John Storthwayt [Storthwaite]*, precentor of Wells M. John Hody*, chancellor of Wells M. Richard Gordon, doctor of laws	Wells, 9 Nov. 1439
49/2441	William [Heyworth], bishop of Coventry and Lichfield	M. Thomas Bekynton [Beckington]*, doctor of laws, canon of Lichfield John Bate*, dean of Tamworth collegiate church	Lichfield, 9 Nov. 1439
49/2442	Chapter of Bath Cathedral	M. John Storthwayte [Storthwaite]*, precentor of Wells F. William Salford, monk of abbey	Bath, 10 Nov. 1439
49/2443	John Martyn, abbot of St Benet of Hulme [LP]	Thomas Kirkeby [Kirkby]*, clerk John Pemberton, clerk	In the monastery, 6 Nov. 1439
49/2444	John [Ousthorp], abbot of Selby	William Babthorp [Babthorpe]*, clerk Richard Selby*, clerk William Normanton*, clerk	Selby, 5 Nov. 1439

49/2445	Edmund [Lacy], bishop of Exeter [LP]	M. William Lyndewode [Lyndwood]*, canon of Exeter M. Peter Stuklegh [Stukeley]*, canon of Exeter Richard Selby*, rector of Stoke [in] Clyunuyslond [Climsland], Cornwall	Our manor of Chuddelegh [Chudleigh], 30 Oct. 1439
49/2446	William [Ardeley alias Hunt], abbot of St John's, Colchester	John Bate* F. John Heyforth, monk of abbey	Colchester, 8 Nov. 1439
49/2447	Thomas [Bristowe], abbot of Malmesbury	Thomas Kirkeby [Kirkby]*, clerk John Louthe [Louth]*	In the monastery, 6 Nov. 1439
49/2448	John Forest, dean of Wells Cathedral [LP]	M. John Storthwayt [Storthwaite]*, precentor of Wells Cathedral	Wells, 9 Nov. 1439
49/2449	John [Cheltenham], abbot of Winchcombe	John Bate*, clerk	Winchcombe, Friday after feast of All Saints [6 Nov.] 1439
49/2450	Chapter of Wells Cathedral	M. John Storthwayt [Storthwaite]*, precentor of Wells M. Peter Stucley [Stukeley]*, treasurer of Wells	Wells, 9 Nov. 1439

PARLIAMENT AT WESTMINSTER, 25 JANUARY 1442

50/2451	[Nicholas Frome], abbot of Glastonbury	M. [Thomas] Bekynton [Beckington]* William Byconyll [Bicknell]*, clerk of parliament Walter Lyhert* John Cammell* F. John Bodbury, monk of abbey [Illegible]	Glastonbury, [Damaged] 1442
50/2452	John [Litlington], abbot of Crowland	Nicholas Dyxson[Dixon]* William Tresham* Thomas Kirkeby [Kirkby]*, clerk John Louth* John Stanlowe [Stanlow]*	Crowland, 13 Jan. 1442
50/2453	[John Kirketon], abbot of Thorney	M. Adam Molens [Moleyns]*, clerk Nicholas Dixon*, clerk William Brewster*, clerk F. John Wisbech, monk of abbey	Thorney, 12 Jan. 1442
50/2454	[John Ousthorp], abbot of Selby	Richard Selby*, clerk Thomas Kirkeby [Kirkby]*, clerk William Babthorp [Babthorpe]* Richard Babthorp [Babthorpe]	Selby, 20 Jan. 1442
50/2455	William [Ardeley alias Hunt], abbot of St John's, Colchester	John Stopyndon*, clerk, keeper of the rolls of chancery Thomas Kirkeby [Kirkby]*, clerk	Colchester, 18 Jan. 1442

393

50/2456	John [Stowe], abbot of Ramsey	William Brewster*, clerk Thomas Kirkeby [Kirkby]*, clerk Walter Tayllard	Ramsey, 22 Jan. [1442]
50/2457	Edmund [Lacy], bishop of Exeter	M. William Lyndewode [Lyndwood]*, canon of Exeter M. Peter Stuclegh [Stukeley]*, canon of Exeter M. John Bate*, canon of Exeter	Our manor of Chuddelegh [Chudleigh], 3 Jan. 1442
50/2458	John [Taunton], abbot of Cirencester	Thomas Kirkeby [Kirkby]*, clerk William Tresham* John Langley*	Cirencester, 19 Jan. 1442
50/2459	Richard [Nottingham], prior of Coventry	M. John Bate*, clerk John Stanley*, gentleman John Broun* William Donyngton [Donnington]* John Norwode [Northwode]	Coventry, 22 Jan. 1442
50/2460	John [Wykewan], abbot of Evesham	Thomas Kirkeby [Kirkby]*, clerk John Throkmarton [Throckmorton]* John Vampage John Andrewes [Andrew]* Thomas Osney*	Evesham, 20 Jan. 1442
50/2461	John Martyn, abbot of St Benet of Hulme	Thomas Kirkeby [Kirkby]*, clerk William Marsshall [Marshall]	In the monastery, 8 Feb. [no year]

50/2462	Richard [Praty], bishop of Chichester	John [Beaumont], Viscount Beaumont Ralph [*Illegible*] de Sideley [Ralph Boteler, Lord Sudeley] M. Thomas Bekynton [Beckington]*, doctor of laws M. John Stokes*, doctor of laws M. Thomas Kirkeby [Kirkby]*, clerk of chancery M. John Frankes [Frank]*, clerk of chancery	Our palace, Chichester, 8 Jan. 1442
50/2463	Thomas [Spofford], bishop of Hereford	William [Alnwick]*, bishop of Lincoln William [Wells], bishop of Rochester William [Aiscough], bishop of Salisbury The Honourable and Magnificent Lord Henry [Percy], earl of Northumberland John [Lord] de Scrop [le Scrope] Henry Shelford*, dean of Hereford	Our manor of Prestbury, 17 Jan. 1442
50/2464	John [Cottingham], abbot of St Mary's, York	John, Lord Lescrop [le Scrope] The Honourable Lord John Stopyngton [Stopyndon]*, keeper of the rolls of chancery M. Thomas Bekyngton [Beckington]*, 'your secretary' D. Thomas Kirkeby [Kirkby]*, master and clerk of chancery	In the monastery, 16 Jan. 1442

PARLIAMENT AT WESTMINSTER, 25 FEB. 1445

| 50/2465 | John, abbot of [*Damaged*] | M. Thomas Kyrkeby [Kirkby]*
[*Damaged*] | Our monastery, 6 Feb. 1445 |
| 50/2466 | Richard [*Damaged*] | William Tresseham [Tresham]*
M. Thomas Kyrkeby [Kirkby]*, clerk of parliament | [*Damaged*] Feb. 1445 |

| 50/2467 | Richard Notyngham [Nottingham], prior of Coventry | John Bate*, clerk
Thomas Bate*, gentleman
William Donyngton [Donnington]*, recorder of Coventry | [Damaged] |

PARLIAMENT AT BURY ST EDMUNDS, 25 FEB. 1447

50/2468	[John Kirketon], abbot of Thorney	Nicholas Dixon* M. Thomas Kyrkeby [Kirkby]* M. William Spaldyng [Spalding]* William Godyng* F. John Ramsey, monk of abbey	Thorney, 26 Jan. 1447
50/2469	Thomas [Bristowe], abbot of Malmesbury	M. Thomas Kirkeby [Kirkby]* John Louthe [Louth]*	[No place], 22 Jan. 1447
50/2470	John [Taunton], abbot of Cirencester	Thomas Kirkeby [Kirkby]*, clerk of parliament	In the monastery, 6 Feb. [no year]
50/2471	John [Cheltenham], abbot of Winchcombe	M. Thomas Kyrkeby [Kirkby]* John Andrews [Andrew]*	Winchcombe, 16 Jan. 1447
50/2472	John [Litlington], abbot of Crowland	Nicholas Dixon*, clerk Thomas Kyrkeby [Kirkby]*, clerk William Tresham* John Louthe [Louth]* Thomas Burgoyn*	Crowland, 30 Jan. 1447

50/2473	John [Wykewan], abbot of Evesham	M. John Kyrkeby [Kirkby]* M. John Stokys [Stokes]*, doctor of laws F. John Vampage, monk of abbey F. Richard Penbrok, monk of abbey	Evesham, 8 Feb. 1447
50/2474	Prior [Thomas Hathwaite] and chapter of Carlisle	M. John Graystok [Graystock]*, bachelor of canon law Thomas Marschall [Marshall], our clerk	Chapter House, 1 Feb. 1447
50/2475	[John Martyn], abbot of St Benet of Hulme	M. Thomas Kyrby [Kirkby]*, clerk of parliament Edmund Clere*, gentleman	In the monastery, 4 Feb. 1447
50/2476	[John Ousthorp], abbot of Selby	Ralph Babthorp [Babthorpe]*, gentleman Richard Selby*, clerk John Lathem, clerk John Cleer, clerk Thomas Kirkeby [Kirkby]*	Selby, 28 Jan. 1447
50/2477	Nicholas [Frome], abbot of Glastonbury	M. Richard Andrewe [Andrew]* Thomas Kirkeby [Kirkby]*, clerk of parliament John Orewell [Orwell]* John Kirkeby [Kirkby]* John Saundres [Saunders]* F. John Ledbury, monk of abbey	Glastonbury, feast of the Purification of the Blessed Virgin Mary [2 Feb.] 1447
50/2478	John [Stowe], abbot of Ramsey	Thomas Kirkeby [Kirkby]*, clerk Robert Stonham [Stoneham]*, gentleman John Styuecle [Stukeley]*, gentleman F. John Berner, monk of abbey	Ramsey, 4 Feb. 1447

PARLIAMENTS OF THE FIRST REIGN OF EDWARD IV (1461–70)

No letters survive for this reign.

PARLIAMENTS OF THE SECOND REIGN OF HENRY VI (1470–1)

No letters survive for this reign.

PARLIAMENTS OF THE SECOND REIGN OF EDWARD IV (1471–83)

No letters survive for this reign.

PARLIAMENTS OF THE REIGN OF RICHARD III (1483–5)

No letters survive for this reign.

PARLIAMENTS OF THE REIGN OF HENRY VII (1485–1509)

No letters survive for this reign.

PARLIAMENTS OF THE REIGN OF HENRY VIII (1509–47)

PARLIAMENT AT WESTMINSTER, 15 APRIL 1523

| 50/2479 | Edmund [Audley], bishop of Salisbury [LP] | Richard [Fox], bishop of Winchester John [Veysey], bishop of Exeter | Our manor of Ramsbury, 1 April 1523 |
| 50/2480 | Robert [Kyrketon], abbot of Peterborough | [John Longland], bishop of Lincoln [Richard Nykke], bishop of Norwich [Nicholas West], bishop of Ely | Peterborough, 7 April [Illegible] |

PARLIAMENT AT WESTMINSTER, 3 NOVEMBER 1529

50/2482	Robert [Sherburne], bishop of Chichester	Geoffrey [Blyth], bishop of Coventry and Lichfield John [Clerk], bishop of Bath and Wells	Our manor of Drogwike [Durringwick], All Saints [1 Nov.] 1529
50/2483	Richard, abbot of [damaged] [LP]	[Damaged], abbot of [Damaged] [Richard Anselm alias Munstowe] abbot of Winchcombe	Chapter House, 25 Oct. 1529
50/2484	Thomas [Skeffington], bishop of Bangor	Cuthbert [Tunstall], bishop of London [John Fisher], bishop of Rochester	[No place], 10 Nov. 1529
50/2485	Robert [Selby alias Roger], abbot of Selby	John Salcot alias Capon], abbot of St Benet of Hulme	[No place], 12 Nov. 1529

50/2486	William [Malvern alias Parker], abbot of St Peter's, Gloucester	Richard [Anselm alias Munstowe], abbot of Winchcombe Thomas [Marshall alias Beche], abbot of Chester	Gloucester, 28 Oct. 1529
50/2487	Thomas Wayford [Weoford], prior of Coventry	Thomas [Grey], marquis of Dorset Clement [Lichefeld alias Wych], abbot of Evesham	Coventry, 29 Nov. 1529
50/2488	Edmund [Whalley], abbot of St Mary's, York	John [Islip], abbot of Westminster	[No place], 24 Oct. 1529
50/2489	[Illegible]	John [recte Cuthbert Tunstall], bishop of London [Blank – Robert Fuller], abbot of Waltham [Illegible – Henry] Pole, Lord Montegue [Montagu]	[No place], 24 Nov. 1529
50/2490	Clement [Lichefeld alias Wych], abbot of Evesham	[John Islip], abbot of Westminster [Richard Anselm alias Munstowe], abbot of Winchcombe	[No place], 12 Dec. 1529

PARLIAMENT AT WESTMINSTER, 16 JANUARY 1531 (SECOND SESSION OF NOVEMBER 1529 PARLIAMENT)

50/2491	[William Marton], abbot of Bardney	[John Islip], abbot of Westminster	[No place], 1 Jan. 1531
50/2492	Cuthbert [Tunstall], bishop of Durham	[Illegible]	Our manor of Aukeland [Bishop Auckland], 7 Feb. 1531
50/2493	William [sic] [Thomas Pentecost alias Rowland], abbot of Abingdon [LP]	[Illegible]	[No place], 6 Feb. 1531

400

PARLIAMENT AT WESTMINSTER, 15 JANUARY 1532 (THIRD SESSION OF NOVEMBER 1529 PARLIAMENT)

50/2494	John [Lawrence *alias* Wardeboys], abbot of Ramsey	John [Salcot *alias* Capon] abbot of Hyde near Winchester	[*No place*], 15 Dec. 1531
50/2495	William [Marton], abbot of Bardney	[John Islip], abbot of Westminster	[*No place*], 20 Jan. 1532
50/2496	John [Essex *alias* Roche *alias* Sturrey], abbot of St. Augustine's, Canterbury	John [Salcot *alias* Capon], abbot of Hyde near Winchester; William [Repps *alias* Rugg], abbot of St Benet of Hulme	[*No place*], 24 Jan. 1532
50/2497	John de Pacicucia [*sic - recte* Hammond], abbot of Battle	John [Islip], abbot of Westminster	Battle Abbey, 3 Jan. 1532
50/2498	Cuthbert [Tunstall], bishop of Durham [*LP*]	Nicholas [West], bishop of Ely; John [Clerk], bishop of Bath and Wells	Our manor of Aukeland [Bishop Auckland], 8 Jan. 1532
50/2499	Thomas Wayford [Weoford], prior of Coventry	[*Illegible*]	[*Illegible*]
50/2500	William [Malvern *alias* Parker], abbot of St Peter, Gloucester	Richard [Camme], abbot of Malmesbury Richard [Anselm *alias* Munslowe], abbot of Winchcombe Thomas [Barton], abbot of St John's, Colchester	[*No place*], 24 Jan. 1532
51/2501	John [Melford *alias* Reve], abbot of Bury St Edmunds	John [Salcot *alias* Capon], abbot of Hyde near Winchester	[*No place*], 11 Feb. 1532

51/2502	John [Chambers *alias* Borowe], abbot of Peterborough	John [Salcot *alias* Capon], abbot of Hyde near Winchester	[*No place*], 7 Feb. 1532
51/2503	Thomas [Pentecost *alias* Rowland], abbot of Abingdon [*LP*]	John [Salcot *alias* Capon], abbot of Hyde near Winchester William [Repps *alias* Rugg], abbot of St Benet of Hulme	In the monastery, 9 Jan. 1532
51/2504	John [Wellys *alias* Bryggys], abbot of Crowland	John [Islip], abbot of Westminster	[*No place*], 8 Feb. 1532
51/2505	[*Space left for name* – Robert Moulton *alias* Blythe], abbot of Thorney	John [Islip], abbot of Westminster Robert [Fuller], abbot of Waltham	[*No place*], 7 Feb. 1532

PARLIAMENT AT WESTMINSTER, 10 APRIL 1532 (FOURTH SESSION OF NOVEMBER 1529 PARLIAMENT)

51/2506	Thomas [Butler *alias* Lorde], abbot of Shrewsbury	Robert [Fuller], abbot of Waltham	London, 24 March 1532
51/2507	John [Hammond], abbot of Battle	John [Islip], abbot of Westminster John [Essex *alias* Roche *alias* Sturrey], abbot of St Augustine's, Canterbury	Battle, 3 April 1532
51/2508	Thomas [Pentecost *alias* Rowland], abbot of Abingdon [*LP*]	John [Salcot *alias* Capon], abbot of Hyde near Winchester William [Repps *alias* Rugg], abbot of St Benet of Hulme	In the monastery, 5 April 1532
51/2509	John [Wellys *alias* Bryggys], abbot of Crowland	Robert [Fuller], abbot of Waltham	Crowland, 21 April 1532

51/2510	Richard [Whiting], abbot of Glastonbury	Glastonbury, 5 April 1532
	John [Islip], abbot of Westminster Abbot of Colchester [*presumably intended to be Thomas Barton, who had died on 25 March 1532*]	
51/2520	Thomas Wyford [Weoford], prior of Coventry	Coventry, 2 April 1532
	John [Veysey], bishop of Exeter George [Hastings], earl of Huntingdon John [Islip], abbot of Westminster	
51/2545	John [Blake], abbot of Cirencester John [Salcot *alias* Capon], abbot of Hyde near Winchester	[*No place*], 28 April 1532

PARLIAMENT AT WESTMINSTER, 4 FEBRUARY 1533 (FIFTH SESSION OF NOVEMBER 1529 PARLIAMENT)

51/2511	John [Hammond], abbot of Battle	John [Salcot *alias* Capon], abbot of Hyde near Winchester John [Essex *alias* Roche *alias* Sturrey], abbot of St Augustine's, Canterbury	In our monastery, 31 Jan. 1533
51/2512	William [Thornton *alias* Dent], abbot of St Mary's, York	John [Chambers *alias* Borowe], abbot of Peterborough [*Space left for name* - William Repps *alias* Rugg], abbot of St Benet of Hulme Robert [Fuller], abbot of Waltham	[*No place*], 28 Feb. 1533
51/2513	[*Illegible*]	[*Illegible*]	[*No place*], 28 Jan. 1533

PARLIAMENT AT WESTMINSTER, 4 FEBRUARY 1536 (EIGHTH SESSION OF NOVEMBER 1529 PARLIAMENT)

51/2514	Richard Rawlyne [Rawlins], bishop of St Davids [*LP*]	John [Stokesley], bishop of London John [Longland], bishop of Lincoln	[*No place*], 6 Feb. 1536

51/2515	Richard [Anselm *alias* Munstowe], abbot of Winchcombe *[LP]*	Robert [Fuller], abbot of Waltham	[*Illegible*], 27 Henry VIII
51/2516	John [Kite], bishop of Carlisle *[LP]*	*No proctors named*	[*No place*], 2 Feb. 1536
51/2517	Clement [Lichefeld *alias* Wych], abbot of Evesham *[LP]*	John [Melford *alias* Reve], abbot of Bury St Edmunds	[*No place*], 8 Feb. 1536
51/2518	William [Marton], abbot of Bardney	[*Space left for name* – Robert Fuller], abbot of Waltham	[*No place*], 24 Jan. 1536
51/2519	Robert [Moulton *alias* Blythe], abbot of Thorney	John [John Salcot *alias* Capon], bishop of Bangor John [Chambers *alias* Borowe], abbot of Peterborough John [Wellys *alias* Bryggys], abbot of Crowland	Thorney, 28 Jan., 1536
51/2521	Thomas Wyford [Weoford], prior of Coventry	William [Boston *alias* Benson], abbot of exempt monastery of St Peter [*location crossed out; see Appendix 3*]	Coventry, 30 Jan. 1536
51/2522	John [Lawrence *alias* Wardeboys], abbot of Ramsey	[*Large space left for proctors, not filled in*]	Ramsey, 15 Jan. 1536
51/2523	Thomas [Pentecost *alias* Rowland], abbot of Abingdon *[LP]*	[William Boston *alias* Benson] abbot of Westminster	[*No place*], 22 Jan. 1536
51/2543	Robert [Sherburne], bishop of Chichester	[*Unfilled space left for names*]	Redingsborn [Easebourne], 28 Jan. 1536
51/2544	Richard [Whiting], abbot of Glastonbury *[LP]*	Ralph	In the monastery, 18 Feb. 1536

SC 10 Appointments by Secular Peers

The following are the appointments in SC 10 which were made by secular peers, comprising the forty-six letters in file 52 and three documents misfiled among the clerical proxies. There are also thirteen letters, five in file 52 and the remainder in the normal clergy sequence, from Thomas la Warre, Lord la Warre, who had an anomalous status as a clerical peer. Two letters cannot be dated with certainty and are placed at the end of this list. For the reign of Henry VIII, the titles of peers have been silently translated into a standard modern form.

PARLIAMENT AT CARLISLE, 20 JANUARY 1307

52/1	John de Beauchamp of Somerset, lord of Hacche *[LP] [F]*	John de Godele, dean of Wells	Estok under Hamedon [Stoke-sub-Hamdon], Somerset, day of the Epiphany [6 Jan.] 1307

PARLIAMENT AT YORK, 6 MAY 1319

52/2	Robert de Veer [Vere], earl of Oxford *[LP] [F]*	M. Oliver de Engham [Ingham]	Kensyngton [Kensington], 1 May 1319

PARLIAMENT AT YORK, 2 MAY 1322

52/3	Robert de Veer [Vere], earl of Oxford [LP] [F]	Thomas de Veer [Vere], 'our son' Robert de Halstede [Halstead], clerk	Our castle of Hengham [Hedingham], 14 April 1322

PARLIAMENT AT SALISBURY, 16 OCTOBER 1328

52/5	Robert de [Veer] Vere, earl of Oxford [LP] [F]	Robert de Bousser	Caumpes [Castle Camps], 28 Sept. 1328

PARLIAMENT AT WESTMINSTER, 9 FEBRUARY 1329

13/601	Robert de Clifford [F]	John de Skipton	Skipton-in-Craven, 7 Feb. 1329

PARLIAMENT AT WESTMINSTER, 26 NOVEMBER 1330

14/672	Robert de Veer [Vere], earl of Oxford [LP] [F]	John de Veer [Vere] Robert de Cheddeworth [Chedworth], 'steward of our lands'	Our castle of Hengham [Hedingham], 22 Nov. 1330

PARLIAMENT AT WESTMINSTER, 30 SEPTEMBER 1331

52/28	William la Zouche of Haringworth [Harringworth] [LP] [F]	M. Amaris la Zouche M. William la Zouche M. Simon de Drayton	Eyton, 22 Sept. [illegible] Edward III

GREAT COUNCIL AT WESTMINSTER, 20 JANUARY 1332

| 52/6 | William la Zouche of Haringworth [Harringworth] *[LP] [F]* | M. Simon de Drayton
M. William la Zouche | Haringworth [Harringworth], 15 Jan. 1332 |

PARLIAMENT AT WESTMINSTER, 16 MARCH 1332

| 52/7 | William la Zouche of Haringworthe [Harringworth] *[LP] [F]* | Sir Michael de Wath
M. William la Zouche | Haringworth [Harringworth], 4 March 1332 |
| 52/8 | Henry [of Lancaster], earl of Lancaster and Leicester, steward of England *[LP] [F]* | M. Richard de Rivers
M. Robert de Hungerford
M. Robert Daston | Leicester, 11 March 1332 |

PARLIAMENT AT YORK, 4 DECEMBER 1332

| 52/9 | William la Zouche of Haringworthe [Harringworth] *[LP] [F]* | M. John de Verdoun [Verdun]
M. Roger la Zouche
Sir Michael de Wath
Richard Luvel [Lovel] | Weston in Arderne [Weston-on-in-Arden], 23 Nov. 1332 |
| 52/10 | John de Warenne, earl of Surrey *[LP] [F]* | M. Ralph de Cobham, 'our dear clerk'
Sir John de Dynyeton | Chastellyon [Holt Castle] in Wales, 28 Nov. 1332 |

PARLIAMENT AT YORK, 20 JANUARY 1333 (RESUMPTION OF DECEMBER 1332 SESSION)

| 52/11 | William la Zouche of Haringworthe [Harringworth] *[LP] [F]* | Sir Michael de Wath
M. William la Zouche | *[Damaged]*, Jan. 1333 |

PARLIAMENT AT YORK, 21 FEBRUARY 1334

| 52/12 | Henry [of Lancaster], earl of Lancaster and Leicester, steward of England *[LP] [F]* | 'Our heir' Henry [of Grosmont], 'our son' | Kenilworth Castle, 8 Feb. 1334 |
| 52/13 | William la Zouche of Haringworthe [Harringworth] *[LP] [F]* | Sir Michael de Wath
M. William la Zouche | Haringworthe [Harringworth], 11 Feb. 1334 |

PARLIAMENT AT YORK, 26 MAY 1335

| 52/14 | William la Zouche of Haringworthe [Harringworth] *[LP] [F]* | Sir Michael de Wath
M. William la Zouche | Haringworthe [Harringworth], 8 May 1335 |

GREAT COUNCIL AT NOTTINGHAM, 23 SEPTEMBER 1336

| 52/15 | William la Zouche of Haringworth [Harringworth] *[LP] [F]* | M. William Deyncourt
Sir Michael de Wath | Eyton, morrow of the Nativity of Our Lady [9 Sept.] 1336 |

PARLIAMENT AT WESTMINSTER, 13 OCTOBER 1339

| 52/16 | Henry [of Lancaster], earl of Lancaster and Leicester, steward of England [LP] [F] | Thomas Wake, lord of Lidell [Liddell] | Leicester Castle, 12 Oct. 1339 |

PARLIAMENT AT YORK, 27 OCTOBER 1400 (DID NOT MEET – PROROGUED TO MEET AT WESTMINSTER, 20 JANUARY 1401)

| 52/16A | Edward Courtenay, earl of Devon [LP] | Edward Charleton [Charlton] Thomas [Berkeley], Lord Berkeley Lord John Haryngton [Harrington] | [Illegible], 1 Henry IV |

PARLIAMENT AT WESTMINSTER, 20 JANUARY 1401

| 52/16B | Edward Courtenay, earl of Devon [LP] | Thomas Camoys, knight Nicholas Bubbewyth [Bubwith]*, clerk | Tyverton [Tiverton], feast of St Hilary [13 Jan.] 1401 |

PARLIAMENT AT COVENTRY, 6 OCTOBER 1404

| 52/17 | Edward Courtenay, earl of Devon [LP] | John Lovel, [Lord Lovel] William Langeton [Langton], clerk | Tyverton [Tiverton], 29 Sept. 1404 |

PARLIAMENT AT WESTMINSTER, 13 OCTOBER 1406 (PROROGUED SESSION OF MARCH 1406 PARLIAMENT)

| 52/18 | Edward Courtenay, earl of Devon [LP] | John [Lovel], Lord Lovel M. William Langeton [Langton], clerk | Our manor of Exminster, vigil of St Matthew, apostle [20 Sept.] 1406 |

PARLIAMENT AT GLOUCESTER, 20 OCTOBER 1407

52/19	Edward Courtenay, earl of Devon [LP]	John [Lovel], Lord Lovel M. Walter Robert, clerk	Tiverton, 4 Oct. 1407

PARLIAMENT AT WESTMINSTER, 27 JANUARY 1410

52/19A	Edward Courtenay, earl of Devon [LP]	Edward Charleton [Charlton], lord of Powys and Charleton [Charlton] M. William Pylton [Pilton]*, archdeacon of Exeter	Exmore [Exmoor], 2 January 1410

PARLIAMENT AT LEICESTER, 30 APRIL 1414

45/2212	Thomas de la Warre, [Lord la Warre]	[D.] John Wakeryng [Wakering]*, 'my clerk' M. Richard Holme*, 'my clerk'	Swineshead, feast of St George, martyr [23 April] 1414

PARLIAMENT AT WESTMINSTER, 16 MARCH 1416

52/20	Thomas, Lord la Warre	John Franke [Frank]*, clerk M. Richard Hulme, clerk John Thoralby*, clerk	Swyneshende [Swineshead], 8 March 1416
52/21	Edward Courtenay, earl of Devon [LP]	Edward Charleton [Charlton], lord of Powys Thomas [Berkeley], Lord Berkeley	Tiverton, 8 March 1416

52/22	Thomas, Lord la Warre	John Franke [Frank]*, clerk M. Richard Hulme, clerk	Swyneshened [Swineshead] Manor, feast of St Michael, archangel [29 Sept.] 1416

52/23	Edward Courtenay, earl of Devon [LP]	Edward Charleton [Charlton], Lord Powys Reginald de Grey, Lord Ruthin	Tiverton, 11 Nov. 1417
52/24	Thomas, Lord la Warre	John Franke [Frank]*, clerk M. Richard Hulme, clerk	Swyneshead [Swineshead] Manor, vigil of St Luke, evangelist [17 Oct.] 1417

46/2294	Thomas, Lord la Warre	John Franke [Frank]*, clerk M. Richard Hulme [Holme]*, clerk John Thoralby*, clerk	Wakirley [Wakerley], 30 Sept. 1419
52/25	Edward Charleton [Charlton], Lord Powys D. Thomas Camoys, Lord Camoys		Tiverton, 10 Oct. 1419
	Edward Courtenay, earl of Devon [LP]		

411

PARLIAMENT AT WESTMINSTER, 2 DECEMBER 1420

52/26	Thomas la Warre, clerk and Lord la Warre	Richard Holme [Hulme], clerk John Franke [Frank]*, clerk John Thoralby*, clerk	Wakirley [Wakerley], 13 Nov. 1420

PARLIAMENT AT WESTMINSTER, 1 DECEMBER 1421

47/2315	Thomas, Lord de la Warr' [Warre]	John Franke [Frank]*, 'my clerk' John Thoralby*, 'my clerk' John Huntyndon [Huntingdon], 'my clerk'	Swyneshenede [Swineshead], 16 Nov. 1421

PARLIAMENT AT WESTMINSTER, 9 NOVEMBER 1422

52/27	Thomas, Lord la Warre	Richard Holme [Hulme], clerk John Franke [Frank]*, clerk Nicholas Dykeson [Dixon]*, clerk	Swyneshened [Swineshead], 20 Oct. 1422

PARLIAMENT AT WESTMINSTER, 30 APRIL 1425

48/2373	Thomas de la Warr [Warre, Lord la Warre]	William Prestewyke [Prestwick]* John [Stafford]*, treasurer	Swyneshened [Swineshead], [Illegible] April 1425

PARLIAMENT AT LEICESTER, 18 APRIL 1426

48/2385	Thomas la Warre, clerk, [Lord la Warre]	John Thoralby*, clerk John Mapilton [Mapleton]*, clerk William Prestwyk [Prestwick]*, clerk	Swyneshenede [Swineshead], 12 Feb. 1426

PARLIAMENT AT LONDON, 15 APRIL 1523

52/46	Thomas [FitzAlan], earl of Arundel	George [Talbot], earl of Shrewsbury Henry [Percy], earl of Northumberland	[*Illegible*], 13 April 1523

PARLIAMENT AT LONDON, 10 JUNE 1523 (SECOND SESSION OF APRIL 1523 PARLIAMENT)

50/2481	Edward Sutton, Lord Dudley	Robert Radclif [Radcliffe], knight, Lord Fitzwalter John Nevill [Neville], knight, Lord Latimer	London, 22 July 1523

PARLIAMENT AT WESTMINSTER, 4 NOVEMBER 1529

52/29	Edward Sturton [Stourton], Lord Stourton	William Saumnes [Saunders], Lord Saunders	[*No place*], 2 Nov. 1529
52/30	Edward Sutton, knight, Lord Dudley	John Tuchet, Lord Audley Thomas [Darcy], Lord Darcy	Hymley [Himley], 3 Nov. 1529
52/31	Henry [Bourchier, earl of] Essex (*to George, earl of Shrewsbury*) [*En*]	George [Talbot], earl of Shrewsbury	[*No place*], 7 Nov. 1529

PARLIAMENT AT WESTMINSTER, 16 JANUARY 1531 (SECOND SESSION OF 1529 PARLIAMENT)

52/33	Thomas [Wentworth], knight, Lord Wentworth	Thomas [Howard], duke of Norfolk Andrew Windesour [Windsor], knight, Lord Windsor	[*No place*], 12 March 1531
52/34	Ralph [Nevill], earl of Westmorland	Thomas [Howard], duke of Norfolk Robert [Radcliffe], earl of Sussex	London, 21 March 1531

PARLIAMENT AT WESTMINSTER, 15 JANUARY 1532 (THIRD SESSION OF 1529 PARLIAMENT)

| 52/35 | George [Talbot], earl of Shrewsbury *(to the earl of Huntingdon) [En]* | [George Hastings], earl of Huntingdon | [*No place*], 15 Feb. 1532 |
| 52/36 | Ralph [Nevill], earl of Westmorland | Thomas [Howard], duke of Norfolk | [*No place*], 25 March 1532 |

PARLIAMENT AT WESTMINSTER, 10 APRIL 1532 (FOURTH SESSION OF 1529 PARLIAMENT)

52/37	John Bourchier, Lord Fitzwarren	[Thomas Vaux], Lord Vaux [Henry Daubeney], Lord Daubeney	[*No place*], 4 April 1532
52/38	Thomas Borough, Lord Borough	William Sandys, Lord Sandys	[*No place*], 25 March 1532
52/39	John Tuchyet [Tuchet], knight, Lord Audley	[George Nevill], Lord Bergavenny William Weston, prior of St John of Jerusalem	[*No place*], 11 April 1532
52/40	Thomas West, knight, Lord la Warr	William Sandys, Lord Sandys	[*No place*], 7 April 1532

PARLIAMENT AT WESTMINSTER, 4 FEBRUARY 1533 (FIFTH SESSION OF 1529 PARLIAMENT)

| 52/41 | William [FitzAlan], earl of Arundel *(to the earl of Wiltshire) [En]* | [Thomas Boleyn], earl of Wiltshire | [*No place*], 1 Feb. 1533 |

PARLIAMENT AT WESTMINSTER, 3 NOVEMBER 1534 (SIXTH SESSION OF 1529 PARLIAMENT)

| 52/42 | John Huse [Hussey], Lord Hussey | Lord [*Illegible*] John [Mordaunt], Lord Mordaunt | [*No place*], 28 Nov. 1534 |

PARLIAMENT AT WESTMINSTER, 4 FEBRUARY 1536 (EIGHTH SESSION OF 1529 PARLIAMENT)

52/43	John Lumley, knight, Lord Lumley	George [Boleyn], Lord Rochford, knight	[No place], 24 Jan. 1536
52/44	John Bowcher [Bouchier], Lord Fitzwarren [LP]	William Sandys, knight, Lord Sandys	[No place], 2 Feb. 1536
52/45	Henry [Percy], earl of Northumberland	Thomas [Boleyn], earl of Wiltshire	[No place], 11 Feb. 1536

LETTERS OF UNCERTAIN DATE

| 52/4 | Robert Fitzwalter, [Lord Fitzwalter] [LP] [F] | Robert [Fitzwalter], 'our son' | [Illegible], 15 Edward II [1321–2] |
| 52/32 | Thomas Vaux, Lord Harrowden | Thomas [Howard], duke of Norfolk Thomas West, Lord de la Warr | [Illegible] March [illegible] Henry VIII |

Appointments in the Journals of the House of Lords, 1510–39

This appendix contains the details of proxy appointments (for both spiritual and temporal peers) found in the Journal of the House of Lords during the period from the start of the surviving journals to the dissolution of the monasteries and the consequent removal from parliament of the heads of religious houses (1510–39). Unfortunately, journals in the Parliamentary Archives only survive for parliaments for which there are no extant letters in SC 10, with the exception of February 1536 where part of the journal has been preserved in the British Library (the appointments contained in this are calendared in Appendix 3). The appointments listed here are taken from volume 1 of the printed edition of Journals of the House of Lords (London, 1767–1830), and the number in the first column refers to the page number in that volume. The second column contains the name of the peer appointing the proctors. The third column lists the names of the proctors. The final column notes the date on which the proxy was recorded in the journal.

PARLIAMENT AT WESTMINSTER, 21 JANUARY 1510

		Leave of absence	
3	[Dafydd ab Owain], bishop of St Asaph		21 Jan. 1510
3	Thomas [Braunche], abbot of St Peter's, Gloucester	Thomas [Ruthall], bishop of Durham	21 Jan. 1510

3	Richard [Holbech], abbot of Thorney	James [Stanley], bishop of Ely	21 Jan. 1510

3	Richard [Holbech], abbot of Thorney	James [Stanley], bishop of Ely [William Codenham *alias* Buntyng], abbot of Bury St Edmunds [Robert Kyrketon], abbot of Peterborough [Richard Bardney], abbot of Crowland	21 Jan. 1510
4	[Dafydd ab Owain], bishop of St Asaph	Edward Vaughan], bishop of St Davids [Thomas Skevington], bishop of Bangor Lord Charles Somerset	22 Jan. 1510
5	[John Dygon], abbot of St Augustine's, Canterbury	[John Islip], abbot of Westminster [Richard Kidderminster], abbot of Winchcombe [George Nevill], Lord Bergavenny	27 Jan. 1510
6	William [Marton], abbot of Bardney	[Robert Willoughby], Lord Willoughby Richard [Bardney], abbot of Crowland	11 Feb. 1510

PARLIAMENT AT WESTMINSTER, 4 FEBRUARY 1512

11	Richard [Camme], abbot of Malmesbury	Miles [Salley], bishop of Llandaff John Newton, abbot of St Peter's, Gloucester	5 Feb. 1512
11	John [Penny], bishop of Carlisle	[Thomas Ruthall], bishop of Durham [Edward Sutton], Lord Dudley	6 Feb. 1512
11	John Broke, Lord Cobham	[Lawrence Champion], abbot of Battle [John Lawrence *alias* Wardeboys], abbot of Ramsey George Nevill, Lord Bergavenny	9 Feb. 1512

12	Ralph Ogle, Lord Ogle	Richard [Fox], bishop of Winchester Lord Henry Scrope of Bolton	10 Feb. 1512
12	[Robert Depyng], abbot of Selby	[Thomas Ruthall], bishop of Durham	16 Feb. 1512
12	John [de Vere], earl of Oxford	Richard [Fox], bishop of Winchester Thomas [Howard], earl of Surrey	16 Feb. 1512
12	[William Pollesworth], prior of Coventry	[Thomas Grey], marquess of Dorset	17 Feb. 1512
13	[Richard Lye], abbot of Shrewsbury	[William Smith], bishop of Coventry and Lichfield [George Talbot], earl of Shrewsbury	23 Feb. 1512
13	[Richard Bardney], abbot of Crowland	[John Lawrence *alias* Wardeboys], abbot of Ramsey [Thomas Howard, earl of Surrey], lord treasurer	25 Feb. 1512

PARLIAMENT AT WESTMINSTER, 5 FEBRUARY 1515

19	[Thomas Hampton], abbot of St Augustine's, Canterbury	[George Nevill], Lord Bergavenny [John Islip], abbot of Westminster	6 Feb. 1515
19	[George Hastings], Lord Hastings	Lord Shrewsbury [*presumably* George Talbot, earl of Shrewsbury] [John Islip], abbot of Westminster	6 Feb. 1515
19	[Lawrence Champion], abbot of Battle	[George Nevill], Lord Bergavenny [Richard Kidderminster], abbot of Winchcombe	6 Feb. 1515

19	[Robert Kyrketon], abbot of Peterborough	[Thomas Wolsey], archbishop of York [Richard Grey], earl of Kent	6 Feb. 1515
19	[Richard Beere], abbot of Glastonbury	[Richard Kidderminster], abbot of Winchcombe [Thomas Stanley], earl of Derby	6 Feb. 1515
19	[William Marton], abbot of Bardney	[Richard Kidderminster], abbot of Winchcombe [Henry Bourchier], earl of Essex	6 Feb. 1515
19	[William Malvern *alias* Parker], abbot of St Peter's, Gloucester	[Thomas Wolsey], archbishop of York [Richard Grey], earl of Kent	6 Feb. 1515
19	[Robert Depyng], abbot of Selby	[Thomas Ruthall], bishop of Durham [Richard Grey], earl of Kent	6 Feb. 1515
19	Abbot of Chichester [*sic*]	[John Islip], abbot of Westminster [Henry Bourchier], earl of Essex	6 Feb. 1515
19	[John Lumley], Lord Lumley	[John Islip], abbot of Westminster [Richard Grey], earl of Kent	6 Feb. 1515
19	[John Wellys *alias* Bryggys], abbot of Crowland	[Richard Kidderminster], abbot of Winchcombe [Robert Willoughby], Lord Willoughby	6 Feb. 1515
19	[Robert Moulton *alias* Blythe], abbot of Thorney	[John Thorne], abbot of Reading [Richard Grey], earl of Kent	6 Feb. 1515
19	Bishop of Oxford [*sic*]	[Richard Fox], bishop of Winchester [John Bourchier], Lord Fitzwarren	6 Feb. 1515

19	[Edward Vaughan], bishop of St Davids	[Richard Nykke], bishop of Norwich [Charles Somerset], earl of Worcester	6 Feb. 1515
19	[Richard Mayhew], bishop of Hereford	[Thomas Ruthall], bishop of Durham [William Atwater], bishop of Lincoln [Charles Somerset], earl of Worcester [George Nevill], Lord Bergavenny	6 Feb. 1515
19	[Edward Stafford], duke of Buckingham	[Richard Fox], bishop of Winchester [John Bourchier], Lord Fitzwarren	7 Feb. 1515
19	[Clement Lichefeld *alias* Wych], abbot of Evesham	[Richard Kidderminster], abbot of Winchcombe [Henry Daubeney], Lord Daubeney	7 Feb. 1515
19	[William Atwater], bishop of Lincoln	[Richard Fitz James], bishop of London [George Nevill], Lord Bergavenny	7 Feb. 1515
20	[Henry Scrope], Lord Scrope	[Thomas Ruthall], bishop of Durham [Thomas Darcy], Lord Darcy	8 Feb. 1515
20	[William Stourton], Lord Stourton	[Thomas Howard, duke of Norfolk], lord treasurer [John Melford *alias* Reve], abbot of Bury St Edmunds	8 Feb. 1515
23	[James Stanley], bishop of Ely	[Richard Fox], bishop of Winchester [Edward Stanley], Lord Monteagle	15 Feb. 1515
24	[John Reding], abbot of St Benet of Hulme	[Richard Nykke], bishop of Norwich [Thomas Howard], earl of Surrey	17 Feb. 1515

| 25 | [Robert Ogle], Lord Ogle | [Richard Fox], bishop of Winchester [Edward Stanley], Lord Monteagle | 23 Feb. 1515 |
| 33 | [Edward Sutton], Lord Dudley | [Charles Somerset, earl of Worcester], lord chamberlain [John Islip], abbot of Westminster | 14 March 1515 |

PARLIAMENT AT WESTMINSTER, 12 NOVEMBER 1515 (SECOND SESSION OF FEBRUARY 1515 PARLIAMENT)

43	Edward Sutton, Lord Dudley	[John Islip], abbot of Westminster [Thomas Fiennes], Lord Dacre	12 Nov. 1515
43	[Robert Moulton *alias* Blythe], abbot of Thorney	[John Islip], abbot of Westminster [Richard Grey], earl of Kent	12 Nov. 1515
43	[John Lawrence *alias* Wardeboys], abbot of Ramsey	[John Islip], abbot of Westminster [Robert Radcliffe], Lord Fitzwalter	12 Nov. 1515
43	[Thomas Hampton], abbot of St Augustine's, Canterbury	[John Islip], abbot of Westminster [George Nevill], Lord Bergavenny	12 Nov. 1515
43	[Richard Camme], abbot of Malmesbury	[Richard Kidderminster], abbot of Winchcombe William Compton, knight [Walter Devereux], Lord Ferrers	12 Nov. 1515
43	[Richard Baker], abbot of Shrewsbury	[Richard Kidderminster], abbot of Winchcombe [George Talbot], earl of Shrewsbury	12 Nov. 1515
44	[James Tuchet], Lord Audley	[Richard Fox], bishop of Winchester [Thomas Brooke], Lord Cobham	14 Nov. 1515

45	[Lawrence Champion], abbot of Battle	[Richard Kidderminster], abbot of Winchcombe [George Nevill], Lord Bergavenny	19 Nov. 1515
46	[William Marton], abbot of Bardney	[Richard Kidderminster], abbot of Winchcombe [William Willoughby], Lord Willoughby	22 Nov. 1515

PARLIAMENT AT WESTMINSTER, 15 JANUARY 1534 (SIXTH SESSION OF NOVEMBER 1529 PARLIAMENT)

58	[Thomas West], Lord la Ware	[George Boleyn], Lord Rochford	15 Jan. 1534
58	[Thomas Weoford], prior of Coventry	[George Hastings], Lord Huntington [William Boston *alias* Benson], abbot of Westminster [John Salcot *alias* Capon], abbot of Hyde near Winchester	15 Jan. 1534
58	[Clement Lichefeld *alias* Wych], abbot of Evesham	[John Chambers *alias* Borowe], abbot of Peterborough [Richard Anscelm *alias* Munslowe], abbot of Winchcombe [Thomas Weoford], prior of Coventry	15 Jan. 1534
58	[Cuthbert Tunstall], bishop of Durham	[John Clerk], bishop of Bath and Wells	15 Jan. 1534
58	[Robert Selby *alias* Roger], abbot of Selby	[William Repps *alias* Rugg], abbot of St Benet of Hulme	15 Jan. 1534
58	[Robert Moulton *alias* Blythe], abbot of Thorney	[Robert Fuller], abbot of Waltham	15 Jan. 1534

58	[Robert Frampton *alias* Selwyn], abbot of Malmesbury	[William Malvern *alias* Parker], abbot of St Peter's, Gloucester [John Blake], abbot of Cirencester	15 Jan. 1534
58	[John Tuchet], Lord Audley	[George Boleyn], Lord Rochford	15 Jan. 1534
58	[John Chambers *alias* Borowe], abbot of Peterborough	[Robert Catton *alias* Bronde], abbot of St Albans [Hugh Cook *alias* Faryngton], abbot of Reading	15 Jan. 1534
58	[John Wellys *alias* Bryggys], abbot of Crowland	[Robert Fuller], abbot of Waltham	15 Jan. 1534
58	[William Thornton *alias* Dent], abbot of St Mary's, York	*No proctors named*	15 Jan. 1534
58	[William Marton], abbot of Bardney	[William Repps *alias* Rugg], abbot of St Benet of Hulme	15 Jan. 1534
58	[Henry Bourchier], earl of Essex	[John de Vere], earl of Oxford	15 Jan. 1534
58	[John Lawrence *alias* Wardeboys], abbot of Ramsey	[John Salcot *alias* Capon], abbot of Hyde near Winchester [William Repps *alias* Rugg], abbot of St Benet of Hulme	15 Jan. 1534
58	[Henry Beeley], abbot of Tewkesbury	[John Salcot *alias* Capon], abbot of Hyde near Winchester [William Repps *alias* Rugg], abbot of St Benet of Hulme	15 Jan. 1534
58	[Edward Stourton], Lord Stourton	[William Sandys], Lord Sandys	15 Jan. 1534

58	[Thomas Pentecost alias Rowland], abbot of Abingdon	[John Salcot alias Capon], abbot of Hyde near Winchester [William Repps alias Rugg], abbot of St Benet of Hulme	15 Jan. 1534
58	[Richard Whiting], abbot of Glastonbury	[John Salcot alias Capon], abbot of Hyde near Winchester [William Repps alias Rugg], abbot of St Benet of Hulme	15 Jan. 1534
58	Abbot of Chichester [sic]	[John Salcot alias Capon], abbot of Hyde near Winchester [William Repps alias Rugg], abbot of St Benet of Hulme	15 Jan. 1534
58	[Edward Lee], archbishop of York	[John Stokesley], bishop of London [Stephen Gardiner], bishop of Winchester [John Clerk], bishop of Bath and Wells	15 Jan. 1534
58	Thomas [Burgh], Lord Burgh	[George Boleyn], Lord Rochford	15 Jan. 1534
58	[Thomas Stanley], Lord Monteagle	[George Boleyn], Lord Rochford	15 Jan. 1534

PARLIAMENT AT WESTMINSTER, 8 JUNE 1536

83	Arthur [Plantagenet], Viscount Lisle	Thomas [West], Lord la Ware Henry [Pole], Lord Montagu	10 June 1536
83	Thomas [Butler alias Lorde], abbot of Shrewsbury	[John Salcot alias Capon], bishop of Bangor [Robert Fuller], abbot of Waltham	10 June 1536

83	Henry Dawbeney [Daubeney], Lord Daubeney	*No proctors named*	10 June 1536
83	[William Marton], abbot of Bardney	[Robert Fuller], abbot of Waltham	10 June 1536
83	Thomas [Marshall *alias* Beche], abbot of St John's, Colchester	[William Repps *alias* Rugg], bishop of Norwich [*not consecrated until 11 June*] [John Salcot *alias* Capon], bishop of Bangor	10 June 1536
83–84	Roland [*sic – recte* John Longland], bishop of Coventry and Lichfield	Thomas [Goodrich], bishop of Ely John [Salcot *alias* Capon], bishop of Bangor	10 June 1536
84	[John Lawrence *alias* Wardeboys], abbot of Ramsey	*No proctors named*	10 June 1536

PARLIAMENT AT WESTMINSTER, 28 APRIL 1539

103	[John Mordaunt], Lord Mordaunt	Thomas [Audley], Lord Audley of Walden, lord chancellor of England	28 Apr. 1539
103	William Weston, prior of St John of Jerusalem	[Thomas Griffin], Lord Latimer [Andrew Windsor], Lord Windsor	28 Apr. 1539
103	[Thomas Butler *alias* Lorde], abbot of Shrewsbury	[Robert Fuller], abbot of Waltham [John Wyche *alias* Wakeman], abbot of Tewkesbury	28 Apr. 1539
103	Arthur Plantagenet, Viscount Lisle	Edward [Seymour], earl of Hertford	28 Apr. 1539

| 103 | William [Sandys], Lord Sandys | William Pawlet [Paulet], Lord St John | 3 May 1539 |
| 103 | Richard [Whiting], abbot of Glastonbury | *No proctors named.* | 3 May 1539 |

Proxy Appointments for February 1536 in the British Library

There is no surviving journal for the eighth and final session of the Reformation Parliament in February 1536 in the Parliamentary Archives. However, some pages of the original journal for this session can now be found in British Library Harley MS 158. It is not clear how they found their way into this manuscript, which is a bound volume containing a miscellaneous assortment of state and parliamentary papers. Folio 143r contains the attendance list for 4 February, and folio 143v the list for 5 February. Folio 144 contains the proxies entered in this session. (The folio numbers have been changed, so in the printed list of Harley Manuscripts, the older, crossed out references are used and these proxies are noted as being on folio 137: Catalogue of the Harleian Manuscripts in the British Museum, 4 vols. (London, 1808–12), vol. 1, p. 48).

This list is of particular interest because it is the only session for which entries survive in both SC 10 and the Journal of the House of Lords, and is therefore the sole occasion in almost three centuries on which the letters in SC 10 can be checked against a corresponding enrolled list. There are more entries in the list than surviving letters: the proxy appointments of the abbots of Shrewsbury and St John's, Colchester, along with those of Lord la Ware and the earl of Arundel, are recorded here, but the original letters of appointment have not survived in SC 10. However, the absence of all the peers for whom there are extant letters in SC 10 (eleven lords spiritual and three lords temporal) is recorded in the journal. It is notable that the names of the proxies entered in the journal do not always match those in the surviving letters of appointment.

The proxy appointments in Harley MS 158 are listed below. The first column refers to the folio number in the manuscript, with the equivalent letter in SC 10 noted in square brackets below (where applicable). The second column contains the name of the peer appointing the proctors. The third column lists the names of the proctors. The names of baronial titles and religious houses have been silently modernised where applicable. The final column notes the date on which the proxy was recorded in the journal.

PARLIAMENT AT WESTMINSTER, 4 FEBRUARY 1536 (EIGHTH SESSION OF NOVEMBER 1529 PARLIAMENT)

f. 144r	[Thomas Butler *alias* Lorde], abbot of Shrewsbury	John [Salcot *alias* Capon], abbot of Hyde near Winchester Robert [Fuller], abbot of Waltham	4 Feb. 1536
f. 144r [51/2523]	[Thomas Pentecost *alias* Rowland], abbot of Abingdon	[William Boston *alias* Benson], abbot of Westminster	4 Feb. 1536
f. 144r [51/2521]	[Thomas Weoford], prior of Coventry	[William Boston *alias* Benson], abbot of Westminster	4 Feb. 1536
f. 144r [52/44]	[John Bouchier], Lord Fitzwarren	Thomas [Mowbray], duke of Norfolk [William Sandys], Lord Sandys	4 Feb. 1536
f. 144r	[Thomas West], Lord la Ware	Thomas Cromwell, king's principal secretary [George Boleyn], Lord Rochford	4 Feb. 1536
f. 144r [51/2543]	Robert [Sherburne], bishop of Chichester	Thomas [Boleyn], earl of Wiltshire	4 Feb. 1536
f. 144r [51/2519]	[Robert Moulton *alias* Blythe], abbot of Thorney	*No proctors listed*	6 Feb. 1536
f. 144r [51/2516]	[John Kite], bishop of Carlisle	William Kingston, knight Cuthbert [Tunstall], bishop of Durham	7 Feb. 1536
f. 144r [51/2522]	[John Lawrence *alias* Wardeboys], abbot of Ramsey	*No proctors listed*	9 Feb. 1536
f. 144r [51/2514]	[Richard Rawlins], bishop of St Davids	John [Stokesley], bishop of London [John Longland], bishop of Lincoln	10 Feb. 1536

f. 144r [52/43]	[John Lumley], Lord Lumley	Thomas Cromwell, king's principal secretary George [Boleyn], Lord Rochford	12 Feb. 1536
f. 144r [52/45]	[Henry Percy], earl of Northumberland	Thomas Cromwell Thomas [Boleyn], earl of W[*damaged* – Wiltshire]	15 Feb. 1536
f. 144v	[William FitzAlan], earl of Arundel	Thomas [Boleyn], earl of Wiltshire Thomas [Boleyn], earl of Wiltshire [*sic*] George [Boleyn], Lord Rochford	22 Feb. 1536
f. 144v	[Thomas Marshall *alias* Beche], abbot of St John's, Colchester	Thomas Audeley [Audley], chancellor of England [John de Vere], earl of Oxford [Robert Radcliffe], earl of Sussex John Melford *alias* Reve], abbot of Bury St Edmunds John Salcot *alias* Capon], abbot of Hyde near Winchester [William Repps], abbot of St Benet of Hulme	22 Feb. 1536
f. 144v [51/2517]	[Clement Lichefeld *alias* Wych], abbot of Evesham	John [Chambers], abbot of Peterborough	22 Feb. 1536
f. 144v [51/2515]	[Richard Anscelm *alias* Munstowe], abbot of Winchcombe	[Robert Fuller], abbot of Waltham	22 Feb. 1536
f. 144v [51/2544]	[Richard Whiting], abbot of Glastonbury	[John Salcot], bishop of Bangor	22' Feb. 1536
f. 144v [51/2518]	[William Marton], abbot of Bardney	[Robert Fuller], abbot of Waltham	24 Feb. 1536

Appointments of Proctors in Episcopal Registers

Comparatively few appointments of parliamentary proctors appear in episcopal registers. This was partly because some bishops were active parliamentarians, yet even for those who did not attend the evidence is sparse. This was perhaps because proctors' powers, though large, were of short duration, and their commissions conferred no increased ecclesiastical authority. The result is that for some dioceses there is no material at all. During many episcopates the writs of summons to parliament would be routinely entered in registers, often among the collection of royal writs. Such entries might be accompanied by notes recording a writ's execution, but there was almost never any mention of the proctors subsequently chosen, whether by the bishop or his diocesan clergy. In large dioceses with well-organised registers the clerks were sometimes unsure where to record the writs of summons. Thus in the registers of both Roger Martival of Salisbury and John Buckingham of Lincoln some writs were entered among the memoranda but many more in the registers of royal writs. Occasionally a reference to proctors' appointments to parliament, as described in a marginal note, turns out, upon closer inspection, to refer to convocation. The quality and variety of material in bishops' registers declined after 1400, with clerical taxation apparently of greater concern than parliamentary representation.

This list is ordered alphabetically by diocese, with the bishops of each diocese then listed chronologically. The register source is listed immediately after the bishop's name, with the page or folio number listed next to each entry of proxy appointments.

BATH AND WELLS

John Droxford (1309–29)
SOURCE: *Calendar of the Register of John de Drokensford, Bishop of Bath and Wells, A.D. 1309–1329,* ed. E. Hobhouse, Somerset Record Society 1 (1887).

1. Council at London, Jan. 1322 (pp. 100, 196).
PROCTORS: John Martel; Robert de Wamberge [Wanborough]; and Nicholas de Bath, clerks.

2. Parliament at Lincoln, 15 Sept. 1327 (p. 273; cf. SC 10/11/529).
PROCTOR: Walter de Hull, canon of Wells.

3. Parliament at York, 7 Feb. 1328 (p. 279).
PROCTORS: John de Brabazon, canon of Wells; Walter de Hull, canon of Wells; and Henry de Fulham, clerk.

4. Parliament at York, 31 July 1328 (p. 290).
PROCTORS: John de Brabazon*; Walter de Hull*; and Walter de Bedwynde.

Thomas Bekynton (1443–65)

SOURCE: *The Register of Thomas Bekynton, Bishop of Bath and Wells 1443–1465*, ed. H. C. Maxwell-Lyte and M. C. B. Davies, Somerset Record Society 49 (1934).

1. Parliament at Reading, 6 March 1453 (p. 200).
PROCTORS: John [Low], bishop of Rochester; Thomas [Bourgchier], bishop of Ely; and Richard [Beauchamp], bishop of Salisbury.
DATED: The Bishop's Inn at London, 1 March 1453.

2. Parliament at Reading, 12 Nov. 1453 (p. 221).
PROCTORS: Thomas [Bourgchier], bishop of Ely; John [Low], bishop of Rochester; John [Stanbury], bishop of Hereford; Robert Botil, prior of the hospital of St. John of Jerusalem in England; and John Stourton, Lord Stourton.
DATED: The Palace, Wells, 3 Nov. 1453.

3. Parliament at Westminster, 14 Jan. 1456 (pp. 264–5).
PROCTORS: John [Low], bishop of Rochester; Reginald [Pecock], bishop of Chichester; Richard [Beauchamp], bishop of Salisbury; James [Blakedon], bishop of Bangor; Robert Botil, prior of the hospital of St. John of Jerusalem in England; John Stourton, Lord Stourton; Master Thomas Lyseux [Lisieux], dean of St. Paul's, London and keeper of the privy seal; M. William Say, canon of Wells; and M. Thomas Boleyn, canon of Wells.
DATED: Banwell, 8 Jan. 1456.

4. Parliament at Coventry, 20 Nov. 1459 (p. 331).
PROCTORS: Richard [Beauchamp], bishop of Salisbury; John [Selwood], abbot of Glastonbury; Robert [Botil], prior of the hospital of St. John of Jerusalem in England; Ralph Boteler, Lord Sudeley, knight; and M. Nicholas Carent, dean of Wells.
DATED: The Palace, Wells, 6 Nov. 1459.

5. Parliament at Westminster, 4 Nov. 1461 (p. 360).
PROCTORS: Walter [Lyhert], bishop of Norwich; William [Grey], bishop of Ely; and George [Neville], bishop of Exeter.
DATED: Wokey [Wookey], 19 Oct. 1461.

6. Parliament at Westminster, 29 April 1463 (p. 385).
PROCTORS: John [Carpenter], bishop of Worcester; Walter [Lyhert], bishop of Norwich; Ralph [Boteler], Lord Sudeley, knight; John [Selwood], abbot of Glastonbury; and M. Robert Stillyngton, archdeacon of Taunton and keeper of the king's privy seal.
DATED: The Palace, Wells, 23 April 1463.

CANTERBURY

SOURCE: The registers of the following two archbishops of Canterbury are unpublished and can be found in Lambeth Palace Library.

Walter Reynolds (1313–27)

1. Parliament at York, 14 Nov. 1322 (Reg. Reynolds, f. 92; letter patent).
PROCTORS: W[alter Stapledon], bishop of Exeter; and J[ohn Hotham], bishop of Ely.
DATED: Wrotham, 9 Nov. 1322

William Whittlesey (1368–74)

1. Parliament at Westminster, 24 Feb. 1371 (Reg Whittlesey, f. 40*v*).
Proctors; [Simon Sudbury], bishop of London; [William Lenn], bishop of Worcester; and [Adam Houghton], bishop of St. Davids.
DATED: Lambeth, 16 March 1371

CARLISLE

John Halton (1292–1324)
SOURCE: *The Register of John de Halton Bishop of Carlisle A.D. 1292–1324*, ed. W. N. Thompson and T. F. Tout, C&Y 12 (1913).

1. Parliament at Westminster, 27 April 1309 (vol. 1, pp. 314–15).
Proctors to represent the diocesan clergy: M. Adam de Appelby [Appleby], clerk; and D. Robert de Meburn, canon of Lanercost.
Sealed with the bishop's seal: Carlisle, 19 April 1309.
The bishop's proctor for the same parliament: M. Adam de Appelby [Appleby].
DATED: Rose, 19 April 1309.

2. Parliament at London, 23 Feb. 1324 (vol. 1, p. 225; cf. SC 10/9/438).
PROCTORS: M. W[illiam] de Kendale [Kendal], rector of [Great] Salkeld; and D. R[obert] Tymparon, rector of Levinton [Kirk Levington], in our diocese.
DATED: Horncastle, 17 Feb. 1324.

John Kirkby (1332–52)
SOURCE: *The Register of John Kirkby Bishop of Carlisle 1332–1352 and the Register of John Rosse Bishop of Carlisle 1325–1332*, ed. R. L. Storey, C&Y 79 (1993).

1. Parliament at Westminster, 3 March 1337 (p. 68).
PROCTORS: D. John de Sampole; and D. Philip de Kyme.
DATED: Horncastle, 19 Feb. 1337

2. Parliament at Westminster, 3 Feb. 1339 (p. 93).
PROCTORS: M. John de Brenkhill, doctor of canon law; and M. John de Stokton [Stockton], clerk.

Gilbert Welton (1353–62)
SOURCE: *The Register of Gilbert Welton Bishop of Carlisle 1353–1362*, ed. R. L. Storey, C&Y 88 (1999).

1. Parliament at Westminster, 23 Nov. 1355 (p. 106).
PROCTORS: Henry de Ingelby [Ingleby] canon of York; William de Burgh; and M. John de Welton.
DATED: Rose, 1 Nov. 1355.

Thomas Appleby (1363–95)
SOURCE: *The Register of Thomas Appleby, Bishop of Carlisle 1363–1395*, ed. R. L. Storey, C&Y 26 (2006).

1. Parliament at Westminster, 1 May 1368 (p.23, with incomplete copy of the entry on p. 36).

Letter patent of the archdeacon of Carlisle appointing as his proctor William de Strickland, clerk.
Sealed with the bishop's seal, with his agreement.
DATED: Carlisle, 18 April 1368.

2. Parliament at Westminster, 27 Jan. 1377 (p. 113; cf. SC 10/31/1533).
PROCTORS: M. Walter Scirlawe [Skirlaw], clerk; D. John Marshall, clerk; John de Kirkby; Thomas de Skelton; and William de Strickland.
DATED: Rose, 8 Jan. 1377.

CHICHESTER

Richard Praty (1438–45)
SOURCE: *West Sussex Record Office, Ep. I/1/2.*

1. Parliament at Westminster, 25 Jan. 1442 (ff. 48, 50 (ink foliation) or 49, 51v (pencil foliation)).
PROCTORS: John [Beaumont], Viscount Beaumont; Ralph [Boteler], Lord Sudeley; M. Thomas Bekyngton [Beckington], doctor of law; M. John Stokes, doctor of law; and Thomas Kirkeby [Kirkby] and John Faukes, clerks in the king's chancery.
DATED: The palace next to the cathedral, 27 Feb. 1442.

COVENTRY AND LICHFIELD

No extant appointments of proctors in the registers of this diocese.

DURHAM

Richard Kellaw (1311–16)
SOURCE: *Registrum Palatinum Dunelmense*, ed. T. D. Hardy, Rolls series (1873).

1. Parliament at Westminster, 8 Aug. 1311 (vol. 1, pp. 86–7).
PROCTORS: M. John Fraunceys; M. Richard Eryum [Airmyn]; and M. John de Sneynton [Snainton].
DATED: 29 July 1311

2. Parliament at Westminster, 18 March 1313 (vol. 1, pp. 301–2).
PROCTORS: William de Rasen; William de Ayremynne [Airmyn]; and Geoffrey de Edenham.
DATED: Stockton, 6 Marcy 1313.

3. Parliament at Westminster, 8 July 1313 (vol. 1, pp. 364–5).
PROCTORS: D. William Rasen; D. William de Ayremynne [Airmyn]; Mr. John de Snaynton [Snainton]; and D. Geoffrey de Edenham.
DATED: Middleham, 1 July 1313.

4. Parliament at Westminster, 23 Sept. 1313 (vol. 1, p. 435).
PROCTORS: D. William de Rasen; D. William de Ayremyn [Airmyn] and Mr. John de Snaynton [Snainton].
DATED: Welehall [Wheel Hall], 12 Sept. 1313.

Richard de Bury (1333–45)

SOURCE: *Richard D'Aungerville of Bury: Fragments of his Register and other Documents*, ed. G. W. Kitchin, Surtees Society 119 (1910).

1. Parliament at Westminster, 18 April 1344 (pp. 56–7; cf. SC 10/23/1136).
PROCTORS: M. Thomas de Bardewardyn [Bradwardine], doctor of theology; M. Richard de Kilvyngton [Kilvington], doctor of theology; M. Stephen de Ketelbery [Kettelburgh], doctor of civil law; D. William de Emelton [Emeldon], clerk; and D. William de Hemyngton [Hemington], clerk.
DATED: Howden, 10 April 1344.

Thomas Langley (1406–37)

SOURCE: *The Register of Thomas Langley Bishop of Durham 1406–1437*, ed. R. L. Storey, 6 vols., Surtees Society 164, 166, 169, 170, 177 and 182 (1956–70).

1. Parliament at London, 27 Jan. 1428 (vol. 3, pp. 69–70).
PROCTORS: John Thoralby, clerk; William Prestwyk [Prestwick] clerk; and Nicholas Dixson [Dixon], clerk.
DATED: Aukland [Bishop Auckland], 21 Jan. 1428.

2. Parliament at Westminster, 22 Sept. 1429 (vol. 3, p. 159).
PROCTORS: John Frank, keeper of the rolls of chancery; William Prestwyk [Prestwick], clerk; and Nicholas Dixon, clerk.
DATED: Howden, 12 Sept. 1429.

3. Parliament at Westminster, 16 Jan. 1431 (vol. 4, pp. 1–2).
PROCTORS: John Frank, keeper of the rolls of chancery; John Thoralby, clerk; William Prestwyk [Prestwick], clerk; and Nicholas Dixson [Dixon], clerk.
DATED: Aukland [Bishop Auckland], 2 Jan. 1431.

4. Parliament at Westminster, 21 Jan. 1437 (vol. 5, p. 8).
PROCTORS: William [*sic, recte* Thomas Brunce], bishop of Norwich; William [Heyworth], bishop of Coventry and Lichfield; Robert Rolleston, keeper of the king's great wardrobe; John Frank, keeper of the rolls of chancery; Nicholas Wymbyssh [Wymbush], master of chancery; and Thomas Holden, the bishop's chamberlain.
DATED: Aukland [Bishop Auckland], 10 Jan. 1437.

ELY

John Fordham (1388–1425)

SOURCE: *Cambridge University Library, EDR, G/1/3 (Reg. Fordham)*.

1. Parliament at Winchester, 20 Jan. 1393 (f. 175).
PROCTORS: Robert de Farrington, canon of York; John Wendlyngburgh [Wellingborough] senior, canon of London; and John Sunderasshe [Sundridge], rector of Doddington parish church, our diocese.
DATED: Our manor of Doddington, 12 Jan. 1393.

2. Parliament at Westminster, 14 Jan. 1404 (ff. 138*v*–139).
PROCTORS: John Rome, 'clerk of this your parliament'; and M. John Bernard, licenciate in laws.
DATED: Our dwelling (*hospitium*) in Holbourne near London, 23 Feb. 1404.

3. Parliament at Westminster, 13 Oct. 1406 (f. 161).
PROCTORS: John Rome, 'clerk of your parliament'; and M. John Bernard, licenciate in laws and dean of royal chapel of Tamworth.
DATED: Downham, 8 Oct. 1406.

4. Parliament at Gloucester, 20 Oct. 1407 (ff. 163*v*–164).
PROCTORS: John Wakeryng [Wakering], keeper of the rolls of chancery; John Rome, 'clerk of your parliament'; and Simon Derby, clerk.
DATED: Our manor of Doddington, 18 Oct. 1407.

EXETER

Walter Bronescombe (1258–80)
SOURCE: *The Register of Walter Bronescombe Bishop of Exeter 1258–1280*, ed. O. F. Robinson, vol. 2, C&Y 87 (1999).

1. Parliament at St. Albans, 7 Dec. 1264 (pp. 13–14).
PROCTORS: M. John Wyger and J[ohn] de Bradley.
DATED: Bishops Nympton, 23 Nov. 1264.
The letter is addressed to H[enry Sandwich] bishop of London and the other bishops of the provinces of Canterbury and York, and to the whole community of the lower clergy.

Walter Stapeldon (1308–26)
SOURCE: *The Register of Walter de Stapleton, Bishop of Exeter (A.D. 1307–1326)*, ed. F. C. Hingeston-Randolph (London and Exeter, 1892).

1. Parliament at Westminster, 20 Oct. 1308 (p. 311).
PROCTORS: John de Brueton [Bruton] and Robert de Stapeldon, canons of Exeter.
DATED: 6 Nov. 1308.

2. Parliament at Lincoln, 23 July 1312 (p. 311).
PROCTORS: J[ohn Droxford], bishop of Bath and Wells; David [Martin] bishop of St Davids; and Thomas de Loggore, canon of Wells.
DATED: Peynton [Paignton], 14 July 1312.

John Grandisson (1327–69)
SOURCE: *The Register of John de Grandisson Bishop of Exeter (A.D. 1327–1369)*, 3 vols., ed. F. C. Hingeston-Randolph (London and Exeter, 1894–9).

1. Parliament at Salisbury, 16 Oct. 1328 (vol. 1, pp. 410–11).
PROCTORS: M. John Bloyton, bishop's official; Walter de Setone [Seton], canon of Lincoln; William de Nassington, canon of Osmortherley [Osmotherley] collegiate church, Yorkshire.
DATED: Lawhitton Manor, 13 Oct. 1328.

2. Parliament at Westminster, 26 Nov. 1330 (vol. 1, pp. 590–1).
PROCTORS: John [Stratford], bishop of Winchester; and Roger [Northburgh], bishop of Coventry and Lichfield.
DATED: Lawhitton, 12 Nov. 1330.
For the same parliament the bishop issued a commission to M. William la Zouche, archdeacon of Exeter, and M. William de Nassington, canons of Exeter cathedral, to excuse him and to take his place there.

3. Parliament at York, 20 Jan. 1333 (vol. 2, p. 680).
PROCTORS: M. Robert de Nassyngtone [Nassington], doctor of canon law; D. Thomas de Evesham, canon and prebendary of Crediton collegiate church; and D. Philip de Nassyngtone [Nassington], rector of Ashcombe, Exeter diocese.
DATED: Chyddeleghe [Chudleigh], 10 Jan. 1333.

4. Parliament at Westminster, 6 June 1344 (vol. 2, pp. 984–5).
PROCTORS: M. Robert Herewarde [Hereward], canon of Exeter; M. John de Northwode [Northwood], canon of Exeter; and Thomas de Crosse [Cross], canon of Crediton collegiate church.
DATED: Clyst, 26 May 1344.

5. Parliament at Westminster, 16 Aug. 1352 (vol. 1, p. 76).
PROCTORS: M. John Lecche [Leech], doctor of laws; and M. Benedict de Paston, clerk.

6. Parliament at Westminster, 6 Oct. 1363 (vol. 1, p. 84).
PROCTORS: William [Wittlesey] bishop of Rochester 'ac nobiles viros Dominos' [*the entry breaks off here*].

Thomas Brantingham (1370–94)
SOURCE: *The Register of Thomas de Brantyngham, Bishop of Exeter (A.D. 1370–1394)*, 2 vols., ed. F. C. Hingeston-Randolph (London and Exeter, 1901–6).

1. Parliament at Westminster, 3 Nov. 1372 (p. 187).
PROCTORS: M. John Wyliet [Wyliot], chancellor of the cathedral, and M. William Byde, the bishop's principal official.

2. Parliament at Westminster, 21 Nov. 1373 (p. 317).
PROCTORS: M. William Byde, the bishop's official, doctor of laws; M. John Schyllyngford [Shillingford], doctor of laws; and D. Walter Aldebury, canon of St Paul's, London.
DATED: Clyst, 4 Nov. 1373.

Edmund Stafford (1395–1419)
SOURCE: *The Register of Edmund Stafford: A.D. 1395–1419: An Index and Abstract of its Contents*, ed. F. C. Hingeston-Randolph (London, 1886).

1. Parliament at Westminster, 3 Nov. 1411 (p. 288).
PROCTORS: John Wakeryng [Wakering]; and John Rome.
DATED: 24 Oct. 1411.

2. Parliament at Westminster, 29 Jan. 1414; later moved to Leicester, 30 April (p. 288).
PROCTORS: John Wakeryng [Wakering], keeper of the rolls; and John Rome, clerk of parliament.
DATED: 6 Jan. 1414.

3. Parliament at Westminster, 16 March 1416 (p. 288).
PROCTORS: John Wakeryng [Wakering], keeper of the privy seal.
DATED: Clyst, 7 March 1416.

4. Parliament at Westminster, 16 March 1416 (p. 288).
PROCTORS: Simon Gaunstede [Gaunstead], keeper of the rolls; and Richard Gabryell [Gabriel], canon of Exeter.
DATED: 3 Oct. 1416.

5. Parliament at Westminster, 16 Oct. 1416 (p. 288).
PROCTORS: Henry Ware, keeper of the privy seal; and Richard Gabriell [Gabriel], canon.
DATED: 17 Oct. 1417.

Edmund Lacy (1420–55)
SOURCE: *The Register of Edmund Lacy, Bishop of Exeter, 1420–1455, Registrum Commune,* 5 vols., ed. G. R. Dunstan, C&Y 60–3 and 66 (1963–72).

1. Parliament at Westminster, 30 April 1425 (vol. 1, pp. 112–13).
PROCTORS: Benedict [Nicolls], bishop of St. Davids; Philip [Morgan] bishop of Worcester; and Richard Betty, canon of St Paul's London.
DATED: Lawhitton, 9 April 1425.

2. Parliament at Leicester, 18 Feb. 1426 (vol. 1, p. 151).
PROCTORS: Philip [Morgan], bishop of Worcester; and M. William Prestewyk [Prestwick], chaplain.
DATED: London, 4 Feb. 1426.

3. Parliament at Westminster, 10 Oct. 1435 (vol. 1, p. 309).
PROCTORS: Philip [Morgan], bishop of Ely; and Peter Stukelegh [Stukeley], canon of Exeter.
DATED: Chudleigh, 2 Oct. 1435.

4. Parliament at Westminster, 21 Jan. 1437 vol. 2, p. 31).
PROCTORS: Mr. Peter Stuklegh [Stukeley], canon of Exeter; Richard Selby, rector of Stoke in Clymmeslond [Stoke Climsland]; and John Wolston of Lansant [Lezant].
DATED: Clyst, 12 Jan. 1437

5. Parliament at Westminster, 12 Nov. 1439 (vol. 2, p. 167).
PROCTORS: Mr. William Lyndewode [Lyndwood], canon of Exeter; M. Peter Stuclegh [Stukeley], canon of Exeter; and M. Richard Selby, rector of Stoke Climsland.
DATED: Chuddelegh [Chudleigh], 30 Oct. 1439.

6. Parliament at Westminster, 25 Jan. 1442 (vol. 2, p. 250).
PROCTORS: Mr. William Lyndewode [Lyndwood], canon of Exeter; Mr. Peter Stuclegh [Stukeley], canon of Exeter; and M. John Bate, canon of Exeter.
DATED: Chudleigh, 2 Jan. 1442.

7. Parliament at Cambridge [prorogued to Bury St. Edmunds], 10 Feb. 1447 (vol. 2, p. 369).
PROCTORS: Walter [Lyhert] bishop of Norwich; M. William Bykenell, doctor of laws, canon of Exeter; D. John Bate, chaplain, canon of Exeter; and Mr. Peter Stukeley (Stukeley), bachelor of canon law.
DATED: Chuddelegh [Chudleigh], 19 Jan. 1447.

8. Parliament at Westminster, 6 Nov. 1449 (vol. 3, p. 48).
PROCTORS: Walter [Lyhert], bishop of Norwich; M. Roger Keys, bachelor of laws, canon of Exeter; D. John Bate, canon of Exeter; and Mr. Peter Stucle [Stukeley], bachelor of laws.
DATED: Chuddelegh [Chudleigh], 14 Oct. 1449

9. Parliament at Westminster, 6 Nov. 1450 (vol. 3, p. 88).
PROCTORS: Walter [Lyhert] bishop of Norwich, M. John Hals, doctor of theology, canon of Exeter; and D. John Bate, canon of Exeter.
DATED: Chudleigh, 19 Oct. 1450.

10. Parliament at Reading, 6 March 1453 (vol. 3, p. 166).
PROCTORS: Walter [Lyhert], bishop of Norwich; M. John Hals, canon of Exeter; and M. Thomas Mannyng [Manning], rector of Cheriton Episcopi [Cheriton Bishop].
DATED: Chudleigh, 20 Feb. 1453.

11. Parliament at Westminster, 26 May 1455 (vol. 3, p. 209).
PROCTORS: Walter [Lyhert], bishop of Norwich; M. Thomas Kyrkeby [Kirkby], keeper of the rolls of chancery; and M. John Hals, canon of Exeter.
DATED: Chudleigh, 20 Jun 1455.

HEREFORD

Richard Swinfield (1283–1317)
SOURCE: Hereford Archives Research Centre, Register of Richard Swinfield.

1. Parliament at Westminster, 12 Nov. 1295 (f. 112).
PROCTORS: [Richard de Hertford], archdeacon of Hereford; and the rector of 'Stretton' [*not identified*].
DATED: Wanetin [Wantage], Salisbury diocese, 10 Nov.1295.

2. Parliament at Westminster, 1 July 1302 (ff. 134–134v.)
PROCTOR: [John de Swinfield], precentor of Hereford.
DATED: Bosbury, 13 June 1302.

3. Parliament at Westminster, 3 March 1308 (f. 160v).
PROCTORS: John de Swinfield, precentor; and Nicholas de Reigate, treasurer.
DATED: Bosbury, 25 Feb. 1308.

4. Parliament at Westminster, Feb. 1312 (f. 173).
PROCTORS: Adam de Herwyntone [Harvington], rector of Awre; M. Adam de Murymuth [Murimuth], doctor of canon law; and R[obert] de la Felde, rector of Staunton in the Forest, Hereford diocese.

5. Parliament at Lincoln, 27 Jan. 1316 (ff. 194–194v).
PROCTOR: Robert de Iklesham [Icklesham], canon of Hereford.
DATED: Bosbury, 20 Jan. [1316].

John Trilleck (1344–60)
SOURCE: *Registrum Johannis de Trillek Episcopi Herefordensis*, ed. J. H. Parry, C&Y 18 (1912).
1. Council at Westminster, 18 April 1344 (p. 6).
PROCTOR: William de Edyndone [Edington], canon of Lincoln.
DATED: Farnham, 18 April 1344.

Thomas Spofford (1422–48)
SOURCE: Hereford Archives Research Centre, Register of Thomas Spofford.

1. Parliament at Westminster, 30 April 1425 (f. 79*v*).
PROCTORS: [Philip Morgan], bishop of Worcester]; [William Heyworth], bishop of Coventry and Lichfield; [William Welles], abbot of St Mary's, York; and M. William Alnewyk [Alnwick], doctor of laws.
DATED: Our manor of Whiteburne [Whitbourne], 11 April [1452].

2. Parliament at Westminster, 21 Jan. 1437 (f. 222).
PROCTORS: [Robert Gilbert], bishop of London; [Thomas Brown], bishop of Norwich; William [Welles], abbot of St. Mary's, York; and Henry Shelford, dean of Hereford.
DATED: Our manor of Whiteburne [Whitbourne], 15 Jan. 1437.

Richard Mayhew, 1504–16

SOURCE: *Registrum Ricardi Mayew Episcopi Herefordensis, A. D. 1504–1516*, ed. A. T. Bannister, C&Y 27 (1919).

1. Parliament at Westminster, 4 Feb. 1512 (pp. 146–7).
PROCTORS: Thomas [Ruthall], bishop of Durham; Edward [Vaughan], bishop of St Davids; Charles [Somerset], Lord Herbert; and George Neville [Nevill], Lord Bergavenny.
DATED: Whitborne [Whitbourne], [*no date*].

2. Parliament at Westminster, 5 Feb. 1515 (pp. 208–9).
PROCTORS: Thomas [Ruthall], bishop of Durham; Charles [Somerset], earl of Worcester; William [Atwater], bishop of Lincoln; and George [Nevill], Lord Bergavenny.
DATED: Whitborne [Whitbourne], 28 Jan. 1515.

Charles Booth (1516–35)

SOURCE: *Registrum Caroli Bothe Episcopi Herefordensis, A. D. 1516–1525*, ed. A. T. Bannister, C&Y 28 (1921).

1. Parliament at Westminster, 15 April 1523, and convocation in St. Paul's Cathedral, London, 20 April 1523 (pp. 138–9).
PROCTORS: Nicholas [West], bishop of Ely; Henry [Standish], bishop of St. Asaph; John [Veysey], bishop of Exeter; and Sir Walter Devereux, Lord Ferrers.
DATED: 2 April 1523.

2. Parliament at Westminster, 15 Jan. 1533 (p. 267).
PROCTORS: John [Longland], bishop of Lincoln; and John [Stokesley], bishop of London.
DATED: Whitborne [Whitbourne], 18 Feb. 1533.

LINCOLN

John Dalderby (1300–20)

SOURCE: Lincolnshire Archives Office, Reg. 3 (Dalderby, Memoranda).

1. Parliament at Westminster, 28 Feb. 1305 (f. 79).
PROCTORS: M. Henry de Stoke, rector of Ravensthorpe; and M. John de Fletburg [Fledborough], rector of Hougham.
DATED: [*Illegible*], Feb. 1305.

2. Letter from the clergy of the diocese (f. 108) testifying to the appointment of
M. Peter de Medbourne, rector of Ingoldsby, doctor of canon law; and John de
Horkstow, rector of Hetherington, as their proctors at the parliament at Carlisle.
DATED: [*Illegible*], 1307.

3. Parliament at Carlisle, 20 Jan. 1307 (f. 110*v*).
PROCTORS: Hugh de Normanton, canon of Lincoln; and Robert de Ashby, rector
of Hale.
DATED: Louth, 8 Jan. 1307.

4. Parliament at Westminster, 27 April 1309.
A (f. 148*v*). PROCTOR: Hugh de Normanton, canon of Lincoln.
DATED: Nettleham, 9 Feb. 1309.
B (f. 153). Letter of authority to Hugh de Normanton and M. Thomas de Bray
canons of Lincoln.
DATED: Nettleham, 16 April 1309
C (f. 153*v*). Notification that Hugh de Normanton is authorised to act as the
bishop's proctor in parliament.
DATED: Nettleham, 18 April 1309.

5. Parliament at Stamford, 27 July 1309 (f. 162*v*).
PROCTORS: M. Thomas de Bray, canon of Lincoln; and Hugh de Normanton,
canon of Lincoln.
DATED: Spaldwick, 26 July 1309.

6. King's council at London, 1310 (f. 190*v*).
PROCTORS: Hugh de Normanton, canon of Lincoln; M. Elias de Muskham, clerk;
and M. Thomas de Langtoft, clerk.
DATED: Liddington, 24 June 1310.

7. Parliament in London, 8 Aug. 1311 (f. 226).
PROCTORS: M. Thomas de Louth, canon of Lincoln; Hugh de Normanton, canon
of Lincoln; and M. Thomas de Langtoft, rector of Hykeham.
DATED: Buckden, 7 Aug. 1311.

8. Parliament at Westminster, 20 Aug. 1312 (f. 260).
PROCTORS: Hugh de Normanton, canon of Lincoln; M. Walter de Warmington,
canon of Lincoln; and M. Thomas de Langtoft, rector of Hykeham.
DATED: Banbury, 16 Aug. 1312.

9. Parliament at Westminster, 18 March 1313 (f. 272).
PROCTORS: Hugh de Normanton, canon of Lincoln; M. Walter de Warmington,
canon of Lincoln; and M. Elias de Muskham, canon of Lincoln.
DATED: Eaton Socon, 16 March 1313.

10. [*Unstated*] Parliament (f. 272*v*).
PROCTORS: M. Roger de Rothwell, archdeacon of Bedford, canon of Lincoln; M.
Gilbert de Middleton, canon of Lincoln; and Hugh de Normanton, canon of
Lincoln.
DATED: Old Temple, London, 3 April 1313

11. Parliament at Westminster, 8 July 1313 (f. 277).
PROCTORS: Hugh de Normanton, canon of Lincoln; M. Walter de Warmington,

canon of Lincoln; M. Elias de Muskham, canon of Lincoln; and John de Buckden, chaplain.
DATED: Sleaford, 28 June 1313.

12. Parliament at Westminster, 21 April 1314 [*otherwise unknown*] (f. 296).
PROCTORS: Mr. Roger de Rothwell, archdeacon of Bedford, canon of Lincoln; Hugh de Normanton, canon of Lincoln; M. Elias de Muskham, canons of Lincoln; and M. Thomas de Langtoft, rector of Hykeham.
DATED: Stow Park, 14 April 1314.
On 8 May 1314 at Stow Park the same three were appointed the bishop's proctors 'at the treaty between the king and the archbishop of Canterbury and his suffragans' (f. 297v).
On 7 May 1314 at Stow Park the same three were appointed to represent the bishop 'to make fine with the king for Scottish service at Berwick on Tweed' (f. 298).

13. Parliament at York, 9 Sept. 1314 (f. 304v).
PROCTORS: M. Roger de Rothwell, archdeacon of Bedford; and M. Thomas de Langtoft, rector of Hykeham.
DATED: Sleaford, 2 Sept 1314.

14. Parliament at Lincoln, 27 Jan. 1316 (f. 338, cf. SC 10/4/196).
PROCTORS: M. Henry de Benniworth, subdean; M. Thomas de Bray, canon of Lincoln; Hugh de Normanton, canon of Lincoln; and M. Thomas de Langtoft, canon of Lincoln.
DATED: Stow Park, 23 Jan. 1316.

15. Parliament at York, 6 May 1319 (f. 416v).
PROCTORS: M. John de Stratford, bishop's official; Sir Simon de Chaumberleyn [Chamberlain], knight; and M. Thomas de Langtoft, canon of Lincoln.
DATED: Buckden, 28 April 1319.

Thomas Bek (1342–7)
SOURCE: Lincolnshire Archives Office, Reg. 7 (Bek, Memoranda)

1. Council on Wednesday after Nativity of Blessed Virgin Mary [10 Sept] 1343 (ff. 41–41v).
PROCTORS: M. Simon Islip, canon of Lincoln; M. John Thoresby, canon of Lincoln; and Walter Grenewyk, the bishop's clerk.
DATED: Stow Park, 5 Sept. 1343.

2. Parliament at Westminster, 7 June 1344 (ff. 57v–58).
PROCTORS: M. John Thoresby, canon of Lincoln; M. John Carlton, canon of Wells; and M. William Burton, rector of Somercotes, Lincoln diocese.
DATED: Thame, 28 May 1344.

3. Parliament at Westminster, 11 Sept. 1346 (f. 85v).
PROCTORS: M. Henry de Chaddesden, archdeacon of Stow; David de Wollore, rector of Elvington; and Walter de Grenewyk, rector of a moiety of 'Causover'.
DATED: Liddington, 7 April 1346.

John Gynwell (1347–52)
SOURCE: Lincolnshire Archives Office, Reg. 9 (Gynwell, Memoranda and Institutions)

1. Parliament at Westminster, 31 March 1348 (f. 35).
PROCTORS: John St Pol, provost of Wells; Walter Power, rector of Leek; and M. Robert Barton, canon of York.
DATED: Eynsham, 29 March 1348.

John Buckingham, 1363–98
SourceL Lincolnshire Archives Office, Reg. 12 (Buckingham, Memoranda)

1. Parliament at Westminster, 4 Oct. 1363 (f. 10*v*; cf. SC 10/29/1411).
PROCTORS: M. William de Thyngehull [Thinghull], doctor of laws, bishop's official; Walter Power, canon of Lincoln; and John de Thorpe [Thorp], canon of St Paul's, London.
DATED: Lidington [Liddington], 26 Sept. 1363.

2. Parliament at Westminster, 23 Feb. 1383 (f. 260; cf. SC 10/35/1709).
PROCTORS: Mr. Walter Skirlaw, treasurer of Lincoln cathedral; and Richard Ravenser, archdeacon of Lincoln.
DATED: Buckden, 18 Feb. 1383.

3. Parliament at Westminster, 20 Oct. 1385 (f. 312; cf. SC 10/36/1757).
PROCTORS: John Waltham, archdeacon of Richmond; Richard Ravenser, archdeacon of Lincoln; M. John Barnet, official of the court of Arches [Canterbury]; and Richard Chesterfield, canon of Lincoln.
DATED: Sleaford, 11 Oct. 1385.

LONDON

Ralph Baldock (1303–13)
SOURCE: *Registrum Radulphi Baldock, Gilberti Segrave, Ricardi Newport et Stephani Gravesend, Episcoporum Londoniensium*, ed. R. C. Fowler, C&Y 7 (1911).

1. Parliament at Westminster, 18 March 1313 (p. 158).
PROCTORS: M. William de Meleford [Melford], archdeacon of Colchester; and M. William de Bray, bishop's official.
DATED: Stepney, 18 March 1313.

NORWICH

No extant appointments of proctors in the registers of this diocese.

ROCHESTER

No extant appointments of proctors in the registers of this diocese.

SALISBURY

Roger Martival (1315–30)
SOURCE: *The Registers of Roger Martival, bishop of Salisbury, 1315–1330*, ed. K. Edwards, C. R. Elrington, S. Reynolds and D. M. Owen, 4 vols., C&Y 57–9 and 68 (1963–75).

1. Parliament at York, 20 Jan. 1320 (vol. 2, pp. 254–5).
PROCTOR: M. Robert de Aylleston [Aylestone], steward of the bishop's lands.
DATED: Potterne, 8 Jan. 1320.

2. Parliament at York, 2 May 1322 (vol. 3, p. 92).
PROCTORS: M. Robert de Ayleston [Aylestone], canon of Salisbury; and John de Blebury [Blewbury], clerk.
DATED: Wymerswold [Wymeswold], 28 April 1322.

3. Parliament at Ripon, 14 Nov. 1322 (vol. 3, pp. 101–2).
PROCTORS: M. Robert de Ayleston [Aylestone], canon of Salisbury; M. John de Blebury [Blewbury], clerk; and M. Simon de Claxbi [Claxby], clerk.
DATED: Potterne, 9 Nov. 1322.

4. Parliament at Westminster, 18 Nov. 1325 (vol. 3, p. 168).
PROCTOR: M. William de Lubbenham [Lubenham], the bishop's household clerk.

5. Parliament at Lincoln, 15 Sept. 1327 (vol. 3, p. 198).
PROCTOR: M. William de Lubbenham [Lubenham].
DATED: Potterne, 1 Sept. 1327.

6. Parliament at York, 31 July 1328 (p. 208).
PROCTOR: M. William de Lubbenham [Lubenham].

Robert Wyvil (1330–75)
SourceL Wiltshire County Record Office, Reg. Wyvil, vol. 1.

1. Parliament at Westminster, 7 June 1344 (f. 124).
PROCTORS: M. John de Offord, canon of Salisbury; and William de Edyndon [Edingdon], canon of Salisbury.
DATED: 'Bourghhildeburg', 29 May 1344.

WINCHESTER

Henry Woodlock (1305–16)
SOURCE: *Registrum Henrici Woodlock Diocesis Wintoniensis A.D. 1315–1316*, ed. A. W. Goodman, vol. I, C&Y 43 (1940).

1. Parliament at Carlisle, 20 Jan. 1307 (pp. 158–9).
PROCTORS: M. Philip de Bartone [Barton], archdeacon of Surrey; M. Gilbert de Middletone [Middleton], clerk; M. John Bloyho, clerk; and M. Richard Woodlock, clerk.

2. Parliament at Westminster, 27 April 1309 (p. 356).
PROCTORS: M. Peter de Gorumville, bishop's official; M. James de Florencia, archdeacon of Winchester; and M. Philip de Bartone [Barton] archdeacon of Surrey.
DATED: Merewell [Marwell], 24 April 1309.

John Stratford (1323–33)
SOURCE: *The Register of John de Stratford, Bishop of Winchester, 1323–1333*, ed. Roy Martin Haines, vol. 1, Surrey Record Society 42 (2010).

1. Parliament or council at Lincoln, 15 Sept. 1327 (pp. 95–6).

PROCTORS: M. Thomas de Louth, treasurer, canon of Lincoln; M. John de Haryngton [Harrington], canon of Lincoln; M. Richard de Stratton, canon of Lincoln; and John de Wyndesore [Windsor], the bishop's clerk.
DATED: Waltham, 11 Sept. 1327.

2. Council at York, 31 July 1328 (p. 398).
Proctors; M. John de Brabazon, doctor of theology; and M. Richard de Byntheworth [Bintworth], doctor of canon law.
DATED: Waltham, 19 July 1328.

William of Wykeham (1367–1404)
SOURCE: *Wykeham's Register*, ed. T. F. Kirby, vol. 2, Hampshire Record Society (1900).

1. Parliament at Shrewsbury, 27 Jan. 1398 (p. 477)
PROCTORS: Richard Felde; Robert Faryngdone [Farrington]; and John de Campeden [Campden].
DATED: Highclere, 20 Jan. 1398.

WORCESTER

Thomas de Cobham (1317–27)
SOURCE: *The Register of Thomas de Cobham Bishop of Worcester 1317–1327*, ed. Ernest Harold Pearce, Worcestershire Historical Society (1930).

1. Parliament at London, 6 Oct. 1320 (p. 103).
The bishop notes that M. Nicholas de Gove, his clerk, will explain that urgent diocesan affairs will probably make it impossible to arrive punctually at parliament. He will arrive as soon as he possibly can and hereby signifies his assent to what may be decided, after due deliberation, before his arrival.
DATED: Bishop's Cleeve [1320].

Wulstan de Bransford (1334–49)
SOURCE: *The Register of Wolstan de Bransford Bishop of Worcester 1339–49*, ed. R. M. Haines, Worcestershire Historical Society 4 (1966).

1. Parliament at Westminster, 20 Jan. 1340 (p. 24).
PROCTOR: M. Robert de Chigewell [Chigwell], canon of London, with the right to appoint a substitute.
DATED: Hartlebury, 9 Jan. 1340.

2. Parliament at Westminster, 29 March 1340 (p. 61).
PROCTORS: M. Robert de Chikewell [Chigwell], canon of London.
DATED: Hartlebury, 22 March 1340.

3. Parliament at Westminster, 12 July 1340 (p. 36).
PROCTORS: M. R[obert] de Chigwell; and Thomas de Evesham.
DATED: Blockley, 3 July 1340.

4. Parliament at Westminster, 28 April 1343 (p. 302).
PROCTORS: M. John de Severleye [Severley], the bishop's chancellor; and D. William de Salwarp, steward of the bishop's household.
DATED: Hartlebury, 22 April 1343.

5. Council at Westminster, 18 April 1344 (p. 305).
PROCTORS: M. John de Thoresby; M. John de Severleye [Severley]; and D. John de Stok [Stoke].

6. Parliament at Westminster, 7 June 1344 (p. 307).
PROCTORS: M. John de Thoresby; M. John de Severleye [Severley]; and D. John de Stok [Stoke].

7. Council ['parliament' in the margin] at Westminster, 3 Feb. 1346 (p. 318).
PROCTORS: M. John de Severleye [Severley]; and D. John de Stoke.
DATED: Alvechurch, 22 January 1346.

Henry Wakefield (1375–95)
SOURCE: *A Calendar of the Register of Henry Wakefield Bishop of Worcester 1375–95*, ed. Warwick Paul Marett, Worcestershire Historical Society, New Series 7 (1972).

1. Parliament at Westminster, 3 Nov. 1391 (pp. 72–3).
PROCTORS: M. Thomas de Stowe, archdeacon of Bedford; and Mr. John Burbache [Burbage], doctor of laws.
DATED: Withington, 28 Oct. 1391.

YORK

Walter Giffard (1266–79)
SOURCE: *The Register of Walter Giffard, Lord Archbishop of York 1266–1279*, ed. William Broun, Surtees Society 109 (1905).

1. Parliament at Westminster, 13 Oct. 1275 (p. 305).
PROCTOR: M. W., bishop's official.
DATED: Bolton in Craven, 7 Oct. 1275

William Zouche (1342–52)
SOURCE: Borthwick Institute, York, Reg. 10.

1. Parliament at Westminster, 14 Jan. 1348 (f. 246).
Proctors M. Ralph [*Damaged*]hull [Turvill], canon of York and Beverley; and M. Gilbert de Welton, canon of York and Beverley.
DATED: Ripon, 4 Jan. 1348

2. Parliament at Westminster 17 March 1348 (ff. 246v–247).
PROCTORS: D. John de St Pol, canon of York; M. Gilbert de Welton, canon of York; and D. John de Wynwyk [Winwick] canon of York.
DATED: Burton by Beverley, 26 March 1348.

3. Parliament at Westminster, 9 Feb. 1351 (f. 249v).
PROCTORS: M. [Gilbert] de Welton, doctor of laws; and D. John de Wynewyk [Winwick], canon of York.
DATED: Ripon, 4 Feb. 1351.

4. Parliament at Westminster, 13 Jan. 1352 (f. 252).
PROCTORS: M. Gilbert de Welton, doctor of laws, canon of York; David de Wollore, canon of York; and Henry de Ingelby [Ingleby], canon of York.
DATED: Ripon 12 Jan. 1352.

Sede Vacante (1405–8)
Source: *The York Sede Vacante Register 1405–1408: a calendar*, ed. Joan Kirby, Borthwick Texts and Calendars 28 (2002).

1. Parliament at Gloucester, 20 October 1407 (p. 52).
Writ addressed to the keepers of the spirituality of the see [the chapter].
Proctors for the chapter: M. John Prophete [Prophet], dean and keeper of the king's privy seal; M. Roger Coryngham [Corringham], archdeacon of York; [John] Wakerying [Wakering], master in chancery; John Rome, master in chancery; Robert Wolveden, canon of York; and Simon Gaunstede [Gaunstead], canons of the cathedral.
Dated: York, 10 Oct. 1407.

York Minster Library MS 22[1]

This formulary was apparently drawn up for the use of Philip Repingdon, bishop of Lincoln November 1404–November 1419. A pencil note on the inside cover says, 'A book of legal formulas formerly belonging to the Lord Fairfax. 135 folios some blank (mainly ecclesiastical)'. On the first parchment sheet is the name William ffothong or Folhong, and on the dorse, in an eighteenth-century hand is the inscription: 'For my good friende Mr. Thomas Thompson keeper of the records att Yorke, from ffairfax.' On folio 5 is a list of the bishops of Lincoln from Hugh Wells to Philip Repingdon. The names of the next three bishops, Fleming, Grey and Alnwick, follow in a different ink.

It seems likely that the need to record these forms for obeying the writs of summons to parliament arose from the practice under Henry IV of proroguing parliaments not only to different times but to different places. The next entries in the manuscript after f. 72v concern the raising of clerical taxes.

Size: 16.5 cm. high x 12.5 cm. wide.

(Headings and margin flags are CAPITALISED. Doubtful readings are <u>underlined</u>. Extensions are in *italics*. Editorial additions in square brackets).

f. 72.

DE EXECUCIONIBUS BREVIUM REGIORUM
EXECUCIO PRO PARLIAMENTO QUO ARCHIDIACONUM ETC.

P etc. archi*diacono* seu eius Offici*ali* salutem etc. Breve domini nostri Regis nuper cum ea qua decuit reverenter recepimus in haec verba, Henricus etc. Execucio-*nem* igitur debite breve predictum in quantum ad nos attinet demandare volentes premissa omnia et singula in eodem brevi contenta premunicionis via ad vestram per presentes deducimus et per vos ad cleri archidiaconatus predicti noticiam deduci, vos volumus et mandamus ut eisdem pareat et pareant facia*tis* et faciant que vobis archidiaconus et eis incumbunt in hac parte quatenus mandatum mandatum [sic] regium antedictum vos et clerum eundem de iure et consuetudine ad id artare poterit seu debebit cite*tis* insuper peremptor*ie* clerum archidiaconatus predicti quod compareat coram nobis aut in nostro in hac parte commiss*ario* in ecclesia etc. die etc. duos procuratores sufficientes et ydoneos una cum clero aliorum archidiaconatuum dicte dio*cesis* in ea parte elect*os* ordinatur*os* et transmis-sur*os* in forma superius annotata, necnon super expen*is* dictorum procuratorum concorditer tractatur*is*, provisur*is* et ordinatur*is* ulterius que securis et receptur*is* quod sit iustum. Et quid fe*ceritis* in premissis etc. Dat' etc.

---

f. 72. DE EODEM DECANO ET CAPITULO

P etc. decano et capitulo ecclesie nostre Linc*olniensis* salutem. Breve domini nostri reg*is* etc. ut supra. Execucioni igitur debite breve predictum in quantum ad nos attinet et demandare volentes premissa omnia et singula in eodem brevi contenta ad vestram et cuiuslibet vestrum via premunicionis noticiam deducimus et deduci, volumus per presentes vobis mandantes ut eisdem pareatis ac cetera faciatis que vobis incumbunt in hac parte quatenus dictum mandatum regium vos et vestrum quemlibet de iure vel consuetudine ad id facien*dum* artare poterit aut debebit die que et loco in brevi predicto assignatis videlicet decanus in propria \vestra/ persona ac vos capitulum per unun procuratorem ydoneum plenam et sufficientem a vobis potestatem habentem intersitis et et [sic] compareatis iuxta eiusdem brevis regii exigenciam et tenorem nos reddentes de omn*nibus* et quod duxeritis facien*dis* in premissis citra festum etc. plenar*ie* certiores litteras vestras paten*tes* haben[?] hunc tenorem etc. Dat' etc.

DECANO ET CAPITULO PROROGACIONE PARLIAMENTI[2]

P etc. decano et capitulo etc. Licet nos nuper auctoritate cuiusdam brevis regii nobis directi vobis per nostras certi tenoris litteras dederimus in mandatis ut vos decano [?] personaliter, capitulum que per unum procuratorem sufficientem et ydoneum, in parliamento apud C tercio die instantis mensis Septembr*is* [sic] prout tunc provisum fuerat et ordinatum interessetis super certis negociis statum et defensionem regni et ecclesie anglican*e* concernentibus tractatur*is*. Quia tamen propter temporis brevitatem inter dictum tercium diem Decembr*is* et festum nat*iv-itatis* domini prox*imum* \tunc/ sequen*tem* necnon negotium in eodem parliamento ventilandorum et discuciendorum ordinitatem dictum parliamentum effectum aliter neque commode eo tempore nequinerat terminari idem que parliamentum usque Crastinum sancti Hillarii promixam [sic] futur*um* apud W deo dante tenendo pro quiete magnatum et aliorum illuc veniencium ac pleniore discussione et terminacione nequorum ibidem terminandorum extitit prorogatum prout in alio brevi regio nobis iam noviter liberato cuius tenorem eo quod in certis contentis in eodem cum tenore [f. 72v] alterius vobis iam predictum ob eandem causam in litteris nostris missi plene concordat ly [sic; concorditer??] miserere [one illeg word] oportet, vobis igitur auctoritate dicti brevis regii atque nostra, mandamus firmiter iniungentes quatinus in parliamento apud W in crastino sancti Hillarii ut premittitur tenendo secundum vim, formam et effectum primarum litterarum nostrarum vobis inde directarum omn*e* excusacione postposita intersit secur*e* et receptur*e* in omnibus et per omnia quod ex communi consilio Regis et regni ad eorum quomodum et utilitatem divina favente clemencia contigerit ordinari. Dat' etc.

f. 72v. ARCHIDIACO DE EODEM

P etc archidiaco etc. Licet nos nuper auctoritate cuiusdam brevis regii nobis directi per nostras certi tenoris litteras tenorem brevis huiusmodi in se contenentes vobis dedeximus specialiter in mandat*is* ut vos archid*iacono* ceterique abbates et priores ac alii ecclesiarum prelati dicti archidiaconatus personaliter clerus que per procuratores sufficientes in parliamento apud C tercio die instant*i* mensis Septembris

---

[2]   This must relate to the parliament summoned on 20 October 1403 to meet at Coventry on 3 December, but which was prorogued to meet at Westminster on 14 January 1404.

etc. ut supra usque h'[sic] verba vobis igitur, auctoritate dicti brevis regii atque nostra, mandamus firmiter iniungentes quatinus in parliamento apud W in crastino sancti Hillarii ut premittitur iam tenendo iuxta unam formam et officium priorum nostrarum litterarum vobis inde directarum, omn*e* excusacione postposita, personaliter intersitis premunientes clerum vestrum archidiaconatus ut procuratores sui ab eisdem una cum clero aliorum archiadiaconatuum nostre dioc*esis* als [?] in tle [?] ecclesia electi dictis die et loco similiter intersint future [?] receptum etc ut *aria*

f. 72v. COMMISSIO AD INTERESSENDUM IN ELECCIONE PROCURATORUM CLERI PRO PARLIAMENTO

P. etc. ad recipiendum certificatoria omnium et singularum archideaconorum sive Offic*iorum* eorundem dicte nostre dioc*esis* de et super mandatis nuper eis directis ad citandum et premuniendum clerum dictorum archidiaconatuum vigore brevis regii eisdem nostris mandat*i* contenti in quantum breve huiusmodi de iure aut consuetudine clerum eundem artare poterit debebit quod die lune proxime futur*e* intersint in ecclesia etc per procuratores sufficientes ad hoc constitutos ad eligend*um* iuxta formam dict*i* brev*is* annotatam duos procuratores qui vice et nomine cleri ipsius die et loco quod brevi eodem designat*os* intersint factur' [?] quod ipsius tenorium [?] exigit et requirit eleccioni que eidem presidend*um* et eam admittend*um* acnon comparentum contumacio*nis* puniend*um* necnon de expensis procuratorum ibidem eligendorum providend*orum* et ordinand*orum* ac moderand*orum* easdem et limitand*orum*. Cetera que exequend*a* et expendiend*a* que in premissis necces*aria* fuerint aut legitime requesita, vobis etc committimus vices nostras cum cuiuslibet cohercionis canonice potestate, mandantes quat*inus* nos de omn*ne* eo quod factum fuerit in premissis una cum certicator*io* supradictis citra festum etc. Certific*etis* etc.

f. 119. PROCUR*ATORES* PRO EPISCOPO IN PARLIAMENTO[3]

Universis pateat per presentes quod nos P etc Linc' episc*copus* ordinamus, fecimus, facimus et constituimus discretos viros A B et C licet absen*tes* tanquam presentes etc procuratores ac dantes et concedentes eisdem procuratoribus nostris et eorum omnilibet etc. <u>specialem</u> potestatem etc. ad comparend*um* et interesend*um* nomine nostro et pro nobis coram in Christo principe etc. rege etc. ac ceteris prelatis, magnatibus, proceribus et aliis de parliamento dicti domini nostri Reg*is* apud Westmon-*asterium* die veneris prox*ima* post festum Sancte <u>Lucie</u>[4] prox*imum* futur*um* celebrand*o* cum contumacione et prorogacione dictorum tunc sequen*tum* et locorum [? illeg.] necnon super negociis quibuscumque <u>statutum</u> dicti regni et ecclesie Anglicane concernen*tis* in dicto parliamento declarand*is*' seu exponend*is*, tractand*is*, et consulend*is* ac etiam ad consensciend*um* hiis que ibidem ex <u>communi</u> deliberacione et consilio dicti regni ad dei honorem et ecclesie ac regni predictorum publicam utilitatem congerit ordinary, absenciam que nostram a dicto parliamento excusand*am* causas que absencie et excusacionis nostrarum huiusmodi propondend*as*, allegand*as* et proband*as* iuramen*tam* que quodnosque in hac parte neccesari*am* et requisitum in <u>animam</u> nostram prestand*am*. Ceteraque omnia et singula facienda,

---

[3] This document is damaged in part of the right-hand side.

[4] If my reading is correct, this is the saint whose feast was on 13 Dec. In 1409 the following Friday would have been 20 Dec., though the parliament was prorogued to 18 December at Westminster. This is the only parliament which seems at all possible.

gerenda, procuranda, et exercenda ac expedienda quod in premissis ac pr?ctum quoque nos ratum, gratum, et simul igitur quicquid per dictos procuratores nostros vel eorum aliquid actum, factum, questum ve fuerit in premissis et quolibet eorundem sub omnia bonorum iuratorum oblicacione et ypotha cautiones que exponimus per presentes. In quorum omnium et testimonium etc.

APPENDIX 6

Proctors of Peterborough Abbey

The Register of Peterborough Abbey during the abbacies of William Genge (1398–1409) and John Deeping (1409–38) is found in the British Library (Add. MS. 25288). It contains fourteen writs of summons to parliament, and in twelve cases this is followed by a record of the proctors appointed by the abbot for the relevant assembly. This register was clearly a fair copy, since it is extremely neat with none of the crossings out and changes of hand which characterise working registers. The fact that the 1419 entry (f. 109) is out of sequence would support this. Most of these entries have equivalents in SC 10, which are noted below, although the two are not always identical. It is also notable that there are letters surviving in SC 10 for which there are no corresponding entries in the register.

William Genge (1398–1409)

1. Parliament at Westminster (14 January 1404).
PROCTORS: M. John Kynlton [Keynton], clerk and F. Thomas Faversham, monk of abbey.
DATED: Peterborough, 11 January 1404
FOLIO REFERENCE: 29*v*–30 [*cf.* SC 10/41/2040].

John Deeping (1409–38)

1. Parliament at Leicester (30 April 1414).
PROCTORS: John Rome*, clerk and F. Richard Harleton, monk of house.
DATED: Peterborough, 1 May 1414.
FOLIO REFERENCE: 60 [*cf.* SC 10/44/2199].

2. Parliament at Westminster (16 March 1416).
PROCTORS: M. David Prys [ap Rees]*, clerk and F. Thomas Fannell, monk of abbey.
DATED: Peterborough, 13 March 1416.
FOLIO REFERENCE: 71.

3. Parliament at Westminster (16 November 1417).
PROCTORS: William Acton [Aghton]*, archdeacon of Bedford and F. Thomas Fannell, monk of abbey.
DATED: Peterborough, 13 November 1417.
FOLIO REFERENCE: 78 [*cf.* SC 10/46/2286].

4. Parliament at Westminster (16 October 1419).
PROCTORS: William Acton [Aghton]*, archdeacon of Bedford, M. Robert Keten [Ketton]* and M. David Prys [ap Rees]*, clerks.
DATED: Peterborough, 11 October 1419.
FOLIO REFERENCE: 109.

5. Parliament at Westminster (9 November 1422).
Proctors: M. Thomas Whiston*, D. William Acton [Aghton]*, archdeacon of Bedford and F. Walter Frysney [Friskney]*, monk of abbey.
Dated: Peterborough, 6 November 1422.
Folio reference: 88*v* [*cf.* SC 10/47/2335].

6. Parliament at Westminster (20 October 1423).
Proctors: M. T[homas] Brouns* and M. David appe Rys [ap Rees]*, clerks, and F. Walter Frysney [Friskney]*, monk of abbey.
Dated: Peterborough, 16 October 1423.
Folio reference: 113 [*cf.* SC 10/48/2352].

7. Parliament at Leicester (18 February 1426).
Proctors: M. Thomas Brouns*, Thomas Smyth* and Thomas Osborne, clerks, F. Walter Frysnay [Friskney]*, monk of abbey, and Ralph Jolyff.
Dated: Peterborough, 14 February 1426.
Folio reference: 128 [*cf.* SC 10/48/2386].

8. Parliament at Westminster (13 October 1427).
Proctors: Nicholas Dykson [Dixon]* and William Prestewyk [Prestwick]* clerks, William Tresham*, and Ralph Jolyff.
Dated: Peterborough, 19 October 1427.
Folio reference: 139.

9. Parliament at Westminster (22 September 1429).
Proctors: D. Thomas Smyth*, clerk, F. Walter Frysney [Friskney]* monk of abbey, Thomas Brigg [Bridge] and Ralph Jolyff.
Dated: Peterborough, 17 September 1429.
Folio reference: 142*v* [*cf.* 13 (16) in File 48].

10. Parliament at Westminster (12 January 1431).
Proctors: William Tresham*, M. John Kyrkeby [Kirkby]*, clerk of parliament, Thomas Brygg [Bridge] and Ralph Jolyff.
Dated: Peterborough, 9 January 1431.
Folio reference: 143*v* [*cf.* SC 10/49/2403].

11. Parliament at Westminster (12 May 1432).
Proctors: Nicholas Dykson [Dixon]* and William Prestewyk [Prestwick]*, clerks, William Tresham*, and Ralph Jolyff.
Dated: Peterborough, 8 May 1432.
Folio reference: 145 [*cf.* SC 10/49/2409].

12. Parliament at Westminster (8 July 1433).
Proctors: William Prestewyk [Prestwick]*, clerk, William Tresham*, F. William Exton, monk of abbey, and Ralph Jolyff.
Dated: Peterborough, 6 July 1433.
Folio reference: 147*v*.

13. Parliament at Westminster (10 October 1435).
Proctors: William Tresham*, William Prestewyk [Prestwick]* and Ralph Jolyff.
Dated: 8 October 1435.
Folio reference: 156–156*v* [*cf.* SC 10/49/2423].

Biographical Details for Proctors

This list gives brief additional details for those proctors marked in the main text with an asterisk, but makes no pretence to be exhaustive; we have tried merely to indicate the types of background from which the proctors were drawn. In seeking to identify individuals we have erred on the side of caution, especially in respect of laymen. Some surnames were too common to be useful in identification, while in many families the same Christian name might be used in several generations, or in different branches of the family. Widely divergent alternative spellings are indicated in brackets, and problematic identifications in *italics*. In the sixteenth century, the proctors were all bishops, abbots or secular peers, whose careers are well known or can be easily traced elsewhere, and therefore they have not been included here.

In addition to the volumes listed below in the abbreviations, the following sources have been consulted: *Calendar of Close Rolls*; *Calendar of Patent Rolls*; J. H. Baker, *The Order of Serjeants at Law*, Selden Society, supplementary series 5 (1984); *The Medieval Court of Arches*, ed. F. Donald Logan, C&Y 95 (2005); *Officers of the Exchequer*, compiled by J. C. Sainty, List and Index Society, special series 18 (1983); *Return of the Name of Every Member of the Lower House of the Parliaments of England, Scotland and Ireland*, vol. I (1878); *List of Sheriffs for England and Wales from the Earliest Times to A.D. 1831*, Public Record Office, Lists and Indexes no. IX (reprinted New York, 1963); *List of Escheators for England and Wales*, compiled by A. C. Wood, List and Index Society 72 (1971); Sir John Sainty, *The Judges of England 1272–1990*, Selden Society, supplementary series 10 (1993); Nigel Saul, *Knights and Esquires: The Gloucestershire Gentry in the Fourteenth Century* (Oxford, 1981); David M. Smith, *The Heads of Religious Houses: England & Wales, III, 1377–1540* (Cambridge, 2008); Chris Given-Wilson, *The Royal Household and the King's Affinity: Service, Politics and Finance in England 1360–1413* (New Haven and London, 1986); Robert Somerville, *History of the Duchy of Lancaster, 1365–1603* (London, 1953); R. L. Storey, 'Gentleman-bureaucrats', in *Profession, Vocation, and Culture in Late Medieval England: Essays Dedicated to the Memory of A. R. Myers*, ed. Cecil H. Clough (Liverpool, 1982), pp. 90–29; T. F. Tout, *Chapters in the Administrative History of Mediaeval England*, 6 vols. (Manchester, 1920–33); John Grassi, 'Royal Clerks in the Diocese of York in the Fourteenth Century', *Northern History* 5 (1970), 12–33; John le Neve, *Fasti Ecclesie Anglicanae 1300–1541*, 12 vols. (revised edition: London, 1962–7); J. H. Wylie, *History of England under Henry IV*, 4 vols. (London, 1884–98); A. L. Brown, 'The Privy Seal Clerks in the Early Fifteenth Century', in *The Study of Medieval Records: Essays in honour of Kathleen Major*, ed. D. A. Bullough and R. L. Storey (Oxford, 1971), pp. 260–81; J. Otway-Ruthven, *The King's Secretary and the Signet Office in the XV Century* (Cambridge, 1939); *Discovery*, the online catalogue of The National Archives; and the card index of chancery clerks in the map room of TNA. In an attempt to compensate for the fact that the magisterial works of Tout (1399) and Wilkinson (1377) end during this period, the receivers of petitions in parliament have been systematically identified.

The following abbreviations are used.

E   A biography appears in A. B. Emden, *A Biographical Register of the University of Oxford to A.D. 1500*, 3 vols. (Oxford, 1957–9).

E:Ca A biography appears in A. B. Emden, *A Biographical Register of the University of Cambridge to 1500* (Oxford, 1963).

HoP   A biography appears either in *The History of Parliament: The House of Commons, 1386–1421*, ed. J. S. Roskell, Linda Clarke and Carole Rawcliffe, 4 vols. (Stroud, 1992), or in *History of Parliament: Biographies of Members of the Commons House*, ed. Josiah C. Wedgwood and Anne D. Holt (London, 1936).

O   A biography appears in the *Oxford Dictionary of National Biography*.

R   Chancery clerk for whom a career summary appears in Malcolm Richardson, *The Medieval Chancery under Henry V* (List and Index Society, Special Series vol. 30, 1999).

W   Chancery clerk for whom a career summary appears in B. Wilkinson, *The Chancery under Edward III* (Manchester, 1929).

Abingdon, John	King's clerk.
Acton, Edward	Sheriff of Shropshire, 1382–3, 1384–5 and 1389–90.
Aghton, William	Chancery clerk; receiver of petitions, 1415; archdeacon of Bedford, 1405–23; R.
Airmyn, William	Chancery clerk (Ayrmyne, Ermyn).
Alderford, John	*Either* (1) chancery clerk *or* (2) MP for Norwich 1406, Feb. 1413, Apr. 1414 and 1427; sheriff of Norfolk, 1428–9; HoP.
Allerthorpe, Laurence	Baron of the exchequer, 1375–1400; treasurer, 1401–2.
Alnwick, William	Archdeacon of Salisbury, 1420–6; king's secretary, 1421–2; keeper of the privy seal, 1422–32; bishop of Norwich, 1426–36; bishop of Lincoln, 1436–49; E; O.
Andrew, John	MP for Cricklade, Wilts., 1378, Jan. 1380, 1381, May 1382, Feb. 1383, April 1384, 1385, 1386 and Feb. 1388; HoP.
Andrew, Richard	King's clerk, 1433; king's secretary, 1442–55; E.
Andrew, Robert [II]	MP for Cricklade, Wilts., 1399; MP for Wilts., March 1416, 1422, 1426 and 1433; HoP.
Appleby, John	Envoy to the curia, 1358–63/5, and to France and Bavaria, 1372; dean of St Paul's, 1364–89; E.
Aston, Thomas	MP for Staffs., Jan. 1380, Apr. 1384, Sept. 1388, 1393, 1399 and 1406; HoP.

Asty, Henry	Serjeant at law, 1373; chief baron of the exchequer, 1375–80; justice of common pleas, 1380–3 (Hasty).
Babington, William	Chief baron of the exchequer, 1419–22; justice of common pleas, 1420–2; chief justice of common pleas, 1423–36; O.
Babthorpe, Ralph	Squire of the king's household, 1451–2 (Babthorpe).
Babthorpe, Robert	Steward of honour of Leicester, 1406–37; controller of the household, 1419–?; brother of William.
Babthorpe, William	King's attorney in common pleas, 1420–9; baron of the exchequer, 1429–43; brother of Robert.
Bacon, John	King's clerk; archdeacon of Richmond, 1383–5.
Baketon, Thomas	Advocate of the court of Arches, admitted 1371, appointed 1382, reappointed 1384; E:Ca.
Barel, John	Envoy to the counts of Holland and Cleves, 1401; E (Barell).
Barnet, John [junior]	King's clerk; chancery clerk of Black prince in Aquitaine, 1363; official of bishop of Lincoln, 1373; E.
Barrow, William	Chancellor of the University of Oxford, 1413–14, 1415–16 and 1416–17; bishop of Bangor, 1418–23; bishop of Carlisle, 1423–9; O.
Barton, Peter	Chancery clerk; greater clerk of chancery, 1376–95; receiver of petitions, 1377–91, 1394 and 1395; W.
Barton, Thomas	Advocate of the consistory court of Wells; E (second entry).
Bate, John	Chancery clerk; clerk of parliament, 1437; receiver of petitions, 1439–47, Feb. 1449, Nov. 1449 and 1450; R.
Bate, Thomas	MP for Warks., 1442 and Feb. 1449.
Bath, John	Secretary of archbishop Arundel, occ. 1412; E (Bathe).
Bealknap, Robert	Chief justice of common pleas, 1374–88; O.
Beaufort, Henry	Dean of Wells, 1396–8; bishop of Lincoln, 1398–1404; chancellor, 1403–5, 1413–17 and 1424–6; bishop of Winchester, 1404–47; papal legate *a latere*, 1417–21; cardinal, 1427–47; O.
Beckingham, Thomas	King's clerk; archdeacon of Northampton, 1402–3; archdeacon of Lincoln, 1403–7; E.
Beckingham, Thomas	MP for Berks., 1419 and 1431; HoP.
Beckington, Thomas	Archdeacon of Buckingham, 1424–43; king's secretary, c. 1438–43; bishop of Bath and Wells, 1443–65; E; O.

Belasis, John	Esquire; commissioned to supervise the repair of Roxburgh castle, 1418 (Belassys).
Belne, Thomas	MP for Worcester, Jan. 1390, 1391, 1393, 1394, 1395, Jan. 1397, 1399, 1402, 1407 and 1410; HoP.
Bernard, John	King's clerk by 1402; E:Ca.
Besford, John	A co-executor of the will of Henry Wakfield, bishop of Worcester.
Beverage, Robert	Chancery clerk.
Bicknell, William	Royal commissioner, 1443 and 1446; E (Byconyell).
Billingford, James	Chancery clerk; chief clerk of chancery, 1396; R.
Bishopstone, John	Chancellor of Chichester, 1371–84.
Blaunchard, John	Commissioner to visit royal free chapel of Hastings, 1361; commissioner of *oyer* and *terminer*, 1383; archdeacon of Worcester, 1371–83; E.
Blodwell, John	Dean of St Asaph, by 1429–?; E.
Bloghwy, John	Landholder by free alms.
Bolton, Richard	Deputy chancellor at Lancaster, 1406; chancery clerk of the second form, occ. 1370s–1413; R.
Boulers, Reginald	Abbot of St Peter's, Gloucester, 1437–50; bishop of Hereford, 1450–3; bishop of Coventry and Lichfield, 1453–9; O.
Bowet, Henry	Bishop of Bath & Wells, 1401–7; archbishop of York, 1407–23; E; O.
Bowland, John	Chancery clerk; receiver of petitions, 1377–85 (Bouland).
Bradshaw, Nicholas	Attorney for Henry Bolingbroke, 1398 (Bradshagh).
Bray, William	E [probably Mag. Wm Bray ii].
Brayton, Robert	Chancery clerk.
Brewster, William	Under-clerk of the kitchen, 1425; clerk of the kitchen, 1430, retired by 1446.
Brinkley, Richard	Examiner-general of court of arches, 1384 and 1397; royal judicial commissioner, 1402x1408; E:Ca (Brinkelee, Brynkley).
Brocas, Arnold	Clerk of the king's works, 1381–8; chamberlain of the exchequer, 1388–95.
Broun, John	MP for Warwick, 1431.
Brouns, Thomas	Subdean of Lincoln, 1414–19; archdeacon of Stow, 1419–?1427; chancellor of the archbishop of Canterbury, 1423–31; archdeacon of Berkshire, 1427–31; dean of Salisbury, 1431–5; bishop of Norwich, 1435–45; E; O.
Bubwith, Nicholas	Chancery clerk; receiver of petitions, Sept. 1397 and 1402–4; archdeacon of Dorset, 1397–1406; archdeacon of Richmond, 1401–2; king's secretary, 1402; bishop of London, 1406–7; bishop of Salis-

	bury, 1407; bishop of Bath and Wells, 1407–24; treasurer, 1407–8; E; O.
Bullock, Walter	Dean of St Asaph, dates unknown [*not known from other sources, but described as such in SC 10 letters from 1420, 1421 and 1422*]; archdeacon of Derby, ?–1431; E.
Burbage, John	Commissioner to hear cases in courts of admiralty and chivalry, 1391; E (Burbache).
Burdet, Thomas	MP for Warks., 1394, 1401, 1406 and 1419; sheriff of Warks. and Leics., 1415–16; HoP.
Burgoyn, Thomas	MP for Cambs., 1442; MP for London, 1445–6 and 1447; HoP (Burgoyne).
Burley, William	MP for Shropshire, 1417, 1419, 1420, May 1421, 1422, 1425, 1427–8, 1429–30, 1431, 1432, 1433, 1435, 1437, 1439–40, 1442, 1445–6, 1449–50, 1450–1 and 1455–6; HoP (Borley, Boerley).
Burstall, William	Chancery clerk; greater clerk of chancery, 1370–81; keeper of the rolls, 1371–81; keeper of the Domus Conversorum, 1371–81; keeper of the great seal, 1371 and 1377; W.
Burton, John	Chancery Clerk; receiver of petitions, 1388–94;W.
Byde, William	Advocate of the court of Arches, 1369; official of Exeter, 1370–91; commissioner to hear appeals in the court of chivalry, 1385; E.
Camme, William	Benefactor of Malmesbury Abbey, occ. 1386.
Cammell, John	Chancery clerk; receiver of petitions, 1442, 1445, Nov. 1449 and 1450; R.
Campden, John	Assistant to William of Wykeham in founding his colleges; E (Campeden).
Carlton, Nicholas	King's clerk; archdeacon of Taunton, 1416–41.
Cassy, John	Chief baron of the exchequer, 1389–1400.
Castell, Robert	MP for Warks., April 1414, 1422; HoP.
Cawood, William	Envoy to Scotland, 1390; commissioner in court of chivalry, 1392; E (Cawode).
Cergeaux, Michael	Dean of the Court of Arches; archdeacon of Dorset, 1396–7; E.
Chamberlain, William	MP for Southampton, 1427, 1429, 1431, 1433, 1435.
Champneys, William	*Either* (1) Life retainer of Henry IV; renewed by Henry V *or* (2) chancery clerk; R.
Charlton, Robert	Serjeant at law, 1383; chief justice of common pleas, 1388–95; O.
Charwelton, Thomas	Abbot of Thorney, 1402–26.
Cheney, William	Serjeant at law, 1412; justice of king's bench, 1415–24; chief justice of king's bench, 1424–38 (Cheyne, Cheyney).

Chesterfield, Adam   Controller of works, Tower of London and Palace of Westminster, 1355–75.

Chesterfield, Richard   Clerk of the exchequer, occ. 1360; under treasurer of the exchequer, 1361–7; canon of Lincoln, 1363–1405; E.

Chichele, Henry   Bishop of St Davids, 1408–14; archbishop of Canterbury, 1414–43; O.

Chitterne, John   Chancery clerk; receiver of petitions, 1393, Sept. 1397, 1399–1413; archdeacon of Salisbury, 1407–19; R.

Clavering, John   Knight; MP for Northumberland, 1406; HoP.

Clere, Edmund   MP for Norfolk, 1447; HoP.

Clerk, John   Chancery clerk, occ. 1396–1415; clerk of the crown 1409; R.

Cliderow, John   Bishop of Bangor, 1423–35.

Cole, James   *One of two men of that name, probably proctor of the court of Arches; E.*

Cole, John   MP for Bridgwater, 1394; HoP.

Colnet, Nicholas   King's clerk and physician to Henry V; E.

Coniston, Richard   Chancellor of the archbishop of York, 1381 and 1400; E (Conyngeston).

Cordon, Richard   Advocate of the court of Arches, 1421; E (*alias* Broune).

Corringham, Roger   Archdeacon of York, 1405–12; king's confessor, 1406–11; E.

Coychurch, Lewis   Archdeacon of Lewes, by 1419–after 1442.

Cyffin, Hywel   Attended the trial of Sir John Oldcastle, 1413; E (Kyffin).

Dalton, Peter   Chancery clerk.

David, John   Chancellor of St Davids Cathedral, 1361–1407.

Dent, John de   Escheator of Yorks., 1384–5.

Derby, William   Baron of the exchequer, 1435–8.

Derham, Richard   Dean of St Martin-le-Grand; E:Ca.

Dighton, William   King's clerk; canon of Salisbury, 1363–91.

Dixon, Nicholas   Clerk of the pipe, 1413–21; clerk of the treasurer, 1421–2; baron of the exchequer, 1423–34.

Dokwra, Roger   Chaplain to Humphrey duke of Gloucester, occ. 1416 [TNA SC 8/229/11410]; E.

Donnington, William   Hosier of Coventry [TNA C 1/43/71]; recorder of Coventry.

Drew, Laurence   MP for Berks., 1385, Feb. 1388, Sept. 1388, 1391, 1406 and Nov. 1414; HoP.

Duffield, Richard   MP for Grimsby, May 1413, Nov. 1414, 1420, Dec. 1421, 1422, 1423, 1425, 1426, 1431, 1432, 1433 and 1435.

Duffield, Thomas	E.
Elmer, John	Advocate of the court of Arches, 1394; commissioner to hear appeals from courts of chivalry, 1390 and 1403; E.
Emond, John	King's esquire, occ. 1409.
Enderby, Albin	Of Somersby and Enderby, Lincs.; the recipient of many local commissions.
Enderby, Thomas	Son of Albin; parliamentary elector of Lincs., 1411.
Esbache, Robert	Commissioner to hear appeal from the court of admiralty, 1409; prebendary of Dasset Parve, Lichfield cathedral, 1387–1413.
Estcourt, John	King's clerk; examiner-general of the court of Arches 1414–21; E.
Everdon, John	Chancery clerk.
Ewen, William	Chancery clerk; R.
Eynsham, John	Abbot of Hyde near Winchester, 1381–94.
Farrington, Robert	Chancery clerk; receiver of petitions Feb. 1383, Oct.1383, April 1384, Nov. 1384, 1385, 1386, Feb. 1388, Jan. 1390, Nov. 1390, 1391, 1393 and 1394.
Felbridge, George	King's yeoman, 1361; king's esquire, 1367.
Felyp, John	MP for Worcs., May 1413; HoP (Phelip).
Field, Thomas	Clerk in the privy seal office, 1404–*post* 1414; dean of Hereford, 1404–19; E (Felde).
Findern, John	Foreign apposer of the Exchequer, 1399–1406 and *c.* 1410–12.
Fleet, William	*Either* (1) One of a family of Boston and London merchants, many of whom were called William *or* (2) clerk in the privy seal office, *ante* 1398–*post* 1422 (Flete).
Flore, Roger	MP for Rutland, Jan. 1397, 1399, 1402, Oct. 1404, April 1414, Nov. 1414, 1415, March 1416, Oct. 1416, 1417, 1419 and 1422; HoP.
Folkingham, John	Chancery clerk.
Ford, Thomas	King's clerk.
Fordham, John	Prebendary of the 'golden' prebend of Mathry, 1376–81; dean of Wells, 1379–81; bishop of Durham, 1381–8; bishop of Ely, 1388–1425; O.
Forest, John	Archdeacon of Surrey, 1414–?; dean of Wells, 1425–46; E.
Forster, Thomas	King's clerk.
Frank, John	Chancery clerk; receiver of petitions, April 1414 and 1415–37; keeper of the rolls, 1423–38; archdeacon of Suffolk, 1421–41; R.
Freton, John	Chancery clerk; archdeacon of Norfolk, 1375–85;

	greater clerk of chancery, 1376–?; receiver of petitions, Oct. 1377 and 1379–84; W.
Frye, Robert	Clerk of the privy seal office, *c.* 1387–*post* 1425.
Fulbourn, William	King's clerk.
Gabriel, Richard	Chancery clerk from 1396; R.
Gare, Robert	MP for Appleby, 1395 and 1402; Sheriff of Yorks., 1409–10; HoP.
Garton, Robert	Chancery clerk.
Gaunstead, Simon	Chancery clerk *c.* 1385–1423; receiver of petitions, Oct. 1404, 1307, April 1414 and 1415–21; keeper of the rolls, 1415–23; R.
Gilbert, John	Bishop of Bangor, 1372–5; bishop of Hereford, 1375–89; chancellor of Ireland, 1380; treasurer, 1386–9 and 1389–91; bishop of St Davids, 1389–97; O.
Gilbert, Robert	Precentor of Lincoln, 1411–20; E.
Gilbert, Robert II	MP for Gloucester, 1415, 1419, May 1421, Dec. 1421, 1422, 1425, 1427 and 1432.
Godyng, William	Chancery clerk.
Golafre, John	MP for Oxon., Sept. 1397; MP for Berks., 1401, Oct. 1404, 1407, 1410, May 1413, April 1414, March 1416, May 1421, 1422, 1426, 1427 and 1429.
Grafton, Richard	Legal advisor to Pershore Abbey, 1406–10; E.
Graystock, John	Envoy of Catherine, the queen mother, to the curia, 1431; E (Graystok).
Grevell, John	MP for Glocs., April 1414, 1419, May 1421, 1422, 1423, 1425 and 1427; HoP (Greville)
Gunthorpe, William	Keeper of the wardrobe, 1366–8; treasurer of Calais, 1368–73; exchequer baron, 1373–87.
Hainton, John	Abbot of Bardney, 1385–1405 (Haynton).
Hallum, Robert	Archdeacon of Canterbury, 1400–6; chancellor of the University of Oxford, 1403–6; bishop of Salisbury, 1407–17; E; O
Hals, John	Justice of king's bench, 1424–34.
Hanworth, Hugh	Archdeacon of Stow, ?1401–19.
Harling, John	King's esquire; usher of the king's chamber, 1375 (Herlyng).
Harlington, John	MP for Hunts., Jan. 1377, Nov. 1384, Sept. 1388, 1394, 1395 and 1399; HoP (Herlyngton).
Harrowdon, John	MP for Hunts., 1376 (Harwedon).
Hartlepool, John	Chancery clerk; receiver of petitions, 1406–13; R (Hertilpole).
Haseley, John	Envoy to Paris on king's business, 1396; E.
Haseley, Thomas	Chancery clerk.

Hawberk, John	E (Hauberk).
Haxey, Thomas	King's clerk; keeper of the rolls and writs of common pleas, 1387–97; receiver of petitions, 1415; R; O.
Henton, William	Proctor-general of the court of Arches, admitted 1424.
Hereford, Nicholas	Former heretic; E; O.
Hervy, John	MP for Beds., 1386; HoP.
Hody, John	E.
Holbache, David	MP for Shropshire, 1406, 1407, 1410, April 1414 and Nov. 1414; MP for Shrewsbury, May 1413 and 1417; HoP.
Holme, Richard	King's clerk by 1397; king's councillor by 1402; king's secretary, 1412; E:Ca.
Horbury, William	Chancery clerk.
Hornby, Thomas	Apprentice-at-law retained by Henry Bolingbroke, 1392–3 (Horneby).
Horsley, Adam	Exchequer clerk; comptroller of the pipe, 1375–82; foreign apposer, 1382–5.
Hovingham, John	Advocate of the court of Arches, admitted 1402; chancery clerk of the first form, 1413; R (Onyngham).
Hugeford, Thomas	MP for Warks., 1425, 1429–30, 1435, 1442 and 1455–6; HoP (Hugford).
Humberston, Alan	King's attorney, occ. 1413.
Hunt, Roger	Baron of the exchequer, 1438–42.
Islip, William	Chancery clerk of the second form, 1415–*c.* 1424; R (Islep).
Judde, John	E:Ca.
Kempston, Simon	Proctor general of the court of Arches from 1410.
Kentwood, Reginald	E (Kentwoode, Kentwode).
Ketton, Robert	Chancellor of William of Wykeham, appointed 1399; councillor of Peterborough Abbey, occ. 1419; E (Keten, Keeton).
Kington, John	Chapter clerk of Lincoln cathedral, 1386–95; chancery clerk; receiver of petitions, 1406 and 1410; keeper of the rolls, 1447–61; E (Kyngton).
Kirkby, Thomas	Chancery clerk; receiver of petitions, 1439 and 1442–53; clerk of parliament, 1439; R (Kyrkeby).
Kyme, John	Deputy steward of honour of Bolingbroke, 1417–20; steward, 1420–1; parliamentary elector in Lincolnshire, 1411 and 1414.
Lacy, Edmund	Dean of the chapel royal, 1414–17; bishop of Hereford, 1417–20; bishop of Exeter, 1420–55; E; O.

Langdon, John	Bishop of Rochester, 1421–34; O.
Langholm, John	MP for Grimsby 1426, 1427, 1429, 1431 and 1433 (Langholme).
Langley, John	MP for Chippenham, 1422; MP for Bristol, 1426; MP for Glos., 1432, 1435, 1437, 1442; HoP.
Langley, Thomas	King's secretary, 1399–1401; archdeacon of Norfolk, 1399–1406; keeper of the privy seal, 1401–5; dean of York, 1403–6; chancellor, 1405–7, 1417–22 and 1422–4; bishop of Durham, 1406–37; E; O.
Lasingby, William	Prior of Guisborough, occ. 1402–5.
Launce, John	Proctor at the Roman curia, 1396; E.
Leche, Roger	MP for Derbys., 1402, 1406, May 1413 and Nov. 1414; HoP.
Lee, Thomas	MP for Herts., 1386; HoP.
Lee, William	MP for Salop, Jan. 1397; HoP.
Lee [II], William	MP for Newcastle-under-Lyme, 1404, May 1413 and Nov. 1414; MP for Staffs., 1420, 1432 and 1435.
Legburn, John	Chamberlain of the exchequer, 1403–13.
Lexham, Thomas	Petition to the pope for a benefice for him was supported by Edward prince of Wales, 1349; E:Ca.
Lincoln, John	Of Grimsby; king's clerk; clerk of the chapel royal; chamberlain of the exchequer, 1386–8; clerk of the signet, 1392–3; king's secretary, occ. 1395–6.
Lisle, Robert	MP for Northumberland, Sept. 1397, Oct. 1404, 1406, Apr. 1414 and 1417; sheriff of Northumberland, 1406–7 and 1415–16; escheator of Northumberland, 1409–10 and 1413–14; HoP.
Littlebury, John	King's knight, 1398–9; chamber knight, occ. 1401; parliamentary elector for Lincolnshire, 1414 (Lyttilbery).
London, Walter	Proctor (not parliamentary) for Llanthony Priory, 1422; E.
Louth, John	King's clerk.
Lowthorpe, George	King's clerk; under clerk of the treasurer, occ. 1398; canon of Salisbury, 1393–1427 (Louthorpe).
Lydford, John	Canon lawyer; archdeacon of Totnes, 1385–1407; E; O.
Lyhert, Walter	Bishop of Norwich, 1446–72; O.
Lyndwood, William	Bishop of St Davids, 1442–6; E; O.
Mackworth, John	Dean of Lincoln, 1412–52; E; O.
Malpas, Henry	Chancery clerk, 1382–1415; receiver of petitions, 1411, 1413, April 1414 and Nov. 1414; E; R. (Maupas).
Malton, Robert	Clerk of the pipe 1397–1413; baron of the exchequer, 1413–26.

Manfield, Robert	Chancery clerk; receiver of petitions, 1386; E.
Mapleton, John	Chancery clerk; receiver of petitions, 1422–5; R. *Two clerks of that name served in the chancery in the early fifteenth century and cannot always be distinguished; R* (Mapilton).
Medford, Walter	Dean of Wells, 1413–23; E.
Melton, Robert	Chancery clerk; under clerk of parliament before 1385.
Merston, Henry	Baron of the exchequer, 1407–21.
Milton, William	Chancery clerk; archdeacon of Buckingham, 1403–24; dean of Chichester, ?1417–24; E.
Moleyns, Adam	Archdeacon of Salisbury, 1439–41; dean of Salisbury, 1441–5; archdeacon of Taunton, 1441–5; bishop of Bath and Wells, 1445–50; E; O.
Mordon, Thomas	Proctor at the Roman curia for the abbot of Glastonbury, occ. 1419; E (*alias* Sottewell)
More, Robert	Advocate of the Court of Arches, admitted 1376.
More, Robert de la	M; official of Henry Wakefield bishop of Worcester.
More, Thomas	Cofferer of the household, 1395–8; keeper of the wardrobe, 1401–5 and 1413; archdeacon of Colchester, 1398–1406.
Morgan, Philip	Archdeacon of Norfolk, 1418–19; bishop of Worcester, 1419–26; bishop of Ely, 1426–35; E; O.
Morpeth, John	Chancery clerk; chancery clerk of the duchy of Lancaster, occ. 1434; R (Morpath).
Morton, Thomas	Chancery clerk.
Muriell, Richard	Commissioner of array in Lindsey (Lincs.), 1392; commissioner of the peace and of *oyer* and *terminer*, 1399.
Muskham, Robert	Chancery clerk; receiver of petitions, Feb. 1383, Oct. 1383 and Nov. 1384.
Nash, Richard	King's serjeant.
Newark, Alan	King's clerk and diplomat from 1390; commissioner to hear appeals from court of chivalry and others, 1391, 1394 and 1395; E.
Newenham, Thomas	Chancery clerk; greater clerk of chancery, 1370–c. 1394; keeper of the great seal, 1377; receiver of petitions, 1377–91; W; O.
Newport, William	MP for Staffs., 1407, 1411 and Nov. 1414; HoP.
Newton, Richard	Serjeant at law; justice of common pleas, 1438–9; chief justice of common pleas, 1439–48; O.
Nicolls, Benedict	Bishop of Bangor, 1408–17; bishop of St Davids, 1417–33; O.
Normanton, William	Under-clerk of the hanaper, 1428–9; chancery clerk; master of chancery, 1450–7; E; R.

Norton, Richard	Justice of common pleas, 1413; chief justice of common pleas, 1413–20; O.
Orwell, John	King's serjeant at arms.
Osney, Thomas	MP for Worcester, 1453–4.
Oudeby, John	Chamberlain of the exchequer, 1396–1414.
Parys, John	E.
Paston, William	Serjeant at law, 1418; king's serjeant, 1426–9; justice of common pleas, 1429–44; O.
Pavy, John	Commissary general of bishop of Worcester, 1406; commissary general of bishop of Hereford, 1408; chancellor of Hereford, 1409; E.
Payn, Roger	Commissioner to hear appeals in court of chivalry, 1393 and 1394; E.
Pelham, John	MP for Sussex, 1399, 1401, Jan. 1404, Oct. 1404, 1406, 1407, 1422 and 1427; HoP.
Petworth, Richard	Chancery clerk, occ. 1417.
Pickworth, Thomas	King's knight, occ. 1399–1403; lieutenant of Calais, occ. 1409.
Pilton, William	King's clerk; keeper of the king's jewels, occ. 1405.
Pinkney, John	E:Ca.
Pirton, Richard	Chamberlain of the exchequer, 1353–65; archdeacon of Colchester, 1383–7.
Pole, Peter de la	MP for Derbys., 1404; HoP.
Popham, Henry	MP for Hants, Feb. 1383, 1385, Feb. 1388, Sept. 1388, Nov. 1390, 1394 and Oct. 1404; HoP.
Prentys, Richard	Clerk of the privy seal office; archdeacon of Essex, 1400–?1406.
Preston, Henry	MP for York, 1420; HoP.
Prestwick, William	Chancery clerk; clerk of parliament, 1424; receiver of petitions, 1425–35; R (Prestwyke).
Pride, Thomas	MP for Shrewsbury, 1378, 1385, Jan. 1390, 1391, 1393, 1394, 1402, Jan. 1404, 1407, 1411, and Apr. 1414; HoP.
Prophet, John	Dean of Hereford, 1393–1407; king's secretary, 1402–6; keeper of the privy seal, 1406–15; dean of York, 1407–17; E.
Pryce, David	See Rees, David ap.
Pygot, John [junior]	King's clerk; chancery clerk; R (Pigot, Picot).
Ravendale, Michael	Chancery clerk; greater clerk of chancery, 1372– ?; receiver of petitions, 1377, Nov. 1380, 1381, May 1382 and Oct. 1382; W.
Ravenser, John	Chancery clerk; keeper of the hanaper of chancery, 1379–93.
Ravenser, Richard	Chancery clerk; keeper of the hanaper, 1357–79;

	treasurer of Queen Philippa, 1362–7 ; greater clerk of chancery, 1363–86; archdeacon of Lincoln, 1368–86; keeper of the great seal, 1377; receiver of petitions, 1377–85; W; O.
Rees, David ap	Advocate of the court of Arches, 1418 and 1419; royal commissioner, 1423; E (Pryce).
Rempston, Thomas	MP for Notts., 1381, May 1382, 1393, 1395, Jan. 1397 and Sept. 1397; sheriff of Notts. and Derbys., 1393–4; constable of the Tower of London, 1399–1406; steward of the king's household, 1399–1401; HoP.
Rishton, Nicholas	Employed on diplomatic missions, 1402–8; attended the council of Pisa, 1409; E (Ryssheton, Ryxton).
Rochford, Ralph	Chamber knight, occ. 1402–6.
Rodbourne, Thomas	Archdeacon of Sudbury, 1414–29; bishop of St Davids, 1433–42; E.
Rokeby, Thomas	MP for Yorks., 1406 and 1423; sheriff of Northumberland, 1405; sheriff of Yorks., 1407–8 and 1411–12; HoP.
Rome, John	Chancery clerk; clerk of parliament, 1384; receiver of petitions, 1399–1413; R.
Rotherham, John	Chancery clerk; receiver of petitions, Jan. 1397–April 1414; R (Roderham).
Russell, John [III]	MP for Herefs., April 1414, 1417, 1419, 1420, May 1421, Dec. 1421, 1422, 1423, 1426, 1429, 1431, 1432 and 1433; HoP.
Ruyhale, Richard	MP for Worcs., Jan. 1397, Sept. 1397 and 1407; HoP.
Ryman, William	MP for Sussex, 1420, May 1421, 1427, 1431 and 1432; HoP.
Saunders, John	MP for Dorchester, 1447; HoP.
Saville, Thomas	King's serjeant at arms (Sayvill).
Scarborough, John	Chancery clerk; under clerk of parliament, 1385–1414; MP for Shaftesbury, 1406; HoP; R (Scardeburgh).
Scarle, John	Chancery clerk; receiver of petitions, Oct. 1382, Oct. 1383, April 1384–Jan. 1397; clerk of parliament, 1384–94; keeper of the rolls, 1394–7; keeper of the great seal, 1394–5 and 1396; chancellor, 1399–1401; O.
Scrope, Richard	Chancellor of the University of Cambridge, 1378; dean of Chichester, 1382–6; bishop of Coventry and Lichfield, 1386–98; archbishop of York, 1398–1405; O.
Selby, Richard	Chancery clerk; R.

Shelford, Henry	Chancery clerk, *c.* 1393–*c.* 1443; receiver of petitions, 1429, 1433 and 1439; dean of Hereford, 1434–46; R.
Shereford, Thomas	Keeper of the spiritualities of Norwich diocese, 1369; E:Ca (Schurford, Shirford).
Shillingford, John	Advocate of the court of Arches, 1369–89; commissioner to hear appeals from the courts of chivalry, 1382–1406; E (Shillyngford).
Skelton, Thomas	MP for Cambs., Jan. 1397; MP for Hants., 1399 and 1406; HoP.
Skipwith, William	Serjeant at law, 1344; king's serjeant, 1354–9; justice of common pleas, 1359–61 and 1376–88; baron of the exchequer, 1361–5; O.
Skirlaw, Walter	Chancery clerk; archdeacon of the East Riding, 1359–85; greater clerk of chancery, 1376–?; receiver of petitions, 1377–Jan. 1380; keeper of the privy seal, 1382–6; bishop of Coventry and Lichfield, 1385–6; bishop of Bath and Wells, 1386–8; bishop of Durham 1388–1406; W; O.
Sleaford, John	Keeper of the privy wardrobe, 1365–78; keeper of the wardrobe, 1371–8.
Smyth, Thomas	Chancery clerk; R.
Southam, John	Archdeacon of Berkshire, 1395–1404; archdeacon of Oxford, 1404–41; E.
Southam, Thomas	Archdeacon of Oxford, 1356–1404; archdeacon of Berkshire, 1404; E.
Spalding, William	Official of the archdeacon of Ely, 1438–44; E:Ca (Spaldyng).
Sparrow, Alexander	Archdeacon of Salisbury, 1426–32; archdeacon of Berkshire, 1432–3; E.
Spert, Thomas	Advocate of the court of Arches, admitted 1367; official of Bath and Wells, occ. 1371–86; E.
Springthorpe, John	Chancery clerk, of the first form by 1405; chancellor of the duchy and county palatinate of Lancaster 1410–13; receiver of petitions, Nov. 1414, 1415, March 1416 and Oct. 1416, 1417–20, May 1421 and Dec. 1421; R (Spryngthorpe).
Stafford, Edmund	Dean of York, 1385–95; keeper of the privy seal, 1389–96; bishop of Exeter, 1395–1419; chancellor, 1396–9 and 1401–3; E; O.
Stafford, John	Archdeacon of Salisbury, 1419–20; keeper of the privy seal, 1421–2; treasurer, 1422–6; dean of St Martin-le-Grand, 1422–3; dean of Wells, 1423–4; bishop of Bath and Wells, 1424–43; chancellor, 1432–50; archbishop of Canterbury, 1443–52; E; O.

Stanley, Thomas	King's clerk, 1370; chancery clerk of the first form, 1386; receiver of petitions, 1390–5 and Sept. 1397–1401; keeper of the rolls of chancery, 1397– *c.* 1401.
Stanlow, John	Treasurer of Normandy, occ. 1446.
Staunton, Thomas	Comptroller of the pipe, 1413–36.
Stokes, John	Chancery clerk; receiver of petitions, 1422, 1423, and 1445; clerk of parliament, 1449; E; E:Ca; R.
Stokes, William	MP for Leominster, 1421; HoP.
Stoket, Nicholas	Envoy to Prussia, 1388; commissioner in appeals from courts of chivalry and admiralty, 1389–94. E.
Stone, John	King's clerk, 1404; king's secretary, 1413–19; E:Ca.
Stoneham, Robert	MP for Hunts., Dec. 1421, 1432, 1435, 1439, 1442 and 1447 (Stonham).
Stopyndon, John	Chancery clerk; king's secretary, 1422; keeper of the hanaper, 1426; receiver of petitions, 1433–47; keeper of the rolls, 1438–47; R.
Stortford, William	Treasurer of St. Paul's, 1387–93; archdeacon of Middlesex, 1393–1416 (Storteford).
Storthwaite, John	Official of the bishop of Bath and Wells, 1422–43; commissioner to hear appeals from courts of admiralty and chivalry, 1434–41; E (Storthwayte).
Stowe, Thomas	Archdeacon of Bedford, *c.* 1375–1405; dean of St Paul's, 1400–5; E.
Strangeways, James	Justice of common pleas, 1429–43.
Stukeley, John	MP for Hunts., 1447, Feb. 1449 and 1450–1; HoP (Styuecley, Stuckley).
Stukeley, Peter	E:Ca (Stewkley).
Stukeley, William	Proctor general of the court of Arches, 1384; official of bishop of London, 1401; commissioner to hear appeals from courts of admiralty and constable, 1400, 1402; E (Styuecle).
Sudbury, William	Monk of Westminster Abbey; refectorer of the abbey, 1391–2; warden and treasurer of Queen Eleanor's manors, 1392–3; E; (Sudbery).
Sydenham, Simon	Lieutenant of the admiral of England, *ante* 1401–3; on diplomatic missions to France, 1401–2; king's clerk, 1405; bishop of Chichester, 1431–8; trier of petitions, 1433 and 1335; E. O.
Symondsbury, John	Crown envoy to the council of Basle, 1431; E (Symondeesburgh).
Talbot, Richard	Dean of Chichester, 1414–17; archbishop of Dublin, 1417–49; justiciar of Ireland, 1420, 1422–3, 1430–1, 1437–8 and 1445–6; chancellor of Ireland, 1423–6, and 1427–31; E; O.
Taverner, William	MP for Leominster, Sept. 1397, 1402, 1406 and

	1407; HoP.
Thelwall, Thomas	Chancery clerk; master of the rolls of Ireland, 1372–5; greater clerk of chancery, 1376–?; chancellor of the Duchy of Lancaster, 1377–8; W.
Thirning, William	Serjeant at law, 1383; king's serjeant, 1388; justice of common pleas, 1388–96; chief justice of common pleas, 1396–1413
Thoralby, John	Deputy chancellor of duchy of Lancaster, 1394, 1395, 1397, 1400 and 1401; chancery clerk, *c.* 1404; receiver of petitions, March 1416, 1425 and 1431; R.
Thornbury, John	MP for Herts., May 1382, Oct. 1382, 1385, Jan. 1390 and 1391; HoP.
Thorp, Adam	Canon and prebendary of York, 1355–84.
Throckmorton, John	MP for Worcs., 1414, 1420, 1422, 1432, 1433 and 1439–40.
Thurgrim, Richard	MP for Worcs., 1394; executor of Henry Wakefield bishop of Worcester; HoP.
Tickhill, Thomas	King's attorney, 1410; apprentice-at-law retained by the duchy of Lancaster, 1411–15.
Tirwhite, Robert	Serjeant at law, 1396; king's serjeant 1398–1408; justice of king's bench, 1408–27; councillor of the duchy of Lancaster (Tirwhit, Tirwhyt).
Tresham, William	MP for Northants., 1423–4, 1427–8, 1429–30, 1432, 1433, 1435, 1439–40, 1442, 1445–6, 1447 and 1449–50.
Tretton, Richard	King's clerk; household clerk of Robert Thorp (chancellor, 1371–2).
Trevor, John	Bishop of St Asaph, 1394–1410; chamberlain of Chester and Flint, 1399–1404; E; O (Trefor, Trevaur).
Turnaunt, Richard	MP for Winchester, Oct. 1416, 1417, 1419, 1426 and 1432.
Tyndale, John	Sheriff of Northants., 1391–2.
Ulston, Richard	Co-collector of tonnage and poundage at Hull, 1415–17 [TNA E 122/60/6].
Usk, Adam	Proctor general of the court of Arches, 1392; advocate of the court of Arches, 1399–1419; chronicler; E; O.
Wace, Thomas	Feodary of the duchy of Lancaster in Lincs., occ. 1408.
Wakering, John	Chancery Clerk; chancellor of the county palatine of Lancaster, 1394/95–9 and 1399–*c.* 1405; receiver of petitions, 1397–1414; chancellor of the duchy of Lancaster, 1402–*c.* 1405; keeper of the rolls,

	1405–15; archdeacon of Canterbury, 1409–15; keeper of the privy seal, 1415–16; bishop of Norwich, 1416–25; R; O.
Walden, Roger	Archdeacon of Winchester, 1387–95; treasurer of Calais, 1387–*c.* 1393; captain of the march of Calais, 1387–91; king's secretary *c.* 1393–5; treasurer, 1395–8; dean of York, 1395–7; archbishop of Canterbury, 1398–9; bishop of London, 1405–6; O.
Waltham, John	Chancery clerk; receiver of petitions, 1380–6; keeper of the rolls, 1381–6; keeper of the Domus Conversorum, 1381–6; archdeacon of Richmond, 1385–8; keeper of the privy seal, 1386–9; bishop of Salisbury, 1388–95; treasurer, 1391–5; E; O.
Waltham, William	Chancery clerk; keeper of the hanaper of chancery, 1393–9; joint keeper of the great seal, 1395.
Wantage, Richard	King's clerk (Wantynge).
Ward, William	Remembrancer of the exchequer, 1419–26; baron of the exchequer, 1426–8.
Ware, Henry	Keeper of the privy seal, 1416–18; bishop of Chichester, 1418–20; E; O.
Warham, Edmund	Notary public by 1385; envoy to Scotland, 1390, envoy to France, 1395; E.
Waryn, Robert	MP for Hunts., 1376, Jan. 1380, Feb. 1383, Feb. 1388, Sept. 1388 and Nov. 1390; HoP.
Wellingborough, John	Clerk of the privy seal office, *ante* 1374–*post* 1399 (Wendeelyngborough).
Westbury, William	Serjeant at law, 1418; justice of king's bench, 1426–45.
Weston, John	MP for Warwick, Jan. 1404, 1406, 1410 and 1411; MP for Worcester, 1410, May 1413, Nov. 1414, 1415 and 1419; MP for Worcs., 1420.
Weston, Thomas	E.
Wetheringsett, Richard	Archdeacon of Ely, occ. 1418–45 (Wetheryngesete).
Whissonsett, John	Under clerk of the chancery, *c.* 1390–*c.* 1420; R (Wyssyngsete).
Whiston, Thomas	E.
Wilcotes, John	MP for Oxon, 1399, 1401, Oct. 1404, 1406, 1407, May 1413, Apr. 1414, Nov. 1414, 1417, 1419 and May 1421; MP for Kent, Mar. 1416; sheriff of Oxon and Berks., 1401–2, 1407–8, 1415–16, 1419–20, 1422; sheriff of Glos., 1420–2; escheator of Oxon and Berks., 1403–4, 1408–9 and 1417–18; HoP.
Wilton, Stephen	E.

Winter, Roger	Teller of the exchequer, 1432–3.
Wisbech, John	E:Ca (Wysebeche).
Woodburn, John	Gentleman; parliamentary elector for Lincs., 1427 (Wodeborn, Wodeburn).
Woodham, John	*King's servant, occ. 1414 (Wodeham).*
Woodhouse, John	Chancellor of the duchy of Lancaster, 1413–31.
Wotton, Nicholas	MP for London, 1406, Nov. 1414, 1419, Dec. 1421, 1425 and 1429.
Wotton, William	Abbot of Cirencester, 1430–40.
Wyche, Richard	Commissioner in appeal from court of admiralty, 1394; lent king £100 for the French war, 1403, E.
Wygge, William	MP for Winchester, Sept. 1388; mayor of Winchester five times, 1388–1413; HoP.
Wykeham, Nicholas	Kinsman of William of Wykeham (bishop of Winchester); co-adjutor to Bishop Wykeham, app. 1403; E.
Wymbush, Nicholas	Chancery clerk, *c.* 1391– *post* 1451; receiver of petitions, 1426, 1427, 1431–9, 1449 and 1450; E; R (Wymbissh).
Wyot, Robert	King's clerk.
Yanworth, Richard	Legal advisor to the abbot of Cirencester.
Zouche, John de la	Bishop of Llandaff, 1403–23.

Indices

Given the amount of material in SC 10, a single index listing everything would quickly prove unmanageable and be of limited use. Five indices have therefore been compiled, the aim being to assist those using these volumes to find specific names, places or other details more readily.

The **Index to Introductions** *covers the introductory surveys found in both volumes. These are paginated separately, with the volumes distinguished in this index by the use of I and II before the page number(s).*

The remaining four indices cover the material found in the SC 10 letters (and other sources calendared in these volumes). Although the amount of material has required two volumes split at 1377, this is a convenient but arbitrary date and the text should be considered as a whole. For that reason, the page numbers of the calendar and appendices run sequentially from the first volume to the second. Entries for pages 1–256 can be found in Volume I, and for pages 257–472 in Volume II.

The **Index of Appointers** *can be used to locate the senders of proxy appointments, wherever these are identifiable. Corporate entities (cathedral chapters and diocesan or archdeaconry clergy) are listed under the relevant place. Individuals are listed under their surnames, where the person is identifiable. However, this index is fully cross-referenced, so titles will direct to the appropriate name(s).*

The **Index of Proctors** *lists all those who are named as a proctor in an SC 10 letter or equivalent document. Proctors often held multiple offices or titles across the course of a career, and it would be impractical to cross-reference all of these in an index of this size. Everyone is therefore listed by name alone, surname first (unless this is not known, in which case a first name plus identifier is used). An exception is made for lay peers, who may be better known by their titles. They are also indexed by name, but cross-references are provided from their noble titles.*

The **Index of Places** *provides all the places named in the dating clauses of documents, as well as those of the benefices of proctors where these are listed.*

Finally, the **Index of Parliaments** *identifies where all the documents pertaining to a particular parliament (or other assembly) can be found. Although the main calendar is arranged chronologically, other material is scattered throughout the appendices, so this index provides a means to locate particular assemblies throughout the volumes.*

INDEX TO INTRODUCTIONS

INDEX OF APPOINTERS

The following abbreviations are used: abt – abbot; abp – archbishop; ad – archdeacon; bp – bishop; CC – collegiate church; clr – chancellor; dn – dean; mstr – master; pr – prior; pcr – precentor; sd – subdean; sp – subprior.
Entries for pages 1–256 can be found in Volume I, and for pages 257–472 in Volume II.

INDEX OF PROCTORS

Entries for pages 1–256 can be found in Volume I, and for pages 257–472 in Volume II.

INDEX OF PLACES

This index includes the places in the right-hand columns, and the parochial and collegiate benefices in the centre columns, except cathedral canonries.

Places (apart from county towns) are identified by the pre-1974 counties. Unidentified places are in single quotation marks. Alternative spellings are in round brackets, and additional information in square brackets.

Entries for pages 1–256 can be found in Volume I, and for pages 257–472 in Volume II.

INDEX OF PARLIAMENTS

The Index of Parliaments identifies the assemblies to which letters relate. While most of the assemblies were parliaments, some letters have also survived for great councils (or other types of council) and convocations, which are identified in the list. The status of some assemblies is unclear or contentious, and some letters pertain to assemblies for which there is otherwise no evidence. More detailed discussion of the assemblies in question can be found, in most cases, in the introductory articles to each parliament in PROME. *The index lists every session of an assembly for which letters survive, and every session is treated independently, even if it was technically a later continuation of a prorogued parliament. It also includes some sessions which did not meet or were postponed, as letters were often sent before the cancellation or prorogation of the assembly. Months are only given when there was more than one session in a calendar year and are the month in which the assembly commenced.*

(GC) – the assembly was a great council or other non-parliamentary assembly.

(CV) – the assembly was a convocation.

Entries for pages 1–256 can be found in Volume I, and for pages 257–472 in Volume II.